MW01058008

First Ladies and American Women

Jill Abraham Hummer

First Ladies
and American
Women

IN POLITICS AND AT HOME

UNIVERSITY PRESS OF KANSAS

Published by the University Press of Kansas (Lawrence, Kansas 66045), which was organized by the Kansas Board of Regents and is operated and funded by Emporia State University, Fort Hays State University, Kansas State University, Pittsburg State University, the University of Kansas, and Wichita State University.

Library of Congress Cataloging-in-Publication Data

Names: Hummer, Jill Abraham, author.
Title: First ladies and American women : in politics and at home / Jill Abraham Hummer.
Description: Lawrence, Kansas : University Press of Kansas, [2017] | Includes bibliographical references and index.
Identifiers: LCCN 2016051183
ISBN 9780700623808 (hardback : acid free paper)
ISBN 9780700623815 (ebook)
Subjects: LCSH: Presidents' spouses—United States—History—20th century. | Presidents' spouses—United States—History—21st century. | Presidents' spouses—United States—Biography. | Presidents' spouses—Family relationships—United States—History. | Women—Political activity—United States—History. | Sex role—United States—History. | United States—Politics and government—1929–1933. | United States—Politics and government—1933–1945. | United States—Politics and government—1945–1989. | United States—Politics and government—1989– | BISAC: HISTORY / United States / 20th Century. | HISTORY / United States / 21st Century. | POLITICAL SCIENCE / Government / Executive Branch.
Classification: LCC E176.2 .H86 2017 | DDC 320.082/0973—dc23
LC record available at https://lccn.loc.gov/2016051183.

British Library Cataloguing-in-Publication Data is available.

Printed in the United States of America

10 9 8 7 6 5 4 3 2

The paper used in this publication is recycled and contains 30 percent postconsumer waste. It is acid free and meets the minimum requirements of the American National Standard for Permanence of Paper for Printed Library Materials Z39.48-1992.

This book is dedicated to my parents,
Tom and Linda Abraham

Contents

Acknowledgments

I am indebted to family, friends, and colleagues, who provided me support and encouragement in writing this book. I gathered the evidence presented in this volume at a series of presidential libraries, whose staffs were always responsive to my many requests. Thanks go to the archivists at the Herbert Hoover Library, Harry S. Truman Library, Dwight D. Eisenhower Library, John F. Kennedy Library, Lyndon B. Johnson Library, Richard Nixon Presidential Materials, Gerald R. Ford Library, Jimmy Carter Library, Ronald Reagan Library, and George Bush Library. Thanks also to the Wilson College librarians, who went to great lengths to acquire materials.

The research in this volume was supported by generous grants from the Herbert Hoover Foundation, Franklin and Eleanor Roosevelt Institute, Harry S. Truman Library Institute, John F. Kennedy Library Foundation, Lyndon B. Johnson Foundation, and Gerald R. Ford Foundation. These grants allowed me to collect materials at their respective libraries. The White House Historical Association also provided funds to defray the costs of research. A research stipend from Wilson College funded the collection of photographs in this volume, as well as the research of my student Christina Gonzalez, who gathered materials for me at the Ronald Reagan Library. A sabbatical leave from Wilson College helped to bring this project to a successful conclusion, and I am grateful to my colleague Kay Ackerman and to Dean Elissa Heil for making that possible.

This volume is the outgrowth of my work as a graduate student at the University of Virginia. Thanks are due to Steve Rhoads, Holly Shulman, and the late James Sterling Young of the University of Virginia and to MaryAnne Borrelli of Connecticut College, who provided mentorship on that initial project. I am also grateful to the editors and staff at the University Press of Kansas, as well as anonymous reviewers, for believing in this project and bringing it to fruition.

Credit especially goes to my family. To my husband, Josh, for his unrelenting commitment to me and support for my project. This book, my first, is dedicated to my parents, in gratitude for my education. To my four children, Scarlett, Abe, Pierce, and Iris, who daily challenged me, "Did you write your words today, Mama?" I share this accomplishment with all of you. Thanks also to many individuals who supported my family while I "wrote my words."

I have no doubt that mistakes, gaps, and misinterpretations cloud this work. It is imperfect as humans are imperfect. And so I urge readers to grant mercy and consider, "Where is the wise man? Where is the scholar? Where is the philosopher of this age? Has not God made foolish the wisdom of this world? For since in the wisdom of God the world through its wisdom did not know him, God was pleased through the foolishness of what was preached to save those who believe" (1 Corinthians 1:20–21).

Introduction

In April 2011, Michelle Obama attended a baby shower for forty pregnant military wives at Camp Lejeune, North Carolina. She came bearing a basket filled with pink and blue White House blankets. She had taken up a gift drive, placing donation boxes all over the East Wing and West Wing. The shower was part of her Joining Forces initiative to ease burdens on military families. Four decades earlier, Pat Nixon traveled to Africa as the nation's official representative. She conferred with heads of state, joined African women in a traditional tribal dance, and visited a school for modern homemaking. Nearly four decades before that, as the country sank deeper into the Great Depression, Lou Hoover took to the airwaves and told women how they could play a part in unemployment relief. She praised American women for making it possible that a child might go to school sufficiently fed and clothed and that a high school girl might finish her course in stenography and bookkeeping.[1]

American first ladies have acted. They have acted in multiple ways and against shifting backdrops. On her Africa trip, Pat Nixon, after a sleepless nine-hour flight and a frantic twelve-hour day of activities, declared that being first lady was "the hardest unpaid job in the world." The first ladyship is a job. It is a peculiar job. Its occupants have worked. They have done duties and performed roles. However, there are no federal guidelines telling first ladies how they must act. They are unelected, having attained their positions by virtue of marriage. Though they have worked, American first ladies have not drawn salaries. Yet, despite the fuzzy role definition and questionable basis of authority, first ladies have acted. This book explores what they have done and why.[2]

First ladies have been intimately connected to American womanhood. A sweeping glance across history reveals this much. The actions and public evaluations of first ladies have been affiliated with women's roles, rights, and responsibilities. These ties are at once intriguing and bewildering. But it is nevertheless clear that the story of first ladies has been linked to the story of women in America. The two cannot be understood apart from each other. This book interweaves these two stories into a single narrative beginning with Lou Hoover and ending with Michelle Obama. Through this knitted narrative, the first ladies' actions and the forces behind them are illuminated and unveiled.

The shifting currents of women's political history structure this book. It is broken into three historical epochs. Though no one first lady has behaved exactly like another, we should see first ladies acting in response to trends that mark and unify each epoch. The first epoch explores the years following women's suffrage, from Lou Hoover through Jacqueline Kennedy. The second examines first ladies' actions during the second wave of the feminist movement, from Lady Bird Johnson through Rosalynn Carter. The third looks at first ladies' actions amid the charged political and partisan environment in the wake of the conservative backlash against feminism after 1980, from Nancy Reagan through Michelle Obama. Each historical epoch contains two chapters. The first chapter within each examines first ladies' actions that stem from women's changing relationship to the state, while the second explores those actions that grew out of shifting debates about women's relationship to the home and family.

Regarding women's changing relationship to the state, after suffrage, first ladies' actions were shaped by women's expanding role as citizens, as voters and participants, and in partisan, professional, reform, and civic networks. During the second wave, first ladies acted in response to women's increasing demands for political and legal equality. And after 1980, they acted to further their respective ideological and partisan positions on domestic and global women's rights and human rights.

On women's shifting relationship to the home, after suffrage, first ladies worked to attain social stability and security by modeling behavior as a wife and mother in the context of depression, war, and postwar uncertainty. During the second wave, first ladies responded to the feminist cry that the personal was political. And after 1980, with family politics at the forefront of the political and cultural debate, first ladies reflected how their administrations valued motherhood.

Though unelected, first ladies have occupied a public post. They have inhabited a government dwelling. Their projects have been supported by federal dollars. They have represented the president in affairs of state. Therefore, it is reasonable to expect a portion of their activities to move in response to women's relationship to the political sphere. Yet, first ladies have also been defined by their wifehood. They have cared for their families. They have fed, clothed, and consumed. They have modeled docility or autonomy in the presidential marriage. They have maintained their government dwelling as a model home. These private sphere activities have also been done on a public stage. Because both public and private roles are wrapped up in the first lady's persona, she, in turn, has been caught up in the evolving societal debates about women's relationship to the state and the home. And understanding how first ladies have moved with these currents of women's political history is essential for attaining a more complete picture of the office.

Sometimes, a first lady's activity, whether her pet project or policy activism, could touch on women's relationships to both the state and home. For example, after suffrage, Eleanor Roosevelt's leadership of the Office of Civilian Defense counts as an example of women's increasing role in government service. However, she also used her post to speak about domestic roles in the context of war preparedness. And while the Equal Rights Amendment (ERA) debate was initially about women's legal equality, it became wrapped up in debates over marriage and the family. We see both elements reflected in first ladies' ERA activities during the second wave. How the presidential administration, press, or others framed an activity; how the public perceived it; what the attributes of the activity itself were; and how it fit into the historical epoch all contribute to whether a first lady activity relates to the state or home.

First ladies have been categorized and sensationalized. Their behind-the-scenes influence has been uncovered. Their personal lives have been scrutinized and political impact analyzed. To some, her position may seem idiosyncratic or given to the whims of the individual occupant. And many works have treated individual first ladies individually. Yet, less attention has been paid to the relationship between first ladies and female politics across modern presidential administrations. This book will illuminate that story, as it unfolds through decades of turbulence, progress, and uncertainty. And so we begin in the 1920s, a time period abounding in all of those qualities.

AFTER SUFFRAGE

*I*n 1923, Lou Hoover, wife of Herbert Hoover, secretary of commerce, urged Republican women assembled at the Ritz-Carlton in Philadelphia to surrender some of the time they devoted to pleasurable pursuits and take an active part in civic affairs. In the roaring twenties, it was the carefree flapper adorned in beads and a henna scarf who epitomized women's new liberties. Many doubted that women's suffrage, won just three years earlier, had mattered. "There is no neutral or passive place for us," she said to the women. "The vote in itself is not a perfect utility. It is perfected in the way in which it is used."[1]

Suffrage raised the possibility that women could enter mainstream politics wholesale. The postsuffrage years were not a period of dormancy in women's politics. A vital network of women's interests—partisan, professional, reform, civic—developed during this time. First ladies were integral actors within this network. This chapter chronicles how first ladies advanced and redefined women's citizenship according to their respective ideologies and highlights how women's political issues and female actors shaped their activities.[2]

LOU HOOVER

In 1928, the National Woman's Party endorsed Herbert Hoover for president. His running mate, Charles Curtis, had introduced its ERA, which proclaimed that men and women should have equal rights, in the U.S. Senate. Though the ERA was on the fringes of mainstream politics, it divided female political actors. After suffrage, women's rights activists were split into two factions: feminists and reformers. Feminists aligned with Republicans, who preached classical liberal values of equality, individualism, and limited government. Reformers sympathized with Democrats, who opposed the exploitation of women in industry and believed that equality would mean the loss of these protections. Feminists believed that women would not be fully citizens until they were treated the same as men in law and policy. Reformers argued that women's special physical constitution, especially their childbearing and maternal roles, necessitated protective legislation.[3]

Lou Hoover considered herself a suffragist but not a militant feminist. Yet, her life before becoming first lady was described as one of the best bits of feminist propaganda the nation had ever seen. She was born Lou Henry on 29 March 1874 in Waterloo, Iowa, her family relocating to California a decade later. In her girlhood, she and her father, a banker, spent their leisure hours hiking and camping along the woods and hills of their home in Monterey. She credited her father with cultivating her love of nature, while also shaping her progressive beliefs about the capabilities of girls and women. In the 1890s, it was uncommon for a young woman to earn a bachelor's degree, which she did in geology at Stanford University. There, she met Herbert Hoover, also a geology student, and in 1899, following a telegrammed proposal, the two were married. A pattern soon emerged where Lou Hoover would organize the distaff side of whatever her husband was working on. They set up their first home in China, where Herbert Hoover supervised a private mining company. During the Boxer Rebellion, the violent Chinese nationalist uprising against foreigners and Christians, Lou Hoover organized the women to ration food supplies. When World War I broke out in Europe and Herbert Hoover chaired the Commission for Relief in Belgium, she served as president of the Women's War Relief Fund. When the United States declared war on Germany and Herbert Hoover directed the Food Administration in Washington, D.C., Lou Hoover ran the Food Administration Women's Club.[4]

Lou Hoover believed that men and women were capable of equal performance in the professions. Though she did not hold a paying job, she and her husband together translated *De Re Metallica* from its original Latin, both of their names and equal credentials appearing on the title page. "I believe that there is a future in anything that one is vitally interested in. It is up to the girl to find the niche in which she thinks there would be the most congenial work, and make her own way into it," Lou Hoover wrote to an aspiring female geologist. When a female collegian asked her to fill out a survey on women in engineering, she answered with similar rugged individualism. To the question, what kinds of engineering do you consider appropriate for a woman? Lou Hoover answered, "Any that she feels capable of and interested in attempting." To the question, do you consider a woman's physical weakness a great disadvantage? Lou Hoover answered, "A woman who has taken correct care of herself all of her life should have <u>no</u> so-called 'physical weakness.'" She wrote these answers, laced with incredulity, in 1921, a time of postwar economic optimism, when suffragists believed a new era of female participation was dawning.[5]

Her attitudes about women in politics mirrored her opinions about women in the professions. Ahead of the 1928 Republican convention, reporter Mary Dougherty inquired, "Mrs. Hoover, what DO you think of women in politics?" They were still a newer phenomenon. "Women in politics do not seem any different to me than men in politics," she replied. "They're just human and voters, and frankly, I don't think they are very different."[6]

During the 1920s, propelled by the power of women's votes, political parties were transformed from all-male bastions. At the grass-roots level, women rapidly entered the organizations. Women became county and precinct leaders. The 1928 election was a turning point in women's political interest and mobilization, with both parties benefiting from an upsurge in women voting. For example, the *Washington Post* reported that the Republican headquarters in Chicago faced unprecedented numbers of women besieging the organization for a share in the campaign. Women party workers plus those who had never voted clamored for campaign work. Women as canvassers, convention speakers, election officers, and party officials became increasingly accepted. The influence of these political women is evident in Lou Hoover's 1928 campaign actions.[7]

Party women wanted to talk about Lou Hoover in their speeches, believing it would cause women to rally around the candidate. For example, a woman from a Republican committee in New York wrote to Lou Hoover to ask for information for speeches she was preparing to deliver before university women's associations. "As you undoubtedly know, the East, in its campaign work of trying to get the women's votes is stressing Mr. Hoover as a person, and as a family man. . . . It is the personal side that the average woman is interested in." As more women went to the polls, wives provided an important link for women to the candidates.[8]

Women's groups wrote to Lou Hoover asking for tokens and mementos to help inspire their volunteer work. For example, the chair of a Republican women's organization in Kentucky wrote asking for a photograph of Lou Hoover, assuring her that her presence on the walls of their headquarters would bring inspiration to their many visitors and workers. Lou Hoover obliged. The delighted chairwoman replied, "The actual good that such a likeness of our next 'first lady' does is difficult to estimate. All women have a natural desire to know something of the one who is to stand for the womanhood of America for the next few years. Needless to say, this charming picture is a delightful 'answer' to their inquiring interest." These party women believed the candidate's wife was important and inspiring because, as a woman, she would represent them in her future White House work.[9]

Lou Hoover politicked behind the scenes. She worked with Caroline Slade, head of the Women's National Committee for Hoover. Lou Hoover forwarded Slade the names of individual connections that would be helpful in particular states and suggested ways to approach them. In Missouri, for example, she referred "the very nice Catholic Mrs. Walsh." In Georgia, she recommended Slade contact Nina Pape, founder of an elite girls' school in Savannah, but suggested that a Southern woman should approach her.[10]

She also made a precedent-setting campaign trip, traveling by train with her husband from Washington, D.C., to their home in Palo Alto, California, for the formal notification ceremony. This was before Franklin Roosevelt made it customary for candidates to accept the presidential nomination at the convention. The press attributed her presence to the importance of the women's vote. The *Christian Science Monitor* narrated her typical train appearance: "Then someone sees a tall, slender, graciously smiling silver-haired woman in the door way of the car. . . . She is recognized. 'Come on out, Mrs. Hoover,' goes up the cry. The applause and cheering is prolonged and enthusiastic. From now on it is her 'show.' Mr. Hoover turns to her with a happy smile." Off the train, she mingled with the crowds. Expectations were shifting. Campaigning was becoming part of the candidate's wife's job description.[11]

Lou Hoover met with numerous women's Republican groups in per-

son. In 1928, for example, she visited a Pennsylvania Republican wom-
en's organization at their headquarters at the Hannah Penn House in
Philadelphia. A decidedly political visit, the group's president assured
her, "I know every one who meets you will become your friend, and a
staunch supporter of the campaign." The *Washington Post* reported that
she greeted 2,300 female Hoover backers in a lengthy receiving line.[12]

After Herbert Hoover's election victory, women of the Republican
National Committee (RNC) sent Lou Hoover a binder filled with reports from across the country, writing that female volunteers would
feel "fully repaid" if Lou Hoover read them. "The interest the women
of the county had in Mr. Hoover was partly a reflected interest in you.
. . . Their knowledge of you . . . and above all your charming personality was an incentive to work on to a successful conclusion of the campaign," they wrote. Their correspondence affirms that the candidate's
wife had the special power to spark women's activism and increase
their knowledge of the candidate.[13]

Lou Hoover was again made aware of the impact she could have in
drawing women into the public sphere when, before the inauguration,
she traveled as part of her husband's delegation on a goodwill tour of
Latin America. "An unexpected result of the visit has been an awakening of interest in and among women," her secretary wrote of Lou
Hoover's presence on the trip. "More pictures of women (those who
entertained her or called on her) appeared in the papers than appeared
during I forget how many past years!" This foreshadowed the first lady's diplomatic role and her ability to uplift international women.[14]

As first lady, Lou Hoover added her voice and influence to the work
of women's physical education advocate Ethel Perrin. She published
the forward to Perrin's 1929 book *Play Day—The Spirit of Sport*. "Play
Days" brought together girls from different high schools and colleges
for athletic matches and emphasized participation over competition.
Lou Hoover wrote, "A team for every one and every one on a team! This
is the aim of the new plan for athletics among girls." Describing these
events as "thoroughly democratic," Lou Hoover and women athletic
leaders were concerned that sports had become too exclusively male,
marked by "over-exertion for a few, bleacher seats for many, and too
strained intentness for all." Lou Hoover believed that when girls exercised as a group, democracy was expanded and women's citizenship

was furthered. She wrote that when members of a community learned to play together, they could understand each other, leading to cooperation on more serious matters.[15]

Lou Hoover also expanded women's citizenship by making inroads into the male-dominated world of radio. On 22 June 1929, Lou Hoover became the first president's wife to deliver a radio address, though it was not the first time her voice was transmitted over the airwaves. Earlier that April, when she picked up a microphone to deliver greetings to the Daughters of the American Revolution, her words were unwittingly broadcast across the eastern United States. Radio, a new technology, marked a turning point for women. It promised less isolation on farms and in homes. Though soap operas flourished, women listeners could also hear programs on politics, economics, and world affairs. The few women who did appear on radio became teachers of the public and voices of authority. So too would Lou Hoover.[16]

Lou Hoover's first intentional address was transmitted over the National Broadcasting Company's coast-to-coast network of radio stations. She spoke from her camp in the Shenandoah National Forest to a 4-H Club meeting taking place nearly 100 miles away at the Department of Agriculture. Arthur Hyde, secretary of agriculture, had invited the first lady to speak to the members, two boys and two girls selected from each state. In her remarks, she singled out the boys for admonishment, and the nub of her remarks questioned gender roles on the farm.

> Girls and boys in home making and farm accomplishment—that is what you are isn't it? I say that very deliberately, especially the juxtaposition of the "boys" and "home making" parts. Girls and women often do much in farming, with the care of the stock and the chickens, with the garden and the berries and the orchard. But even more does every boy and man help or hinder in home making. Just stop and think what home is to you, boys. Is it simply a place where mother and the girls drudge a good part of the day in order that father and the boys may have a place to come to eat and sleep?

Divisions of labor were not as clear as they thought, she explained, while urging boys to be cheerful in helping with homemaking.[17]

Though she was initially aghast when the secretary assigned her twenty full minutes of airtime, Lou Hoover's speech rolled. Near the end she exclaimed, "I think of so many things I want to talk with you about, that I wish I had twenty minutes every day for a week!" Her speech was well received. But in the interwar years, women graced radio frequencies only infrequently. Those who did pioneered new territory. Broadcasters believed that soprano voices sounded shrill and jangly. After her broadcast, the *Washington Post* editorialized, "Not three women in possibly a hundred or more we have heard . . . have a radio voice as pleasing, in our opinion, as has Mrs. Hoover. If most women could hear their radio voices they probably would never face the microphone again."[18]

Perhaps this aversion to women on the airwaves explains why Lou Hoover had voice tests made over a sound newsreel apparatus set up in the White House. Newspapers revealed that she desired to "adopt permanently a method of speech and intonation" for future talks on broadcast media. Reportedly, she thought her voice sounded husky and difficult to understand. The voice tests indicated she wanted to blend more harmoniously into this male-dominated territory.[19]

Lou Hoover also expanded women's citizenship through her traditional entertaining role. The most controversial episode of her first ladyship was the DePriest tea incident. In April 1929, Oscar DePriest, the first black congressman since 1901, was sworn in. He had a wife named Jessie. As Herbert Hoover recounted, "Mrs. Hoover insisted upon inviting the Negro's wife equally [to the annual tea for congressmen's wives] with the others." Lou Hoover's racial politics did not go unnoticed. Racist lawmakers took stabs at her. The Texas legislature passed a resolution condemning her. Lou Hoover was wounded by the hostility, but she had made an important statement about the social equality of the races.[20]

The DePriest tea incident also raises the point that women's expanding citizenship was not relevant to all women. Many of the inroads made after suffrage were relevant to middle- and upper-class white women, leaving out racial and ethnic minorities. While Lou Hoover's invitation was a progressive one, black women were regarded as second-class citizens in White House society.

The onset of the Great Depression would build on Lou Hoover's campaign role and these initial undertakings, while drawing upon her previous work with the Girl Scouts. She was elected second vice president of the Girl Scouts in 1917 and president in 1922. As first lady, she served as honorary president. According to Herbert Hoover, "She gave a large part of her spare energies to [the Girl Scouts] during the twelve years we were in Washington and long afterwards. She raised over $2,000,000 of funds and built it up ultimately to a million girls and made it into a potent agency for good."[21]

Lou Hoover made the Girl Scout focus on pioneer-like preparedness, survival skills, and citizenship relevant to the Great Depression. In the years after suffrage, Girl Scout leaders believed they could transform women's social and political roles to meet the new opportunities accorded by the franchise. It was a school of citizenship that prepared girls for a lifetime of meaningful democratic engagement and that modeled problem solving, parliamentary procedure, and leadership. Lou Hoover's speeches reflected this postsuffrage citizenship training. For example, to a Girl Scouts convention in 1931, she remarked that when a Girl Scout became a grownup, she would "be ready to take on her citizenship duties better . . . by reason of having met her troop obligations, and of having long participated in the representative government of her troop and camp." Scouting was serious, she said, because it trained young women to be community leaders.[22]

Women's agencies in the federal bureaucracy needed to reach women during the Great Depression. Lou Hoover became a conduit between the executive branch and the nation, addressing her audiences as a woman and a Girl Scout. On 23 March 1931, she gave a radio address under the auspices of the Woman's Division of the President's Emergency Committee for Employment. Speaking from a White House desk and flanked by two Girl Scouts, Lou Hoover praised the work of the girls and women in meeting and overcoming the disastrous conditions. She prescribed for women a plan of action, rooted in conservative values of individual responsibility, private charity, and localism. She said women should first look for opportunities to help in their own neighborhoods, for example, by giving coal to those in dire straits. When they have reached the end of their own "pocketbooks and flour bins," they should look to the national charities, such as the Red Cross. Afterward, Arthur Woods, chair of the committee, wrote to her, "You have no idea what a lift [your address] has given to the work. The

. . . picture you gave of general cooperation was most stimulating." Lou Hoover had inspired women's relief work.[23]

Not only did she preach private charity, Lou Hoover practiced it. During the Great Depression, requests to the first lady for material assistance, such as clothing, work, and money, had become so onerous that she personally employed two secretaries to resolve them. Her secretary Philippi Harding Butler recorded the process: "For the great number of questions and appeals of various kids, we contacted friends all over the country who were located in an area from which a letter had come, or committees which had been formed by various organizations." Then they would report back to Lou Hoover. For example, the General Federation of Women's Clubs reported on the case of a Miss Jean Collins from Pennsylvania: "Asks employment; says she has held position as secretary, secretarial companion, managing housekeeper; asking for almost any kind of work. Referred to Mrs. John A. Frick, Allentown, Penn., who has gotten in touch with Miss Collins and promises to do everything in her power to help get her a position." In the case of an ill widow with a dependent child, it was determined that "she is much better off than many in the community and at any rate she will not be allowed to suffer; that the community will take care of her." These responses reflect the harsher side of individualism, as well as Republican reliance on the local community.[24]

Depression conditions continued to worsen, and Herbert Hoover's reelection prospects appeared dim. For the 1932 campaign, West Virginia suffragette Lenna Lowe Yost directed the RNC Women's Division. She and Lou Hoover strategized behind the scenes. For example, Lou Hoover provided Yost with a list of female speakers. They discussed organizational matters, such as a board of counselors for the Women's Division. Lou Hoover tried to get high-profile women, such as the wife of Henry Ford, to join. Yost wanted diversity on her board, asking Lou Hoover, "Can you suggest a prominent German or Jewish woman?" She also kept the first lady apprised of the Women's Division policy work. "We are having three new leaflets printed—one on Tariff, one of the Reconstruction Finance Corporation, and one on the Home Loan Bank. Copy of the first is enclosed and the others will follow when they are off the press," Yost wrote, so that Lou Hoover could be prepared.[25]

The first lady's public campaign role was expanding. In 1932, Lou

Lou Hoover, standing beside Herbert Hoover, waves to crowds aboard the 1932 campaign train. Courtesy Herbert Hoover Presidential Library.

Hoover traveled extensively with her husband, appearing with him in street parades and mass meetings, while meeting with Republican women's organizations on her own. According to Nancy Beck Young, she gave pseudo-speeches, mostly directed to women's and children's interests. This was the first time a first lady spoke to crowds on behalf of a presidential candidate, thereby infusing the role with substantive responsibility. Between 1928 and 1932, women were further mobilized to vote. The perceived benefits of participating in the franchise increased between these years. Women were speaking at national conventions, in party meetings, and in their own campaigns for office. Lou Hoover's brief campaign speeches were an outgrowth of these trends, as well as of her own experience speaking to the public during her tenure.[26]

After Franklin Roosevelt defeated Herbert Hoover, Lou Hoover gave a final radio address, this time under the auspices of the National Woman's Committee of the Welfare and Relief Mobilization of 1932, of which she had been appointed honorary chair. Not wavering in her beliefs in private charity and localism, she urged women to find out "whether Mrs. Neighbor who is keeping up such a brave front, though her husband has been out of work for months, is really as assured as she seems on the surface." She told women to go on fact-finding missions about the hospitals in their communities. If they found the facilities to be inadequate, any woman could "add her insistence to any movement, legislative or otherwise, that is designed to keep up those essential services during this emergency." She urged women to guard against idleness and pursue recreational activity. In this final address, which was a call to action, she fused together conservatism and Girl Scout beliefs to promote women's citizenship, while illustrating the first lady's new role as a citizen educator.[27]

ELEANOR ROOSEVELT

Eleanor Roosevelt's work to expand women's citizenship as first lady cannot be understood apart from her earlier involvement in the Progressive movement. Among the factions of women's activists after suffrage, Eleanor Roosevelt sided with reformers. Though she was a debutante from a long line of New York aristocrats, her reform impulses were stirred as she attached herself to female domains within the Progressive movement. Her work with other elite women provided an entrée into efforts to improve living and working conditions.

She was born Anna Eleanor Roosevelt on 11 October 1884 in New York, New York. Her mother died when she was eight, and her father, an alcoholic, died when she was nine. Eleanor and her two brothers were left to the care of her imposing maternal grandmother. During her girlhood, Eleanor Roosevelt's education under Marie Souvestre of the exclusive Allenswood Academy in London, England, from 1898 to 1902 significantly impacted her worldview. Souvestre lectured on social movements and instilled within her pupils a deep sense of public duty. Eleanor Roosevelt's grandmother then insisted she return to New York City, where she was introduced into society. At the time, two-thirds of New York City residents lived in dilapidated tenements. Eleanor Roosevelt joined the ranks of other debutantes actively working with the Junior League for the Promotion of Settlement Movements. Women of the settlement movement were troubled by the problems of urbanism and industrialism. Many felt a needling sense of uselessness in elite society and wanted to do something important. Eleanor Roosevelt worked at a settlement house on Rivington Street, where she taught calisthenics and dancing. This was her first real exposure to the plight of the working poor.[28]

The settlement movement was part of a reform network that included the National Consumers League, which Eleanor Roosevelt joined as an investigator. She was horrified when she witnessed kindergarten-age children dropping from fatigue while working around sweatshop tables. The National Consumers League lobbied for the abolition of child labor, as well as for equal pay for equal work, a minimum hourly wage, and limits on workday hours.[29]

She married her fifth cousin Franklin Delano Roosevelt in 1905. Five years later, he was elected to the New York State Senate. She found the political atmosphere of Albany stimulating, and the swirl of New York Democratic politicians contributed to her political education. When FDR served as the assistant secretary of the navy during World War I, she threw herself into war work—running Red Cross canteens and knitting for the navy. Meanwhile, between 1906 and 1916, Eleanor Roosevelt bore six children, one dying in infancy.[30]

In the decade after suffrage, Eleanor Roosevelt embodied women's expanding citizenship. She joined the League of Women Voters and worked for better labor conditions, children's rights, and political reform. In the 1924 presidential campaign, she worked for the Women's Division of the New York State Democratic Committee. At its convention she gave a speech seconding the nomination of candidate Al Smith. She gave radio addresses presenting women's point of view on legislative matters and began a lucrative career writing for magazines. In 1928, in *Redbook Magazine* she wrote about how women were frozen out of the inner sanctums of decision making. She pointed to widespread male hostility toward sharing power with women. She argued that women must learn to play the game of politics as men do—by working hard, mastering the social sciences, and backing women party bosses. Four years later, she would assume the role of women's de facto party boss.[31]

By FDR's inauguration, Eleanor Roosevelt was the nucleus of a network of journalists, educators, reformers, and party workers dedicated to a New Deal for women. When the Roosevelts went to Washington, so did a flock of women reformers. Eleanor Roosevelt was determined to get women their share of patronage appointments in the swelling government apparatus. The essence of patronage is rewarding individuals, especially by giving them government jobs, for faithful service to a candidate or party. Together with Mary (Molly) Dewson, head of the Democratic National Committee (DNC) Women's Division and longtime friend of the Roosevelts, she created a patronage pressure system directed to FDR and DNC chair James Farley. [32]

Molly Dewson worried that the traditional trappings of the first ladyship might constrain Eleanor Roosevelt's work for women's patronage. On 3 April 1933, Dewson wrote to her, "Jim [Farley] told me whatever you want for the women goes and since you are the 'key' woman I hope you are not held back by also being the president's wife. Otherwise it's quite an awkward situation for the handful of women who did the outstanding work." Dewson's fears were eventually dispelled, as patronage was meaningfully extended to women for the first time during the 1930s, largely because of Eleanor Roosevelt's leadership. But it did not happen without a fight.[33]

Eleanor Roosevelt and Molly Dewson had a plan in place from the beginning. "The big idea was that the women who worked for you and me—the Women's Division—were to have a few jobs on our recognition," Dewson wrote to the first lady on 15 May 1933. Dewson's initial list had 124 names on it. She was relentlessly committed to her list.[34]

Dewson recognized that male politicians wanted to keep patronage appointments for themselves. She wrote to Eleanor Roosevelt on 27 April 1933 that because the men were so tenacious, continuous pressure would have to be brought on Farley. "I mean continuous in the sense of pressure on behalf of one woman one day and another woman another day." Though the pair did exert this day-to-day pressure, they were not always successful. "The men are taking all the positions we want," an exasperated Dewson wrote to the first lady on 15 May 1933.[35]

Molly Dewson was vexed when Cordell Hull, secretary of state, wanted to give a woman named Lucille McMillin a lesser position than Dewson believed she deserved. She wrote to Eleanor Roosevelt on 29 April 1933:

I realize I may be asking more from you than is possible at this stage of woman's development, but certainly the Democrats never would have carried some of the key Western states if the women had not worked in an organized fashion. Why doesn't Mr. Hull send Mrs. McMillan [sic] to some foreign country? Benton McMillan [sic] would probably have been given a high position in the Foreign Service. Why not Mrs. McMillan [sic]? Please do not think I am getting to be an old crank, but I think that the women who have shown they will be of value in the Party in the 1934 and 1936 campaigns because they did such excellent vote-getting in this campaign are the ones to be rewarded.[36]

Lucille McMillin was eventually appointed to the Civil Service Commission.

And so the process went. Dewson cajoled. Roosevelt hounded. The following are some characteristic excerpts of their patronage pressure system:

Molly Dewson to Eleanor Roosevelt, 27 April 1933: Another place where nothing may be done unless you come into the picture is the case of Mrs. Spann of Nevada. . . . She might be a Trade Commissioner at Havana, Montevideo or Caracas, Uruguay. I am sure there are some such jobs in the State Department.

Molly Dewson to Jim Farley, 16 September 1933: You wrote you would speak to the "Boss" about Lavinia Engle. Mrs. Roosevelt has already. Talk to her too. I hear Lewis Pope of Tennessee was just appointed to the Parole Board but dramatically refused. Why was he preferred to Lavinia? She qualifies as an expert.

Eleanor Roosevelt to Harold Ickes, 13 December 1933: Is it possible to be sure that the assistant commissionership of education which is now held by a woman will be retained by a woman, and that women will receive half of the jobs under [the] plan for employing unemployed teachers?[37]

They also had successes. Mary Ward was appointed commissioner of immigration. Sue Shelton White was appointed to the National Recovery Administration, as was Emily Newell Blair. Nellie Tayloe Ross became director of the Mint. Florence Kerr became an administrator in the Works Progress Administration, and Hilda Smith and Ellen Woodward were appointed to the Federal Emergency Relief Administration.[38]

Eleanor Roosevelt also brought a New Deal to newspaperwomen. On 6 March 1933, just two days after becoming first lady, Roosevelt held the first of 348 weekly Monday morning press conferences for female reporters. Thirty women reporters attended Roosevelt's first press conference, growing to 130 until just before the United States entered World War II. The conferences were informal. Eleanor Roosevelt spoke from a settee, with reporters crowded around her, many seated on the floor. No men were allowed. The conferences were intended to protect newspaperwomen's jobs, which were vulnerable in the Great Depression, by feeding them nuggets of information not available to the men. For example, Ruby Black, the first woman to be hired by United Press after Eleanor Roosevelt insisted on a women-only admission policy, said that the best story from the 29 January 1934 news cycle came from the first lady's press conference. The District of Columbia had just repealed its ban on liquor. Raymond Muir, the chief usher, gave a statement that wine, but not distilled liquor, would be served at the White House. "She brought jobs to jobless newspaper women, raises to some who had been poorly paid, recognition to those who had been shoved in a corner, stimulus to every one," Black wrote of Roosevelt.

Eleanor Roosevelt stated that she would not discuss legislative or political questions at her press conferences but would stick to women's issues and social life. Yet her press conferences over the years included numerous policy statements on issues such as low-cost housing, equal pay for women, old-age pensions, minimum wage and maximum hours laws, child labor, and the Neutrality Act of 1939. She often brought in female New Deal bureaucrats and Women's Division organizers to promote their work.

She invited newswomen to informal White House affairs, such as Sunday night suppers, thereby giving them the opportunity to talk to FDR and overcoming a belief common among publishers that only male correspondents could have inside access to FDR. Moreover, Roosevelt believed a newspaperwoman's role was to interpret for the women of the country what went on in legislative and national life, thereby inspiring their thought formation. Therefore, through the newswomen, she equipped American women with greater insight into civic affairs.[39]

The policy problems surrounding married women and paid employment occupied Eleanor Roosevelt during the Great Depression. When the country debated whether married women should work for pay, the first lady weighed in. She believed that women's wage work should depend upon family needs but affirmed women's right to pursue professions beyond the home. "All men and women have the right to work," she told a radio audience. "Whether they have money or not, those who feel the need and want to do it, should I think be allowed that privilege without question."[40]

Eleanor Roosevelt's bigger concern, though, was for women who were unemployed. On 2 November 1933, she convened the White House Conference on the Emergency Needs of Women in order to glean ideas for possible work projects for women. At the time, between 300,000 and 400,000 women needed help, but only 50,000 had relief jobs. Many relief jobs were heavy construction labor designed by and for men. The conference discussed women's potential jobs in sewing rooms, canning centers, and clerical fields. Many of the projects suggested at the conference became part of women's relief during the remainder of the Great Depression.[41]

The Civilian Conservation Corps (CCC) was started in 1933 for unemployed, unmarried men. On 30 April 1934, Eleanor Roosevelt convened the White House Conference on Resident Schools and Educational Camps for Unemployed Women to gather ideas for a similar women's program. After the conference, the Federal Emergency Relief Administration made funds available, and by the end of the year, twenty-eight schools and camps, enrolling about 2,000 women, were running. Nine schools concentrated on workers' education, four offered vocational training in household management, and the rest offered a general program of recreation, health education, and vocational training. In July 1935, the camps became part of the National Youth Administration. Forty-seven camps enrolling 3,000 students were established in twenty-seven states.[42]

Eleanor Roosevelt believed that beyond providing relief, the camps enhanced women's contribution to democratic society. The camps developed women's knowledge and intelligence by facilitating current-events discussions in a group setting. Women could better see "the whole picture," and this was of tremendous "good to any community to which they return."[43]

Eleanor Roosevelt kept New Deal programs for unemployed women up and running, lobbying Harry Hopkins, director of the Federal Emergency Relief Administration, for continuation of the schools and camps. However, the camps were discontinued in 1937 due to lack of funds, even as the CCC camps for men continued until 1942. But in a testament to her role in assuring the federal government paid attention to unemployed women, Ruby Black wrote to her on 18 August 1946, "I know, too that if you had never lived in the White House, thousands of women would have gone on in misery, and the position of all women would have been further degraded during this passing period of economic stress, as it has in nearly all the countries of the world."[44]

Economically distressed women wrote to Eleanor Roosevelt, as they did to Lou Hoover, asking for material assistance. But unlike Hoover, who funneled requests through a network of women's organizations and private charities, Roosevelt forwarded her relief mail to Florence Kerr and the Works Progress Administration. By piping requests through New Deal agencies, Roosevelt encouraged women to look to the government for solutions. One sample report on her mail from February and March of 1939 stated that all letters "were written by women or were concerned with women's problems." The majority, 850 letters, pertained to employment and were forwarded to state agencies. Over 300 letters requested direct relief, especially hospitalization, and were forwarded to appropriate relief agencies. Over 100 writers asked the first lady to donate money, send discarded clothes, provide hope chests, or advise on personal problems.[45]

Black women were especially distressed. In 1936, Mary McLeod Bethune, a leader in the black woman's club movement and founder of the National Council of Negro Women, was appointed director of the Division of Negro Affairs of the National Youth Administration. Eleanor Roosevelt backed Bethune. On 4 April 1938, Roosevelt convened the Conference on Negro Women and Children in Federal Welfare Programs. Bethune made a presentation to Roosevelt and women administrators of government agencies—sixty-five black women leaders attended—arguing for greater representation of black women across the federal bureaucracy. This call was revolutionary, as black women had never held these positions, nor would they for another generation, providing further evidence that minority women lagged behind white women's expanding citizenship. Still, Roosevelt's conference too was revolutionary. While Lou Hoover introduced a black woman into the White House social sphere, Roosevelt provided the first presidential platform through which black women could air substantive political concerns.[46]

While Eleanor Roosevelt fought for a New Deal for women, she simultaneously fought against the ERA. She lent her weight to keeping the ERA off the Democratic platform in 1940. That year, Republicans became the first party to endorse the ERA. On the eve of the 1940 convention, Dorothy McAllister, chair of the DNC Women's Division, sent an urgent telegram to Roosevelt, asking her for a statement opposing the ERA to be read before the platform committee. Roosevelt responded that until women were unionized to a far greater extent, the ERA would be a great hardship on industrial women workers. The ERA was not included in the 1940 Democratic platform.[47]

Eleanor Roosevelt also tried to sway public opinion against the ERA. In 1944, she condemned the ERA at one of her press conferences. Following her comments, the National Woman's Party, aware of the first lady's influence, asked for the chance to present its case for the ERA. She agreed and invited them and representatives from the Women's Trade Union League to her New York City apartment for a debate. A railroad clerk, a bookbinder, and a test pilot testified against protective laws, while a restaurant worker, war worker, and department store clerk argued for protective laws. The first lady remained unmoved.[48]

Eleanor Roosevelt was not overly concerned about the ERA because she believed it would take a long time to ratify. Her prediction would prove correct. At the time, she took what would later become the conservative position, arguing that a survey of discriminatory and protective laws should be made, and that there should be an effort to get rid of the former and strengthen the latter. She wrote on 11 February 1944, "Women are more highly organized, they are becoming more active as citizens, and better able to protect themselves, and they should, in all but very certain very specific cases which are justified by their physical and functional differences, have the same rights as men." She believed women's physiological differences, especially the maternal function, justified protective laws.[49]

By 1944, concerns about women turning out in droves for Republicans outweighed Eleanor Roosevelt's anti-ERA arguments, and the Democratic platform supported the measure. At this time, however, the ERA was still off the radar of most male politicians. Just three decades later, the ERA would roil the country, especially around the question of whether women should be drafted into military service. Militant pro-ERA activists argued that they should. As the United States was preparing to enter World War II, Eleanor Roosevelt also argued that they should. When she began a question-and-answer column in the *Ladies' Home Journal* in May 1941, she devoted her first article to this question. Though never advocating full combat roles for women, she wrote that girls between the ages of eighteen and twenty-four should be conscripted for one year. Roosevelt wrote that girls "should be placed on exactly the same footing as men, and they should be given the same subsistence and the same wage." At the heart of her argument was women's citizenship. She wrote that military service would "give girls a good opportunity for understanding what democracy really means." Roosevelt was also bothered by women's increasingly "placid acceptance" of men's defense of them in wars. Conscription required women to "stand side by side with the men" and accept part of the burden for defending freedom.[50]

Eleanor Roosevelt's proposal startled many. Some believed she wanted women to join Nazi-style forced labor camps. Roosevelt, though, maintained that her proposal was pragmatic. She also clarified that the compulsory year of service would be most useful for poor, rural girls, who were apt to face dead-end jobs. Even for the wealthy and educated, conscription would allow them to "develop a sense of responsibility for democratic citizenship." Furthermore, since both poor and wealthy women had to face a cold reality of not being cared for by men, Roosevelt believed that conscription would give women a competitive advantage if they had to become breadwinners.[51]

In May 1941, at the same time she was writing about the role of women in the national emergency, Eleanor Roosevelt was considering her own role. That month, FDR established the Office of Civilian Defense (OCD), with Fiorello La Guardia, mayor of New York City, its part-time director. FDR appointed his wife assistant director. He was glad for her to be productively occupied, as many New Deal programs would have to be swept aside, and she believed the OCD could be used to promote social reform ideals during wartime. Before and after her appointment, Eleanor Roosevelt was critical of La Guardia, particularly his focus on creating militaristic volunteer positions, such as air-raid wardens and aircraft spotters. FDR eventually replaced him. Eleanor Roosevelt served in her post for only about five months, from September 1941 to February 1942. Criticism over the jobs and high salaries of several of her OCD appointees, who were also Eleanor Roosevelt's friends, prompted her resignation. Though her OCD appointment was a failure, it marked the first time a president's wife held an official governmental appointment, a position requiring presidential approval. Though it raised questions about the wisdom of a president's wife serving in an official post, for a brief moment she lived out that which she had been advocating all along: women in government service. Her appointment simultaneously set the precedent for the president's wife to serve in an official capacity and caused many to question whether presidential wives should act in this way.[52]

Beyond the volunteer realm, World War II forced many women into the paid labor force. Eleanor Roosevelt added her voice to a patriotic chorus of government and media encouraging women to enter the workforce. Over 6 million women took jobs, wages increased sharply, and women's unionization quadrupled. World War II caused an enormous change in women's economic status.[53]

The change did not come all at once. In the fall of 1942, Eleanor Roosevelt embarked on a month-long alliance-building trip to Great Britain. She left amid a stateside manpower crisis. Surveys of factories in 1942 showed that American plant managers were reluctant to hire women. Overseas, she observed British women doing male industrial labor. Upon her return, she recorded a propaganda piece for the Office of War Information to help end sex discrimination in employment. She said that British "management and labor will tell you that there are some types of work that women do better than men and there are no occupations, except those which require great physical exertion, where women are not being used and used successfully." In Britain, she witnessed women in every type of war production plant, in shipyards, and in the military auxiliary services. Women were accepted as shop stewards and management and labor committee members. In the British military, she saw a twenty-three-year-old woman directing the planes on patrol over the English Channel in an area where they often met enemy planes. This woman would send warnings to towns she thought might be blitzed. Roosevelt wanted American women in similarly substantive jobs.[54]

As the manpower crisis intensified in 1942 and 1943, the government tried to coax married women into war work. But with married women came married women's problems. Women had high rates of turnover and absenteeism. Jobs did not free them from their household responsibilities. Eleanor Roosevelt believed the country had neglected these problems, so she called for more day nurseries for little children. She was disturbed by reports of babies being locked in automobiles, while mothers tried to steal glimpses of their offspring out factory windows. She stated that the United States should adopt the British restaurant idea, whereby municipalities and the Ministry of Food cooperated to set up restaurants to provide one three-course meal per day at a reasonable price, thereby lifting the burden of cooking from women. In her speeches and remarks, she tried to move public opinion to support greater social services for female workers.[55]

When the end of World War II was in sight, Eleanor Roosevelt argued that men and women should have equal roles in shaping the postwar world. Not long before Allied forces landed in Normandy, she argued for equal representation of women in delegations to peace conferences. "This is not only a question of the recognition of women, it is a question of education for citizenship," she wrote. On 14 June 1944, she convened 200 women for the White House Conference on How Women May Share in Post-War Policy Making. Prominent female leaders appealed to women to prepare themselves to serve as decision makers on national and international councils. Just as women stood with men in production lines and the fighting services, so they must work side by side in reconstructing a war-torn world. The conference resolved to take every step to further the "active participation of qualified women in positions of responsibility pertaining to the conduct of public affairs, national and international." And so Eleanor Roosevelt concluded her first ladyship as she started it—arguing that women should get their share of government appointments.[56]

BESS TRUMAN

During the postwar years, women received little recognition from Congress, despite their war work and growing influence within the electorate. It fell to the White House to do something for the women. Political women pressed for recognition through appointments to policy-making posts, and Harry Truman complied. Bess Truman was key to maintaining friendly appreciation within women's political networks, making women feel close to the administration and of value in political life.[57]

Bess Truman is known as a reluctant first lady. She made her distaste for White House life evident to the press and public. When Bess Furman, a reporter covering the White House women's beat, wrote to ask the first lady whether she would have gone to the White House on her own free will, she replied, "Most definitely, would not have." When Furman asked whether being the president's wife was enjoyable, Truman replied, "There are enjoyable 'spots,' it's true, but they are in the minority." A 1952 article in *Collier's* entitled "The Riddle of Mrs. Truman" puzzled over the enigma she remained even after eight years in office. She often looked bored. She rarely gave press interviews. She was unable to relax before strangers. The writer noted that she could not fully retreat from the demands of her office without failing her husband. "She must stay in the picture of the Truman administration." And she did stay in the picture. Female political actors drew her out and kept her active.[58]

Bess Truman's background helps to explain her circumspection. She was born Elizabeth Virginia Wallace on 13 February 1885 in Independence, Missouri, a town of about 3,500 the year of her birth. Though rural, Independence was not an unenlightened backcountry. Her family was well to do, though not wealthy. They moved near the top of elegant society. As a teenager, she benefited from women's movement into interscholastic competitive sport. In high school, she earned a reputation and built confidence as a good tennis player, ice skater, and equestrienne. In 1905, she enrolled in the Barstow School in Kansas City, a college preparatory academy. At Barstow, she earned top marks and was the star forward on the basketball team.[59]

Bess Wallace did not follow her classmates into higher education.

Her father's suicide had turned her mother, Madge Gates Wallace, into a hermit, and Bess moved home to look after her, an occupation that would last until her mother died in the White House. Bess Wallace lived the life of a typical Independence woman, organizing bridge clubs and making clothes for the poor with the Needlework Guild. Women's suffrage was not a popular idea in Missouri, and Harry Truman and Bess Wallace did not count themselves among its proponents.[60]

After a nine-year courtship, Harry Truman and Bess Wallace were married in 1919. He was thirty-five and she was thirty-four, and both were anxious to have children. She suffered a devastating miscarriage during their first year of marriage and then gave birth to her only child, Margaret, at the age of thirty-nine. She became a politician's wife when her husband was elected judge of Jackson County in 1926. While he was out politicking, she stayed home.[61]

When they moved to Washington in 1935 for Harry Truman's first term in the Senate, Bess Truman played the typical role of a senator's wife. With loyalty to her mother pulling her westward, she split her time between Washington and Independence, a routine she continued during the White House years. She also worked as a part-time staffer in her husband's Senate office—first informally, signing letters and reading correspondence. But in August 1941, he put her on the payroll at $2,400 per year, to make up for Harry Truman's meager salary. When Washington became the epicenter of war strategy, she answered Eleanor Roosevelt's call to volunteerism, weekly handing out coffee and donuts at the Washington USO.[62]

When she became first lady, outside forces drew Bess Truman into the administration's work of providing status and recognition to women. India Edwards was a primary force. Edwards, a former newspaperwoman, became politically active after her nineteen-year-old son was killed in World War II. While searching for something to fill the void, she became incensed by Clare Boothe Luce's 1944 Republican convention speech criticizing Roosevelt's war preparedness and decided to work for the Democratic Party. During the 1944 campaign, she did public relations for the DNC Women's Division, writing news releases and speeches. During the Truman administration, she directed the Women's Division and was appointed DNC vice chair in 1950.[63]

Unlike the Roosevelts, who had a wide circle of female activist

friends ripe for political appointment, the Trumans' inner sanctum
did not include such women. Edwards took it upon herself to work for
their appointments. Edwards believed that Bess Truman was the reason the president was open to women appointees. "I never could have
sold him on the idea that we needed women in government if it hadn't
been that he had a smart wife," she stated. For example, Edwards got
Frieda Hennock appointed to the Federal Communications Commission in 1948 and Edith Sampson appointed as delegate to the United
Nations in 1950. She was persistent, even watching out for death notices of federal appointees and then rushing to Harry Truman with a
woman replacement. Edwards often ran up against male opposition.
For instance, she tried to get Florence Allen appointed to the Supreme
Court when a vacancy opened. Truman seriously considered it, but he
reported back to Edwards, "No, the justices don't want a woman. They
say they couldn't sit around with their robes off and their feet up and
discuss their problems." But, overall, Edwards was happy with his record. "He appointed an awful lot of women," she said. Between 1945
and 1952, Truman appointed eighteen women to posts requiring Senate confirmation. Nine of these were to jobs women had never held.
Counting members of commissions, Edwards tallied that he appointed
more than 250 women to substantive positions.[64]

Bess Truman—largely because of Edwards's urging—recognized
the women who received presidential appointments. For example,
Bess Truman was the featured guest at a women-only reception at the
Carlton Hotel to honor appointees Perle Mesta, ambassador to Lux-
embourg, and Georgia Neese Clark, treasurer of the United States.
Edwards organized the gathering. According to one press account, Truman "mingled informally with the guests . . . seeming to enjoy the part
immensely and obviously was in no hurry to depart." Another report
characterized the event as "a celebration for the entire ever-increas-
ing role of women in the American Government" and a "field day for
woman officials."[65]

Though Bess Truman was known for her reluctance, in her letters
she often seemed happy to meet with women's groups. For example,
Edwards threw a reception for Eugenie Anderson, ambassador to Denmark. Edwards chose a Saturday afternoon, since that was the easiest
day for women who work to attend a party. Bess Truman said it would

Bess Truman pays homage to Democratic women. From left to right: Perle Mesta, Bess Truman, Georgia Neese Clark, India Edwards, and Gladys Tillett. Carlton Hotel Photo, Julia King, Courtesy Harry S. Truman Presidential Library.

give her great pleasure to receive with Edwards. After the event, she wrote to Edwards, "I am sure you feel that your tea for Mrs. Anderson was a great success. It undoubtedly <u>appeared</u> to be—and I enjoyed receiving with you."[66]

During the social season, Bess Truman did do a good deal of receiving. On a typical day at the White House, between the hours of four and six in the afternoon, she hosted teas. Notably, the first lady gave Edwards and the Women's Division the privilege of suggesting names of women to be invited to these receptions. Edwards thanked Truman for her "never-failing cooperation and courtesy" in things such as issuing invitation cards for Democratic women to tour the White House. The value of these events was, of course, in rewarding those who sacrificed for the Democratic Party.[67]

Bess Truman's presence did a great deal to bolster Democratic women. Gladys Tillett, vice chair of the DNC, wrote to Bess Truman on 13 February 1947, thanking her for joining them for luncheon. "A number of the government women spoke to me after the luncheon and some of them later called me on the telephone to say how much it had meant to them. . . . You were so very kind to express interest in all that was being accomplished by these women." Tillett also enclosed a list of government women and the positions they held. The next day, Bess Truman replied, "It was not only a delightful one, with so many congenial people there, but also a most interesting one. I learned a great deal about what women are doing in the government and what important cogs they are in the machinery." She also said that she was "delighted" to have the list of government women and was trying to commit to memory what each one did. In all of the above examples, Truman seemed a willing, not reticent, supporter of government women and demonstrated that she was undergoing an education about women in government.[68]

Edwards would sometimes write to Bess Truman to vent about DNC problems. Bess Truman would pass Edwards's concerns on to her husband, thereby acting as a channel of access between the Women's Division and the president, as Eleanor Roosevelt was. For example, Edwards once wrote that she was tired of having to fight with male DNC officers and threatened to resign. Bess Truman handed the letter to her husband, prompting Harry Truman to reassure Edwards that he was anxious for her to stay in her position. And when Harry Truman was dithering about whether to make a Democratic Women's Day speech, Edwards had tea with Bess and told her what the women's vote would mean to the president. He made the speech.[69]

In the spring of 1946, Edwards sponsored a five-part speakers' school for Democratic women, including cabinet and congressional wives. At the request of Gladys Tillett, Bess Truman greeted the participants at the White House for its final session. Edwards told the first lady that most of the women were working hard and enthusiastically at honing their new skills. She held out the fifth session with the first lady as a carrot. She withheld tickets from freeloaders, saying, "I do not feel that they are entitled to go to the White House if they have not attended the other meetings." Here again, the first lady played a role in Edwards's rewards system for political women.[70]

The speakers' school and Bess Truman's role in it were parts of a larger trend. Edwards schooled wives in political rhetoric to get them ready to help their husbands in the 1946 congressional election. After World War II, wives became increasingly important to the success of their husbands' campaigns. Beginning in the 1946 campaign, political wives began to specialize in making appeals to women voters in an unprecedented, overtly public way. To this end, the women party workers began to serve as the wives' handlers.[71]

India Edwards claimed responsibility for getting Bess Truman on the 1948 campaign train. She hounded the DNC chair, telling him that the president had to take his wife and daughter with him. Edwards claimed she was the first female politico to ride on a campaign train. Her connection to Bess Truman gave her access. "I went along to look after the women, and I did," Edwards said. On the train, Edwards wrote speeches. Harry Truman would try them out on his wife, who would critique them. Harry Truman relied greatly on his wife's judgment. Edwards regarded her as one of the best politicians she had ever known.[72]

Bess Truman was deployed on the 1948 campaign train to court the women's vote. Edwards believed that women could decide the election because of their numerical strength combined with the importance of three vital women's issues: peace, prices, and places to live. Under Edwards, the Women's Division was also a publicity machine, creating Truman car decals and organizing grassroots volunteers to ride on housewives-for-Truman trailers. Edwards helped Bess Truman greet those volunteers both on and off the train. Women came aboard to visit with her. She disembarked to attend local women's receptions. In a *Louisville Times* story about one such event, Edwards is photographed peering over the shoulders of a smiling Bess Truman, as she received hundreds of Democratic women workers.[73]

While Bess Truman did accommodate many of Edwards's requests, she declined a number as well. For instance, on the occasion the 1946 Democratic Woman's Day, Edwards arranged for a national broadcast to urge women to register and vote, as she believed American women neglected this right. Edwards implored Bess Truman to speak on the broadcast, saying, "I believe firmly that to have you address Democratic women even for a minute will be of inestimable value to our party. I shall be awaiting your reply with fingers crossed the same way in which I used to cross them when I wanted something very much when I was a child!" But Bess Truman wrote that her husband rejected the plan, saying, "He doesn't think it would be a good thing to do, in view of the fact that I have refused a countless (at most) number of others and shall continue to refuse them." Such a visible appearance crossed the limits of Bess Truman's politicking.[74]

One final act attests to her loyalty in honoring Democratic Party women workers. On 5 December 1952, Bess Truman's mother died in her White House bedroom. That same day, the first lady honored her commitment to receive Women's Division volunteers. After this visit, the women party workers wrote to Edwards of the honor they felt. "The distaff side of the National Committee is deeply appreciative of the opportunity afforded us today to be received by Mrs. Truman at the White House. We know that it was through your efforts that this was brought about and we are most grateful. . . . Friday's visit was a highlight for all of us, and the graciousness of Mrs. Truman, especially under the trying circumstances, [is] something to be long remembered." Undersigned were the names of dozens of women party workers.[75]

That the feting of Democratic women by Bess Truman ever took place is remarkable for another reason. The day before the event described above, an enraged India Edwards had written to Harry Truman to complain that she had been excluded from a White House meeting to which lower-level DNC male officials had been invited. She wrote, "If it is correct that women voters this year turned to the Republican Party, perhaps action of this sort on the part of our men leaders might be one reason for women's interest in a change of administration. . . . As a woman, I resent the continual, whether intentional or thoughtless, by-passing of women when policy is being discussed, and I know millions of women share this resentment." Though Edwards had made many inroads, women still had a way to go in reaching the innermost sanctums of politics.[76]

On 27 January 1953, the DNC announced that the Women's Division would be dissolved. Officials believed it would give Democratic women the opportunity to achieve their postsuffrage goal of equal status with men in party work. "I was told, not consulted," Edwards wrote to one party woman about the abolition of the Women's Division. While Edwards liked the theory underlying the plan, she believed that neither men nor women were ready for it. "We will have to be like the boy who is thrown into the deep water and has to swim or be drowned," she wrote. Edwards said that the decision meant women would no longer be planning and educating. They would not have a budget or make important decisions. It would also have implications for the first lady's role.[77]

MAMIE EISENHOWER

At the time the DNC Women's Division was abolished, the RNC Women's Division was also on the chopping block. The diminishing role of these divisions dovetailed with another trend. By the 1950s and 1960s, the candidates' wives had supplanted female party workers as the most prominent campaigners for the party ticket and were recognized as important to the success of their husbands' campaigns. Mamie Eisenhower's expanded campaign role reflects these trends.[78]

In 1952, for the first time since women won the right to vote, women were given credit for working together to elect a president. A highly visible campaign—launched by the still functioning RNC Women's Division, the Citizens for Eisenhower grassroots organization, and local and national Republican women's clubs—was instrumental. Prominent Republican women went on speaking tours, while countless ordinary women addressed envelopes, campaigned door to door, and arranged cooperative child care so that more women could volunteer. The hordes of women who worked on the campaign were imbued with a sense of civic responsibility and general purpose. They were defining a public role for themselves. These trends also raised the campaign profile of Mamie Eisenhower.[79]

Born Mamie Geneva Doud on 14 November 1896, she was the last first lady born in the nineteenth century. Her father made his money in meatpacking and was a millionaire by age thirty-six. He relocated the family—Mamie, her mother, and Mamie's three sisters—from her birthplace in Iowa to Colorado, where they integrated into Denver high society. From 1914 to 1915, she attended Miss Wolcott's School, a finishing school. Mamie never did undertake rigorous academic study, and her father did not care about grades. He thought Mamie should learn how to run a large home with servants. She took ballroom dancing and learned how to sew and embroider, preparing items for her hope chest. Though Colorado extended the franchise to women three years before Mamie Eisenhower was born, the Doud women were aloof from politics.[80]

The Douds wintered in San Antonio, Texas, where Mamie made her society debut in 1915. There she met Dwight Eisenhower, who was stationed at an army base nearby. Her parents approved of Eisenhower but warned their daughter that she would never have the lifestyle to which she was accustomed. But Mamie did not care. "I wanted that man," she said.[81]

As an army wife, she lived in temporary housing all over the United States and abroad—Panama, Kansas, Texas, the Philippines, Paris, and Washington. She believed that her job was to make a nice family life for her husband and her son. She did this by separating home life from work life. "You see, when we were first married, a wife never went near headquarters. You never went to his place of operation. You were not allowed in that building. I suppose that started me out early on that course," she recalled. Nor did Dwight Eisenhower bring his problems home to Mamie. Recalling the impact of her upbringing on her first ladyship, she said, "In all of the eight years that Ike was President, I don't think I ever went to his office over three times, and I was invited each time. It never occurred to me just to run over there off-hand, because I wasn't brought up that way."[82]

Mamie found companionship with other military wives, especially during World War II, when Eisenhower was overseas for three years and eventually was appointed supreme commander of the Allied forces. She and other army wives lived at the Wardman Park Hotel in Washington. Citizens would write her letters, and Mamie would answer them. The press also hounded her. Her celebrity was rising along with her husband's.[83]

The heart of the 1952 campaign was an eight-week, forty-five-state whistle stop tour. Inside the campaign train, Mamie Eisenhower's role was to greet Republican committeewomen and local volunteers. Katherine Howard, secretary of the RNC and Eisenhower campaign strategist, also traveled on the train. As Howard described her own role, "I was part of the policy staff but also I had responsibility for meeting and greeting all of the women who came on, and taking them in to see Mrs. Eisenhower." Howard shuffled groups back and forth to Mamie Eisenhower all day, every day. Howard was impressed by how Mamie Eisenhower charmed the women. "She's awfully good, you know. Army wives get to be this way, chatty, and she could chat and make conversation and make them all comfortable and happy," Howard said. Howard recalled a time she pointed out a mother whose son had died in the war, and Mamie Eisenhower took the woman aside and had a special word with her. These personal interactions won her many admirers.[84]

The women's conversations with Mamie Eisenhower were not political, however. Finding out what women were "stewed up about" was Howard's job. When the women climbed aboard to see Mamie Eisenhower, they would usually "bring her flowers or a cheese or apples or something" and they would chat about "what a pretty country it was." Light, local topics were Mamie Eisenhower's specialty.[85]

Mamie Eisenhower did some whistle stop campaigning on her own once when her husband branched off for a three-day stretch. Howard recalled that Mamie was the first candidate's wife to ever campaign on a train alone. When she stepped off the platform to greet a cheering crowd, she said, "Didn't you know Ike isn't here?" They replied, "Yes, we did, we came down to see you." She chatted with the people, signed autographs, and handed out Ike buttons. The candidates' wives were indeed becoming more and more important.[86]

Like Bess Truman, she also mingled with party women off the campaign train. For example, Mamie Eisenhower and Pat Nixon, wife of the vice presidential candidate, received 3,000 women at a tea put on by the Women's Republican Club of Massachusetts. "They'd look at Mamie and they just seemed to be sort of transfixed, her personality was such, and Mamie would shake hands with them and chat with them, and then they'd go on and they'd be in sort of a daze and they didn't half see Mrs. Nixon . . . they were still so overcome by Mamie," Katherine Howard recalled. At this particular reception, Howard's job was to keep the line moving along, but Eisenhower admonished her, "Don't do that, Katherine. I want to talk to them." Howard was so astonished, she said, "Mamie, I think you could shake hands with 3,000 women and make them all feel that you care." To which Mamie replied, "Why, Katherine, I do."[87]

In January 1953, Bertha Adkins was appointed director of the RNC Women's Division. During the Eisenhower years, Adkins was the primary person to further women's political integration. Though the RNC Women's Division dissolved later that year, Adkins was appointed assistant chair of the RNC. In that position, she encouraged women to pursue political careers and orchestrated regular breakfast sessions between Dwight Eisenhower and female leaders. As India Edwards had done, Adkins urged Eisenhower to appoint well-qualified women to high-ranking posts. She also encouraged grassroots canvassing and fundraising as a way to bring emerging political women into contact with the candidates and public.[88]

"It was my responsibility to work with [Mamie Eisenhower] in bringing women's groups for tea and receptions in the White House," said Adkins. That this was part of her portfolio shows that Mamie Eisenhower's teas and receptions were not just social affairs. They were intended to reward women's political work and goad them into future service. This language of political repayment and stimulation is peppered throughout correspondence between Mamie Eisenhower, Adkins, and women's political groups.

In her receptions as on the campaign train, Mamie Eisenhower was grace and charm personified, according to Adkins. Adkins recalled how at one such reception, a female guest told the first lady it was her birthday. The first lady leaned over and kissed her on the cheek and wished her a happy birthday. "Oh, this woman was just on cloud nine," Adkins recalled. Mamie Eisenhower was master of the warm, spontaneous gesture.[89]

Press accounts regularly tabulated the number of hands Mamie Eisenhower shook. For example, *U.S. News and World Report* estimated that during her first social season she shook hands with an average of 600 to 700 people per day. At the Daughters of the American Revolution reception, she shook 2,000 hands. At the reception for wives of the U.S. Chamber of Commerce reception, she shook 1,600 hands. The press gave her high marks. "For each caller she has or contrives a bright, seemingly-individual smile. Her handclasp is firm. She often adds warmth to it by placing the left hand over the right." Women's goodwill toward the administration was transmitted through these handshakes.[90]

In the spring of 1953, Mamie Eisenhower's warm handshakes were extended to 1,400 members of the RNC's women's conference, a political and policy training camp coordinated by Adkins. Following the visit, Adkins wrote to Mamie Eisenhower, "Without a doubt, visiting the White House was of special interest to the women and they left with a feeling of friendship that comes only from personal contact." She noted that every woman delegate expressed appreciation for the first lady's cordiality and deemed it a "highlight" of their program.[91] The first lady had created a welcoming link to the White House for these female party workers. Contrary to insinuations that hard-working party women were bitter about the glamorization of campaign wives, Mamie Eisenhower's correspondence indicates that female politicos were thrilled and inspired by her attention.[92]

Mamie Eisenhower personally tended to the receiving line details. She was petite in stature, and she wanted to be set apart so her guests could see her. She tried various arrangements. Chief Usher J. B. West and the carpenters constructed a small platform for her to stand on. She also tried standing on the bottom step of the grand staircase. According to West, she delighted in these receptions and could charm anybody she met. "If there were a thousand people going through the line she'd have a thousand little items of small talk for them," he said.[93]

Receptions for women's groups marked Mamie Eisenhower's typical afternoon during her first year in office. The groups were diverse, ranging from farming women to women with doctoral degrees to Illinois Republicans. She did this because she wanted to meet the president's constituents, and they wanted to see her. She did not serve them food or cocktails, aside from occasional liqueurs with coffee. Sometimes she would have large teas. The groups were so large that she used the Green Room, Blue Room, and Red Room to greet them. "It gave me insight into the people of the United States, because there are all types, and to me that was interesting," she explained. She also said that the receptions were her own initiative. When asked if her husband coordinated her liaison work she replied, "Oh, no! No, these were women that came to see me. . . . I was the hostess to these ladies. Ike was working over in his side of the building."[94]

Their spheres, however, were actually not as separate as she claimed. Mamie Eisenhower's receptions were pure constituent relations. She functioned as the White House public liaison to women's groups. In 1954, Charles Willis, assistant to Sherman Adams, chief of staff, even suggested that Mamie Eisenhower hire a new staff person, complete

with an office in the Executive Office Building, to work as liaison between the first lady and women's clubs. Adams dismissed the idea, so
the proposal went nowhere. But that the idea was even circulated in
the West Wing shows how political her links to women had become.[95]

The West Wing actually did coordinate with the first lady to bring
women's groups to the White House. For instance, Wilton Persons,
Dwight Eisenhower's congressional liaison, at the request of Francis
E. Dorn, congressman from New York, worked with the first lady to
bring twenty-four female party workers to the White House. Dorn
considered these women important and told the West Wing staffers of
their wish to meet the first lady. Persons, at the behest of Olin Teague,
congressman from Texas, also arranged for Mamie Eisenhower to greet
twenty-three South American women who were on an agricultural tour
of the United States so that they could bring favorable reports back
to their countries. Persons also arranged for Mamie Eisenhower's visit
with the Women's Republican Club of Middlesex County, New Jersey,
which was credited with helping Eisenhower win the normally Democratic county. Though the West Wing coordinated their visits, it was
not the president these women were interested in seeing. They specifically requested an audience with the first lady. They were interested in
her, and she inspired their work.[96]

Since it was the job of the congressional liaison to move forward
Eisenhower's legislative program, visits with Mamie Eisenhower were
sometimes a reward for favorable votes. William H. Ayers, congressman from Ohio, wrote to Jack Martin of the congressional liaison staff
to request that sixty "hard-working gals" in his campaign organization
greet the first lady so that they would be encouraged to "go back home
and push even more doorbells." When Martin urged the first lady to
accept the invitation, he noted that Ayers had made a speech on the
House floor changing his position on a recent tax bill to line up with the
president. Mamie Eisenhower received them.[97]

Though Bertha Adkins was primarily interested in rewarding Republican women, she coordinated with other groups as well. For example, Adkins arranged for the Maryland branch of the National Woman's
Party to greet the first lady. The pattern was always the same: Adkins
petitioned, Eisenhower accepted, accolades followed, political women
left inspired.[98]

Ahead of the meeting, the National Woman's Party had forwarded ERA literature to Mamie Eisenhower. Dwight Eisenhower supported equality in the abstract but did not want to be perceived as meddling in social reform. His support for the ERA remained tepid, though both Republican and Democratic platforms endorsed it in 1952 and 1956. But on 25 October 1956, in front of a packed house at Madison Square Garden, President Eisenhower promised to "assure women everywhere in our land equality of rights." Republican women were very pleased with this statement.[99]

Though first ladies of this era mainly liaised with middle- and upper-class white women, Mamie Eisenhower was attuned to the budding civil rights movement. When she reinstituted the White House Easter Egg Roll, which was paused during World War II, she made sure that it was racially integrated for the first time. She hosted a White House reception for the National Council of Negro Women, of which she was an honorary member. Eleanor Roosevelt facilitated the conference that included them, but it was not held at the White House. Mamie Eisenhower welcoming them into the head of state's house was an important symbolic move. She also invited Lucille Ball to the White House while she was on Senator Joseph McCarthy's list of suspected communist sympathizers. *I Love Lucy* was one of Mamie Eisenhower's favorite television shows. On 19 January 1953, over 2 million more people watched Ball's television birth than tuned into Eisenhower's inaugural address the next day. This was during a time when CBS would not allow the word "pregnancy" to be broadcast. Similarly, when Mamie underwent a hysterectomy in 1957, it was considered a private matter and referred to in the press as an operation "typical of women her age." Yet, as Ball's television birth indicates, change was afoot.[100]

In the 1954 campaign season, Mamie Eisenhower campaigned for Ellen Harris, a female congressional candidate from Denver, Colorado. Harris chartered a bus and hung an elephant's trunk from its front and a tail from its back and painted blue eyes on the windshield. Mamie Eisenhower followed the bus in a Chrysler limousine. When the bus parked, the first lady climbed aboard for some retail politicking. She pinned a Harris-for-Congress button on her coat, ate donuts, and greeted constituents, mostly housewives, who came onto the bus. Eisenhower even slipped her arm around Harris's waist and said to her audience, "Ladies, I hope you'll all vote for her. We women have to have a voice in things." Harris lost her uphill battle to unseat the Democratic incumbent. However, a record seventeen women were elected that year, up 25 percent from the previous session and nearly 50 percent from ten years prior. Mamie Eisenhower understood that women were making inroads to elected office, and she supported their efforts.[101]

Mamie Eisenhower also acknowledged women's increasing leadership in the public arena. She wrote a letter to the winners of the *Woman's Home Companion* awards for the most successful women. Among the honorees were a poet, teacher, actress, clubwoman leader, cancer research scientist, and United Nations delegate. She wrote, "It is most appropriate in the middle of our century that the work of the distaff side of American leadership be recognized and applauded. . . . We can all take pride in the forward steps women have taken during our own generation to a role of leadership in community and even national affairs." She further noted that their accomplishments attested to women's increasingly important place in American life.[102]

Mamie Eisenhower's congratulatory letter touched on important changes in women's lives in the 1950s. Women sought to have an identity outside the home, especially after their child-rearing years had passed, and they continued to enter the job market. Forty percent of all women over age sixteen held a job. The proportion of working wives had doubled from 15 percent in 1940 to 30 percent in 1960. During this time span, the number of mothers at work jumped from over 1 million to over 6 million. Educated, middle-class wives spearheaded this growth. With inflation and consumerism on the rise, these women workers labored for luxuries, such as new homes, children's college tuition, restaurant meals, and household equipment. Plus, many women enjoyed the socialization and recognition work outside the home provided. Mamie Eisenhower understood women's need for self-expression, as well as budgeting difficulties and the desire for extra luxuries that characterized the 1950s. Consistent with Republican beliefs, she felt that the decision to work was entirely up to the individual woman.[103]

Eisenhower's record on women appointments was solid for the time. It exceeded Truman's, with twenty-eight women named to posts requiring Senate confirmation. Including members of commissions, Eisenhower's female appointees numbered over 400. With a movement for more women in government underway, pressure was also mounting on the first lady to do more. "A lot of people of course thought Mamie ought to do conferences and big luncheons at the White House," said assistant White House press secretary Anne Wheaton. The first lady would soon be swallowed up in this push for bigger roles for women in government.[104]

JACQUELINE KENNEDY

While Jacqueline Kennedy did not take up the mantle of putting on big White House conferences and luncheons, her tenure did embody shifting roles for women. She was born Jacqueline Bouvier on 28 July 1929 in Southampton, New York into a world of privilege. Her parents, John and Janet Lee Bouvier, divorced when she was young. Her mother, who remarried wealthy stockbroker Hugh Auchincloss, raised Jacqueline and her sister, and the family split its time between estates in Rhode Island and Virginia.

Jacqueline Kennedy's official 1962 White House biography listed her hobbies. These included painting, reading, collecting art books, photography, and sports such as riding, tennis, swimming, and water skiing. These aristocratic avocations were developed during her formative years and impacted her first ladyship. She attended Miss Porter's School in Farmington, Connecticut, from 1944 to 1947 and then Vassar College from 1947 to 1949, spending her junior year at the Sorbonne in Paris, France, where she studied languages and art history. She finished her education at George Washington University, graduating in 1951. While there, she won *Vogue* magazine's competitive "Prix de Paris," for which she designed an original magazine issue. The reward was a year-long position as a junior editor for the magazine. Her mother, however, made her turn it down. After college, Jacqueline Kennedy got a job as an inquiring photographer for the *Washington Times-Herald* and covered the coronation of Queen Elizabeth II. In 1953, she married Senator John F. Kennedy.[105]

Though these biographical bullet points seem straightforward, there were many contradictions playing out behind the scenes. Intellect collided with femininity among college-educated women of her generation. These women were encouraged to work hard and get good grades but also not to appear overly brainy and scare off prospective beaus. Jacqueline Bouvier was intellectually curious and capable. Yet, in public, she often put on an air of docility. If she seemed to dither between these qualities, she was no different than other educated women of her era. Female college graduates in the 1950s also did not easily shift into domestic life. When she could have led a postcollege life of leisure, Jacqueline chose to take a newspaper job earning just $42 per week. Even women with small children often desired to put their knowledge and skills to use.[106]

In the 1960 campaign, Jacqueline Kennedy was pregnant again. She had suffered a miscarriage in 1955 and delivered a stillborn daughter in 1956. Her daughter, Caroline, was born in 1957. Though the role of candidates' wives had expanded, Jacqueline Kennedy could not endure the physical strain of campaign travel. At the same time, Democratic women had lost their influence and access to the candidate. Previously, the candidate's wife had provided party women with the access to campaign travel and, thus, the candidate. But JFK, preferring his male advisors, refused to allow Margaret Price, who was coordinating women's activities at the DNC, to travel with the campaign. India Edwards remarked that under JFK no one at the DNC had any real influence on women's affairs.[107]

"America's women are evidencing such heartening interest in issues and personalities of national import," Wade Nichols, editor of *Good Housekeeping* magazine, wrote to Letitia "Tish" Baldrige, Jacqueline Kennedy's social secretary, on 21 February 1962. With the magazine having a total circulation of 12 million women, he would know. He cited the magazine's "campaigns for water fluoridation, pre-marketing proof of drug efficacy, and sane nutritional and diet programs" as proof. He wanted Jacqueline Kennedy to contribute columns on international affairs, education, and literature to his magazine. Women were becoming interested in policy, and the first lady was being coaxed into the arena.[108]

By the 1960 campaign, not even Jacqueline Kennedy's pregnancy could exempt her from the policy arena. Though she never became a *Good Housekeeping* columnist, during the campaign she did pen a regular column called "Campaign Wife," which connected women with New Frontier policy proposals. A product of the DNC publicity division, the columns were made available to newspapers. This marked the first time a candidate's wife promoted candidates and campaign themes.

"This week I decided one way to keep from feeling left out was to talk through this column to the friendly people all over the country I would have met while campaigning," Jacqueline Kennedy wrote in her first "Campaign Wife" column on 16 September 1960. She related how anxious she felt watching the convention vote on television and said that she was reading several newspapers every day to keep up with her husband's activities. She told readers that her obstetrician firmly objected to her going on the campaign trail. Active campaigning was now expected of a wife, and Jacqueline Kennedy needed to provide a doctor's excuse for her absence.[109]

Jacqueline Kennedy also bolstered the work of the Women's Committee for the New Frontier, an arm of the campaign charged with calling women's attention to policy proposals. Eleanor Roosevelt was a member along with leading women experts in various policy areas. At her Georgetown home, she held panel discussions. "Our discussions and recommendations will serve as a continuing source of information for my husband," she wrote in "Campaign Wife."[110]

In October 1960, the campaign launched Calling for Kennedy, an initiative to gauge and then highlight issues of particular concern to women. Volunteer teams went door-to-door administering a questionnaire. Jacqueline Kennedy launched the campaign. Before a meeting of 200 Virginia precinct workers convened at an Arlington Holiday Inn, she telephoned chairs of Calling for Kennedy programs in states across the nation to kick off the drive. "One woman is worth 10 men in a campaign!" she told the volunteers, echoing her husband. The thousands of forms collected by the volunteer canvassers were then analyzed by the DNC. A special daytime television broadcast, "Coffee with Senator and Mrs. Kennedy," aired on 2 November 1960. During the first part of the show, Jacqueline Kennedy showed family pictures, and then she asked her husband some of the questions the women had returned on the Calling for Kennedy surveys. She also reported the results of the survey. She said that women were foremost concerned about peace. Next came education, medical care for the aged, and cost of living. Listening parties were organized around the country for women to gather together in living rooms and watch the program. Jacqueline Kennedy attended one, hosted by her mother.[111]

As radio had done, television opened a new avenue for women to hear about public affairs in their homes. Jacqueline Kennedy sponsored listening parties for the Kennedy-Nixon presidential debates, the first ever to be televised. Organized by Margaret Price of the DNC, listening parties were not intended to be mere social gatherings. Jacqueline Kennedy and others used the slogan "Join in the great debate" to encourage women to attend. Fact sheets about the four issues identified as of particular concern to women—peace, education, cost of living, and medical care for the aged—were furnished to sponsoring groups and served as the basis for discussion. For the first debate, Jacqueline Kennedy gathered national committeewomen and their husbands in her Hyannis Port, Massachusetts, home. "I wanted to hold the first listening party to encourage people around the country to do the same. . . . There has not been an encounter like this since the Lincoln-Douglas debates and all good citizens should watch it. Every woman who comes promises that she will hold a listening party of her own for one of the next three debates and ask 10 friends," she wrote in "Campaign Wife." She hosted another listening party for the second debate and was with her husband in New York for the third.[112]

Jacqueline Kennedy used her experience as a mother as an entrée into policy discussion. For example, in her 6 October 1960 edition of "Campaign Wife," she confessed her worries over where to send Caroline to school and lamented the overcrowded classrooms in schools around the nation. "It does seem imperative that the federal government step in and do its share," she wrote. In her column, she also advocated higher pay for teachers and touted her husband's legislative record on education.[113]

In 1960, Benjamin Spock was the country's most famous doctor. In 1946, he published *The Commonsense Book of Baby and Child Care*, and in the following six years it sold 4 million copies to anxious postwar parents. The care he prescribed emphasized the child's psychological state and deemphasized rigidity, urging parents to relax and trust their instincts. "Along with most mothers in the country, I have read his books and admire him greatly," Jacqueline Kennedy wrote in "Campaign Wife." Spock had stopped by her Georgetown home near the end of the campaign. They talked policy. "He is most anxious that there be immediate legislation to build more schools and provide for higher salaries for teachers. I'm glad to say, he believes that Jack is the man best qualified to build on a realistic program in these fields," she told readers. Spock's seal of approval meant something to mothers nervous about the health and safety of their children.[114]

In 1960, the issue of medical care for the aged had reached a tipping point. Jacqueline Kennedy told her readers that many citizens had written her on the issue. In October 1960, the Women's Committee for the New Frontier issued a report on medical care, and Jacqueline Kennedy related its findings. "The report stressed the importance of paying for increased medical care through the social security system rather than requiring that older people pass an income or means test in order to get medical benefits," she wrote. She explained that this was a way for people to contribute to their own care while they worked, making it sound like less of an entitlement program. Such policy statements were new for a candidate's wife.[115]

Seventeen days after her husband's narrow victory, Jacqueline Kennedy gave birth to her son John Fitzgerald Kennedy Jr. via cesarean section. She spent the transition recovering in Palm Beach, Florida. Just after she was discharged from the hospital and before she left for Palm Beach, Mamie Eisenhower gave her the customary tour of the White House. What she saw surprised her. The pieces in the public rooms did not date earlier than the major renovation that occurred during the Truman administration. When the Truman renovations were winding down, just $210,000 remained in the funds for decorating sixty-six rooms. So when high-end New York City department store B. Altman & Co. offered the Commission on the Renovation of the Executive Mansion to provide furniture, rugs, draperies, and accessories for the White House at absolute cost, plus provide interior decorating services for free, they accepted. Even before the Truman renovation, nothing in the State Rooms, save for a set of candlesticks, two clocks, and some paintings, had remained from the first 100 years. Some objects from presidential households had been relegated to basement obscurity. Others had been given away, auctioned, sold, or had vanished. Many former White House treasures were nestled in private homes, inns, and taverns across the country. For Jacqueline Kennedy's Palm Beach reading, she requested books on the White House interior from the Library of Congress. After the inauguration, she continued her childbirth recovery in the White House, keeping a sparse public schedule but reading and studying in her upstairs bedroom, crosschecking references to White House furniture and bibelots. Her plan for a White House restoration project was taking shape.[116]

As in the practice of public policy, Jacqueline Kennedy began by identifying a problem and studying it, then articulating a goal or vision, devising a solution, and finally executing a plan. One month after the inauguration, she announced the establishment of the bipartisan Fine Arts Committee for the White House, a subset of the federal Fine Arts Commission. Jacqueline Kennedy said the purpose of the committee was to locate authentic period pieces and raise funds to purchase them, whereupon they would be permanently placed in the White House. No furniture was to be placed in the executive mansion until it had been selected, authenticated, and photographed by the bodies of experts.[117]

"It would be sacrilege merely to 'redecorate' it—a word I hate. It must be *restored*—and that has nothing to do with decoration. That is a question of scholarship," Jacqueline Kennedy told Hugh Sidey, who wrote a feature on the restoration for *Life* magazine. Sidey noted that she "assigned herself" the restoration as the "major task of her career." He referred to Jacqueline Kennedy as a detective and a spelunker, her work as shake down, her demeanor as calculating. His descriptions portray professionalism. Jacqueline Kennedy's depict substance.[118]

The Fine Arts Committee had trouble acquiring furniture at first. Jacqueline Kennedy recounted in a letter to Arthur Schlesinger that all the potential sellers or donors were "scared it would be mistreated or disappear—until we got that law passed." The first lady here is referencing Public Law 87-286, which she pressed members of Congress to adopt. The law established the White House Historical Association. A West Wing press release crediting the first lady for establishment of the association stated that its mission would be to enhance visitor understanding, appreciation, and enjoyment of the White House. The law required the principal corridor on the ground floor and its public rooms to be preserved and curated as a museum. Furthermore, it ordered that articles of furniture, fixtures, and decorative objects of historic or artistic interest be considered the inalienable property of

Jacqueline Kennedy opens the newly restored Treaty Room. From left to right: Senator Everett Dirksen, Jacqueline Kennedy, Vice President Lyndon Johnson, Senator Mike Mansfield, Maureen Hayes Mansfield, and archivist of the United States Wayne C. Grover. Abbie Rowe, White House Photographs, Courtesy John F. Kennedy Presidential Library and Museum.

the White House. In other words, nothing could be sold or given away. When historic objects were not on display or in use, they had to be transferred to the Smithsonian Institution for exhibition or storage.[119]

Jacqueline Kennedy initiated and helped author the first White House guidebook, *The White House: An Historic Guide*. She told Arthur Schlesinger that the guidebook was "desperately important," and she pushed for it against a tide of opposition and apathetic support staff. Some members of the public and the executive branch believed it sacrilegious to have money change hands in the White House. She recalled, "And so, when I told Jack that, you know, he'd had more opinions saying not to do it, but he listened to me and said, 'All right, go ahead.'" Restoration could not go on without money. Jacqueline Kennedy wrote to Arthur Schlesinger, "We have to get this finished soon so it can be printed by this spring and we can make some money—it is where all our funds will come from—more hemming and hawing has gone on for a year with everyone thinking someone else was doing it." She got especially frustrated with Lorraine Pearce, the first White House curator, because, according to Jacqueline Kennedy, she would always go off "to have tea with other curators" instead of sitting down to work on the project. The first lady and Schlesinger worked together to get the book in print. Jacqueline Kennedy agonized over every detail, hunting for examples in guidebooks for Mount Vernon and the Palace of Versailles. She was also not above receiving credit for the guidebook. Pearce had drafted the first introduction, which the first lady characterized as "ghastly—uncoordinated and conceited." As Jacqueline Kennedy wrote to Schlesinger, "JFK says that I should write short introduction—then I don't have to be mentioned in the text—which I find offensive." She told Schlesinger, "I so badly want it to be something we can be proud of—that scholars will want instead of students."[120]

JFK was interested in his wife's restoration project. Jacqueline Kennedy said that after the tours started going, he would come home and rave about the masses of people coming through. He was "riveted," she said, when she uncovered, from beneath a muddle of electronic equipment in the White House broadcast room, the Victorian desk made from the oaken wood of the HMS *Resolute*. It was a gift sent by Queen Victoria in 1880 for the recovery and safe return of the British ship abandoned in the Arctic. "I was so happy that I . . . could do something that made him proud of me," she said. As she conceived it, this was her first job since the start of her marriage.[121]

The restoration project was an innovation to the first lady's role. Jacqueline Kennedy lobbied Congress and her husband and influenced legislation. She acquired funds and used government money to solve a problem. She worked with a presidential commission and West Wing staffers. She put to use her education and expertise. The first lady's work was expanding into the public domain along with women in the country.

Jacqueline Kennedy, however, did not build on the public liaison activities of Mamie Eisenhower. She had no desire to meet Democratic women and felt no need to supercharge their labor with a handshake and smile. "If she had one failing—not actually a failing but, but let's call it a lack of enthusiasm—it was a reluctance to spend a lot of time with women's groups," Letitia Baldrige, her social secretary, wrote. Women's groups constantly badgered Baldrige for a White House reception. Baldrige would beg Jacqueline Kennedy to comply. Kennedy would hedge. If a group was large enough, she would sometimes acquiesce. But then she would often cancel at the last minute, claiming sudden ill health. Baldrige "lived in fear that the press would catch her playing hooky, riding her horse out in Virginia, when she should be at one of these women's receptions." Baldrige's number-one substitute was Lady Bird Johnson. The first lady's staff dubbed her "Saint Bird" because she would always rearrange her schedule to help them out.[122]

One reason Jacqueline Kennedy could get away with spurning women's groups was that the Women's Divisions were no longer a force in party politics. There was no India Edwards to educate and needle her about the importance of Democratic women's groups. Letitia Baldrige, her closest White House aide and gatekeeper of her calendar, was not a party woman. Baldrige, who came from family of Republicans and was a registered Republican, had met the future first lady at Miss Porter's School, and the two attended Vassar together.

Jacqueline Kennedy also considered her restoration work to be of real importance, and she was adamant about prioritizing it. Her 8 June 1962 letter to William Walton is illustrative. She was trying to convince Walton to head the Fine Arts Commission and advising him on how to lessen the administrative headaches of the position. Citing her own experience, she wrote, "I just told Tish—who nearly died from the shock—that I would NEVER go out—lunches, teas, degrees, speeches, etc. For 2 months there was a flap—Now it is a precedent established." She also advised Walton to appoint a deputy to do the ceremonial things like going to museum dinners. As an example, she said the president of France did the wreath laying, which freed the prime minister to do "all the vital things." She advised that some "pushy creative" would adore being so deputized. Furthermore, Jacqueline Kennedy wrote to Walton, "To save the old and to make the new beautiful is terribly important." These were her priorities. Restoration was the vital thing. Receptions with women's groups were ceremonial fluff, tantamount to wreath laying, something to be delegated to a subordinate.[123]

It was first substitute Lady Bird Johnson, not Jacqueline Kennedy, who hosted the reception for the delegates of the President's Commission on the Status of Women after their first meeting. Though Jacqueline Kennedy's White House years did reflect women's expanding sphere, she did not have much to do with the commission, her husband's most important legacy on women's rights. Having Lady Bird Johnson receive the group was fitting. Though JFK authorized the commission, it was Lyndon Johnson who had more vocally supported its objectives and regularly attended its functions.[124]

Secretary of Labor Arthur Goldberg, who recommended the president establish the commission, wrote that women were "combining activities in the home with outside work to an increasing degree," noting that over twenty-four million women had jobs outside the home. He stated that women's earnings were lower than those of men, an average of $3,300 annually in 1960, or about three-fifths of men's wages. Women were not able to make full use of their skills, creative ability, or professional training. Women's situations had changed greatly since they won the right to vote in 1920. According to Labor Department statistics, in 1920, there were over 8 million women workers; in 1960, there were over 22 million women workers. In 1920, the average woman worker was single and twenty-eight years old; in 1960, she was married and forty years old. In 1920, women earned 16,642 bachelor's degrees, 1,294 master's degrees, and 93 doctoral degrees; in 1960, they earned 132,000 bachelor's degrees, 23,600 master's degrees, and 1,000 doctoral degrees. The numbers of stenographers and saleswomen had increased, while women farm workers had sharply declined. Women were moving into a variety of occupations. They were becoming nurses, office workers, researchers, technicians, librarians, and social workers.[125]

On 14 December 1961, JFK issued an executive order establishing the commission, proclaiming that prejudices and outmoded customs acted as barriers to the full realization of women's basic rights. He appointed Eleanor Roosevelt chair and Esther Peterson, head of the Women's Bureau in the Department of Labor, its executive vice chair. Its prominent members were old reformers. JFK charged the commission with making recommendations on laws affecting women. In its final report, the commission recommended the elimination of sex bias in the civil service, as positions could be labeled "men only" or "women only." It denounced discrimination against women in private employment, endorsed the maintenance and expansion of protective labor legislation, recommended an extensive day-care program, and affirmed women's need to expand their horizons through education. It also ruled that, since the Constitution already embodied equal rights, the ERA was unnecessary. Eleanor Roosevelt died before the final report was presented, which was on her birthday and just forty-two days before JFK was assassinated.[126]

After the assassination, Jacqueline Kennedy took up residence at 3017 N Street in Georgetown. It was to this address that Lyndon Johnson sent her an invitation to a reception for newly appointed women in government. Johnson, acknowledging her hard work and expertise, had appointed her a member of the Committee for the Preservation of the White House. He wrote, "It is because you make women stand taller in the eyes of the world that we hope you can be with us on this occasion." As the reception heralding government women and Jacqueline Kennedy's invitation indicate, change was happening, and the Johnson administration was capitalizing on it. A movement for women's full political and legal equality was rumbling underfoot, soon to burst forth into a full-fledged movement.[127]

CHAPTER TWO *The Stable Society*

66 Since the family is the basic social unit of our national life, it naturally follows that that which is good for the family is good for the nation," wrote M. S. Wilson, head of the New Deal Subsistence Homestead Program, in 1935. Alongside their citizenship activities, first ladies bolstered the home and family. These actions highlight responses to different trends in women's political engagement. This chapter explores how first ladies acted through their roles as wives, mothers, housekeepers, and consumers in the conditions of depression, war, and postwar uncertainty. Through their actions, first ladies sought to bring about social consolidation, stability, and security.[1]

LOU HOOVER

The name of Hoover used to be synonymous with food security. After Germany invaded Belgium in 1914, Herbert Hoover commanded food relief efforts, saving millions of Belgians and French from starvation. After the United States declared war on Germany in 1917, he was appointed food czar in Woodrow Wilson's new Food Administration. Lou Hoover made speeches persuading housewives to economize on food in the national interest, an effort that became known as Hooverizing. She was credited with creating the Hoover apron, a cotton housedress worn over an everyday dress and designed to lower laundry bills.[2]

The autumn of 1929 began the first full formal social season of the Hoover administration, and fashion fads and clothes plans were on the minds of Washington women. Just weeks before the stock market crash, Washington was aflutter with the official visit of Ramsay MacDonald, British prime minister. The style pages delighted over Mrs. Hoover's soft blue velvet gown with a two-foot train.[3]

The fashionable flapper disappeared from popular culture as the country entered a new politics of scarcity. The Great Depression sparked renewed debate about private matters, including family dynamics, household work, and personal life. There was great concern that families might fall part, destabilizing social foundations on top of an already crumbling economy. The need for a labor-intensive family economy emphasized the housewife who did it all herself. Saving the family required enhancing the emotional well being of spouses and children, while salvaging family finances required competency in housekeeping. Lou Hoover's public housekeeping during this time of insecurity reflected those needs.[4]

Lou Hoover used her Girl Scout platform to instruct the nation in homemaking. While scouting emphasized citizenship preparedness on the one hand, it also taught girls homemaking skills. As Louise Stevens Bryant, secretary of the Girl Scouts, wrote:

> Do you believe that girls should like to work at home, to cook and clean house and mind the baby? Do you believe that a girl should like to take care of her clothes and be able to make them; that she should know how to be thrifty and conserve the family money in buying and using food and clothing? If you do, you believe in the Girl Scouts, for in this organization the girls learn all these things in such a happy way that they *like* to do them.

According to Bryant, the top five Girl Scout badges awarded from 1919 to 1920 were home nurse, laundress, first aid, needlewoman, and child nurse. These emphases were also evident in Lou Hoover's educational actions.[5]

Homemaking instruction was centered in the Girl Scouts Little House in Washington, D.C. Its purpose was to provide hands-on instruction in child rearing, cooking, and gardening. Lou Hoover ceremonially broke ground for construction of the Little House, built in 1923 to commemorate Better Homes in America Week. When it had to be relocated off government property a few years later, she personally paid the moving expenses. As first lady, she continued her support, planting a rock garden and donating plants and flowers. She connected its work to women-focused government agencies. For example, Lou Hoover attended a Little House meal planned by food specialists of the Bureau of Home Economics in the Department of Agriculture. Intended to publicize low-cost food guidelines, the meal cost less than twenty-four cents per person. Lou Hoover once characterized the Little House as the halfway house between the playhouse of childhood and the home every girl hopes to achieve. She believed that the Little House could gratify "the feminine urge, which begins way back in the mud-pie days, for domesticity, cooking, playing with dolls, for having one's own spot where mothers may be imitated in every household pursuit." Her patronage caused the idea to spread. Approximately seventy other such houses were operating by the early 1930s.[6]

Lou Hoover believed the Girl Scouts' homemaking education could be put to use in crisis situations. Before an audience of Red Cross volunteers, Hoover boasted about the heroic homemaking of Girl Scouts after a recent California earthquake. She recalled how Santa Barbara housewives tried in vain to get breakfast cooking on front yard campfires until the Girl Scouts appeared "like a flying squadron of kitchen coaches." She said that "in almost every yard a uniformed Scout could be seen building the fire in regulation manner, frying the bacon and boiling coffee." Furthermore, she believed that Girl Scouts could benefit from Red Cross training and that its emphasis on home hygiene and care of the sick would offer "an ideal opportunity for the development of her womanly qualities."[7]

While Lou Hoover did not make herself readily available for press interviews, she broke this rule during the annual Girl Scout conventions. In an interview during the 1930 Indianapolis convention, she told reporters that the housewife who stands at the kitchen sink washing dishes three times a day is no less courageous than the big game hunter. Encouraging steadfastness in the midst of domestic chores was intended to buoy those who might be lured away by the outdoor adventure the Girl Scouts also promoted.[8]

Women during the Great Depression had to adapt how they ran households and cared for families. Local support networks affected levels of family hardship. As breadlines lengthened, Lou Hoover called on troops to take stock of the service side of scouting. To the 1931 Girl Scout convention, she praised troops for "holding sewing and knitting meetings" and "canning and drying fruits and vegetables for winter consumption of the poor in their neighborhood," as well as "holding rummage sales . . . for their community chest." She praised Girl Scouts for providing wholesome activities for children and the unemployed. Responding to material and mental needs fortified the family against a deteriorating economy.[9]

In a press interview after her speech, she urged American women, the family purchasing agents, to keep spending money, lest they throw the whole economic machine out of gear. Applying her own economic recovery theory, she said, "The White House windows will need new curtains within the next year or two. I suppose the frayed edges might be cut and made to do. But the man in Washington who would make the new curtains is having a difficult time. An order for curtains for the White House windows—they are so awfully big—would be of considerable help to him." Her White House actions were intended to give guidance to female purchasing agents across America.[10]

Lou Hoover's fashion choices were even tied to economic recovery. A style columnist reported that Washington women were following Hoover's lead by patronizing home industries. Hoover had made it a practice to wear gowns that were made in America and fashioned from American goods, such as the black velvet dress she wore to an army and navy reception during the 1931–1932 social season.[11]

Proficient with the knitting needle, Lou Hoover made headlines when she contributed five warm woolen dresses, several children's sweaters, and a pair of soft woolen sleeping boots to the Needlework Guild of America in the late autumn of 1932. A press report connected this to her welfare work, noting that the first lady was practicing what she was preaching about relief work.[12]

In a radio address to 4-H boys and girls on 7 November 1931, Lou Hoover issued a call to action for children to enhance the emotional stability of their families. Amid the widespread agricultural and industrial problems, she said, "Indeed some of us will find the greatest problem is the problem of our own family." She told the children to cheerfully do without and not give in to worry. She said that children's attitudes could either help or hamper efforts to survive the coming winter months. "There is nothing much more discouraging than a moody complaining child," she admonished. She told them to take notice of neighborhood need, tactfully share toys and goodies, and increase dinner invitations.

Your one time calf may have reached the stage of being a milk cow this year, and you may have a quart or more of milk every day to take to the family whose baby or old grandmother actually needs it. You may have apples or root vegetables of your own which will keep well, or fruit or green vegetables which you have canned, which you can share with someone less well provided. . . . Or you girls who know how to sew may help remodel or make new garments for, <u>or with</u>, those who are not going to be able to buy new ones this year.[13]

The tone and message of this 4-H address was notably different from her pre-crash one, in which she urged boys to take an interest in home-making. When she addressed the Girl Scouts in October 1932, she also echoed the themes of family stability. Once again praising the contributions of the Girl Scouts, Lou Hoover told her audience assembled in Virginia Beach, "In many homes the morale of the family has been buoyed up by the cheerfulness and confidence of Girl Scouts." The radio transmission of her address ultimately failed, however, because of a break in the long-distance telephone line, minimizing any electoral impact it may have had.[14]

ELEANOR ROOSEVELT

While many families turned inward for sustenance during the Great Depression, uncertainties swirled around the family unit. Birth rates declined. Miseries abounded. The basic problem of the family revolved around the question of how to reestablish security. The New Deal was a seminal moment in the history of the American family because for the first time the federal government became a major guarantor of family welfare.[15]

While Eleanor Roosevelt encouraged women's citizenship outside the home, she always said family came first. Between 1900 and 1920, domestic help was becoming rare. A widespread "mother's movement" restructured women's domestic roles according to new professional and scientific standards. This movement gained national recognition when Eleanor Roosevelt's uncle, Theodore Roosevelt, hosted the White House Conference on Child Welfare in 1909, prompting the adoption in 1914 of the Smith-Lever Act, which provided funding for home demonstration agents to train housewives in scientific methods of homemaking. Concurrently, the Progressive movement, to which Eleanor Roosevelt had hitched herself, initiated a variety of measures intended to help the family adjust to modern conditions. Its buzzwords included education, government regulation, and professional expertise. The government was granted new authority to stabilize marriage and the family, a power that Eleanor Roosevelt's first ladyship would come to embody. This section illustrates how Eleanor Roosevelt, through her public speaking and writing, instructed women to be stabilizing forces in their families.[16]

Weeks before FDR's inauguration, Eleanor Roosevelt took to the airwaves to urge women to view government as housekeeping on a larger scale, so that they would understand that "taxes are the key note to the results which come through government and actually touch their homes." A mother should know about government services and whether they are services for which she is willing to pay taxes, she said. The vigilant housekeeper should become interested in schools, health, sanitation, and the environment, she argued as she sought to make the connection for American women between their homes, children, and the state.[17]

In 1933, Roosevelt published a book entitled *It's Up to the Women*. Part encouragement, part admonition, and part instruction manual, Roosevelt explained how women should bear their privations with pilgrim-like fortitude while carrying on the work of their homes. To the rich woman who lost her luxuries, she wrote, "If you have never sewed except to give your idle hands some occupation, it is somewhat disconcerting to find that . . . your sewing must serve some useful purpose such as mending a frock or darning your stockings." To the majority of women, who were living on moderate incomes and enduring wage cuts, she said that the crisis "may not mean actually less food, but it does mean cheaper food" and "endless little economies and constant anxiety [about] the family budget." But having little money, she wrote, caused families to draw closer together and sacrifice for one another. The "clan spirit" fostered when families clung together was a great force, protecting both family and country from threats inward and outward.[18]

She filled her book with housekeeping tips. She provided daily sample menus and recipes used at the White House. For example, for a Monday breakfast, she recommended whole-wheat toast with butter, milk for children, and coffee for adults. For lunch, she recommended meat loaf, creamed potatoes, a lettuce salad, stewed prunes, whole-wheat bread with butter, and milk for children. On the dinner menu, she placed scalloped tomatoes with cheese, whole-wheat bread with butter, Scotch wafers, and cocoa, giving only weak cocoa to young children. On clothing, she advised women to buy investment pieces. "For instance, for me it pays to buy a rather expensive tailored suit, made to order," she wrote, "as I am not a size for whom it is easy to buy ready-made things, and I wear it a long time." On children's health, she declared that every young person should have a periodic examination by a doctor and daily recreation out of doors. She told families with young children not to economize on milk.[19]

Eleanor Roosevelt believed child labor prohibition and minimum-wage and maximum-hour laws promoted the health of the modern industrial family, as reformers and home economists believed harsh labor conditions caused physical and mental strain to the family unit. In the early 1930s, there were over 2 million children at work in fields ranging from agriculture to domestic service. She raised awareness about these conditions, such as boys as young as six years working twelve-hour days stripping tobacco. She chided American women for not paying enough attention to the issue, saying, "I wonder if the women of America have really ever faced this problem which is after all fundamental to the growth of our country mentally and physically?" She lobbied for a constitutional amendment banning child labor. Though that was never adopted, the Fair Labor Standards Act of 1938 eventually regulated child labor.[20]

Eleanor Roosevelt lobbied housewives to spend more rationally. Recognizing that women purchased the vast majority of goods and that manufacturers marketed products to appeal to them, Roosevelt believed that women had the power to revive industry. As a reformer, she instructed women to find out under what conditions goods were made and refuse to buy things that were made under poor conditions. On the matter of clothes, for example, she urged women to look beyond garments that were cheap and appealing and instead buy simpler clothes with good workmanship that did not "represent the grinding down of our sisters." Both the national consumer consciousness and women's working conditions impacted family security.[21]

Farm families were especially vulnerable during the Great Depression. While the New Deal created a vast system of farm relief, Eleanor Roosevelt addressed the plight of farm homemakers. In her extensive travels around the country, she saw many worn-out women aged beyond their years because of hard farm living. Many farms lacked running water and electricity. Women scrubbed dirt-caked farm clothes and soiled diapers on washboards and boiled them in vats. Farm wives hauled logs from outdoor piles for woodstove cooking. Homemakers were simultaneously responsible for onerous housework, child care, and fieldwork. The Great Depression caused young women to migrate to the cities. Unable to find work, many returned disgruntled at the prospect of life as an overworked, unpaid farm laborer. Roosevelt counseled farm mothers and fathers to "make their homes centers" where young people could enjoy simple recreation, taking assistance from government-sponsored home demonstration clubs.[22]

Eleanor Roosevelt believed cooperative homesteading could help families. Her Arthurdale, West Virginia, resettlement community was the ultimate manifestation of this belief. Interested in how West Virginia coal mining families were falling far short of minimum standards for security, in August 1933 Eleanor Roosevelt drove alone to Scott's Run, a formerly prosperous mining community with large families of eleven or twelve children. The community was idle, its workforce devastated by the Great Depression. FDR believed the West Virginia miners and those similarly situated could be helped through the Subsistence Homestead Program, for which the National Recovery Act had appropriated $25 million. Rural industrial communities and partial-subsistence homesteads were regarded by some as the greatest potential contribution that the New Deal made toward solving the problem of American families at the intersection of agriculture and industry. Planning and cultivating family gardens, for example, provided interesting constructive occupation and psychological benefits. Work centers for handicraft production for family use and exchange provided a forum for esthetic expression.[23]

After FDR had delegated the Arthurdale homestead to his wife, it

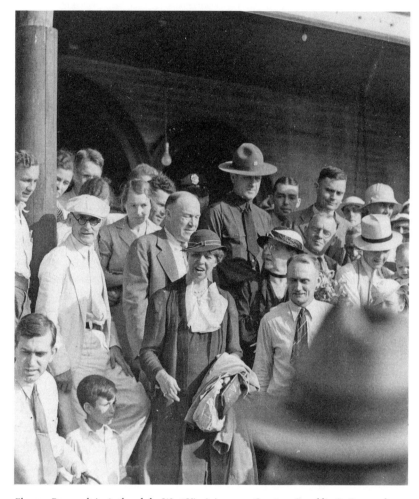

Eleanor Roosevelt in Arthurdale, West Virginia, 1933. Courtesy Franklin D. Roosevelt Presidential Library and Museum.

quickly became her so-called baby. Resettling its first residents in November 1933, she dedicated substantial effort to the project, immersing herself in every detail and commuting there often. She wrote about Arthurdale in her "My Day" syndicated column. For example, on 3 December 1936, she reported that the chicken farm was doing well, the entire output of eggs sold to the state sanitarium. The pig cooperative had also done well, she reported, and the dairy cooperative was about to commence. She wrote of the craft shop, where she bought Christmas presents, and of the tearoom, where she lunched. The latest forty prefabricated houses were delightfully livable, she proclaimed. She concluded that Arthurdale was a shining example for preplanned communities across the nation.[24]

There were many mistakes in Arthurdale. The prefabricated houses had deficiencies and drew fire. Money was spent wastefully. Critics harped on every blunder, the first lady's presence magnifying negative publicity. Yet, for all it lacked, Eleanor Roosevelt believed it served its main purpose, which was to give its 200 families real security.[25]

Then as war became increasingly inevitable, Eleanor Roosevelt's speaking and writing on families shifted to maintaining stability amid international turmoil. In September 1941, she wrote that the primary role of women in national defense was to see that their homes met the demands of the national emergency. They must encourage the men, whether they were serving in the military or working in the fields, that they were saving the American way of life from the totalitarian rule of Hitler. They must be conscious consumers, educating themselves and organizing against inflation. They must help in nutrition programs, disseminating knowledge about what families should eat.[26]

Eleanor Roosevelt believed that women were more responsible than men for building the morale of the nation because they could instill democratic values at home. But if women were to challenge their families to make wartime sacrifices and endure hardships, then, according to Roosevelt, they must understand that which they defend, which was a government responsive to the will of the people and resolved to the pursuit of happiness for every individual. In 1940, she published another book, *The Moral Basis of Democracy*, to help women understand why democratic government was worth defending. A fusion of history, philosophy, and religion, her brief treatise traced the development of democracy from the Magna Carta, while championing individual liberty and defending a Christlike love for neighbor against totalitarianism. Only with this understanding of democracy could women strengthen families and, by extension, national morale.[27]

Not only were women primarily responsible for the family's emotional health, Roosevelt said that women's other main wartime objective was to keep their families physically well. This entailed choosing food for its nutritional value and carefully buying and skillfully preparing it. She told women to be sure all family members got sufficient sleep. She believed that every woman should take Red Cross nursing courses, which provided the knowledge of sanitation needed to prevent epidemics.

Homemakers were primarily responsible for coping with wartime shortages and rationing, and they were barraged with advice on how to conserve. Roosevelt advised every woman to sign the U.S. government's Consumer's Pledge. "I will buy carefully. I will take good care of the things I have. I will waste nothing," it read. Modeling responsible homemaking for the nation, Roosevelt took the Consumer's Pledge together with her White House staff. In "My Day," she reported head housekeeper Henrietta Nesbitt's plan to take the food left over after big parties and deliver it to a farm cooperative, where it could be used to feed animals. She said every woman must participate in war drives to collect scrap metal, rubber scrap, and tin cans. These materials—even lipstick containers—could be used to build tanks and ships. And every woman must put 10 percent of her income into war savings stamps and bonds as a way of sharing in national defense.[28]

To purchase war bonds, she instructed women to give up little luxuries—a bar of candy, an ice cream soda, cigarettes, or a trip to the theater. Pennies invested during wartime meant arms and ammunition, tanks, airplanes and guns, thereby promoting the safety of military family members. She addressed war bonds and stamps in a radio broadcast in the fall of 1942 after she returned from Great Britain. She praised the work of one British women's organization near Canterbury, where every member assessed herself a threepence per week to buy wool to knit for the merchant marines, saved sixpence a week for stamps, and allotted the remainder to charities. To Roosevelt, British women provided an example of rationing and privation in civilian defense their American sisters should emulate.[29]

The British Women's Voluntary Service for Civil Defense coordinated the country's domestic war work. Eleanor Roosevelt envisioned that the Office of Civilian Defense (OCD) could perform a similar role. While Roosevelt's job at the OCD was the first time a president's wife held an official government appointment, it was simultaneously an outgrowth of her efforts to organize the government to promote family security, this time in the context of war preparedness. Eleanor

Roosevelt envisioned that she would take charge of recreation, health, welfare, family security, education, and other community services, putting people to work in places like nursery schools and homes for the elderly. Though she directed her charges to men, women, and children together, she believed women had a particular role in civilian defense. And many of her civilian defense efforts, before, during, and after her tenure at the OCD, were directed to women specifically through their roles as homemakers.[30]

"You are a very important part of the defense of our nation when you contribute to the well-being of your home," Eleanor Roosevelt stated a radio address to the Camp Fire Girls. She encouraged the girls to find meaning in their homemaking projects by tying them to civilian defense. Growing your own food and preserving it for later use, she said, is an example of civilian defense. She told them that there was nothing more important they could do to strengthen their community, and therefore the nation, than to improve their homes—making them more attractive, restful, and pleasant.[31]

In 1944, with Allied victory on the horizon, many began to ask the first lady what would become of the female industrial workers. Many doubted whether there would be enough jobs for both the women and returning veterans. Eleanor Roosevelt believed that after the war the main job of the average American woman would be what it always had been—to marry and nurture a home and children. She said that women in trades and professions, if they were married, would have to either subordinate their desires for work outside the home or arrange for proper child care, though she doubted anyone could replace a mother. Reflecting a concurrent trend, Roosevelt also maintained that it would be acceptable for some women to work if their families needed the money. With inflation and consumerism on the rise, society justified wives working if their employment was primarily directed to helping the family. Nevertheless, as reflected in the concerns citizens expressed to the first lady, World War II had opened a new area of potential activity to women, thereby creating new anxieties about families in postwar America.[32]

BESS TRUMAN

World War II both strained American families and reinforced government responsibility for American family life. When soldiers returned, new physical, economic, social, emotional, and psychological challenges appeared. Couples got married younger and had more children. The white middle class moved to single-family homes in the suburbs, thereby weakening kinship ties. Women refocused on childrearing and homemaking. As one psychologist wrote, "The focal point of life after the war will be the home. . . . If happy adjustments can be made at the family level, happiness will flow through all the affairs of the country. If the family fails, it might well be impossible for industry and government to succeed." This philosophy guided the actions of postwar first ladies.[33]

The presidential family modeled the successful, stable family unit. India Edwards understood this. In the November 1948 edition of the *Democratic Digest*, she wrote that since the Good Neighbor policy was the foundation of international relations, to have a family in the White House that could be genuinely described in this manner was an asset to the whole nation. The Trumans were just the kind of family you would like to have next door, wrote Edwards, as she tried to convey their friendliness and hospitality. For example, she detailed how the Truman women graciously sampled local delicacies they were offered at campaign stops, from Colorado brook trout to Nevada peaches. She told readers they were much better looking in person than in photographs. With the presidential family front and center, appearance and personalities mattered. Edwards described Bess Truman as "more retiring and shy by nature than her husband or daughter" but "nonetheless friendly and charming."[34]

Bess Truman struggled to balance public demand for personal information about the first lady with her own desire for privacy. In her memoir Edwards wrote that Bess Truman was "a lady in the old-fashioned sense, belonging to the school who believed that it was permissible to have one's name in the paper only when one was born, married, and died." Bess Truman also had not trusted the press since her father's suicide by gunshot made front-page news. The *Jackson Ex-*

aminer recounted the gruesome details, including how the bullet had passed through his head and landed in the bathtub.[35]

In the postwar years, there was incessant demand for the minutiae of presidential family life. This was a new phenomenon, driven by postwar readjustment. For example, around this time, *Good Housekeeping* ran a series of articles highlighting the intricacies of wives of men in public life. One such article, entitled "If You Were Mrs. Eisenhower," stated, "Your wedding ring is platinum with diamonds going halfway round. On your left arm you wear a wrist watch, on your right a gold charm bracelet. . . . The charms make a complete history of your husband's career; among them dangle a shield, a helmet, a gas mask." Also, your husband "will eat anything but parsnips" and is "allergic to fish," though he "eats onions, in the raw, between two slices of bread. Likes them, too." The press wanted such information from Bess Truman.[36]

Postwar prosperity required new guidance for middle-class, particularly white, women. The press hounded Bess Truman's staff for tidbits, begging for interviews and dispatching questionnaires. Personality stories on the president's wife were in high demand, and reporters wanted to zero in on the intricacies of White House life, such as these excerpts from inquiries made by reporter Dorothy Williams: About what time does Mrs. Truman get up? Is she an early riser, like the president? Breakfast in bed or where? What is a typical breakfast menu? To what extent does she check over housekeeping problems with the staff? Does she ever suggest the china for the functions smaller than state dinners? Does she ever say that blueberries and cream would be a good breakfast fruit now that blueberries are in season? What sweets does she prefer? Does she ever shun sweets because of calories? Would she tell us roughly what she weighed when she entered the White House and what she weighs now? Does the family ever lunch together? After dinner, are there any opportunities for family evenings? Does she knit or sew?[37]

Despite the constant barrage, Bess Truman remained tight-lipped, frustrating women reporters. In an article entitled, "Behind Mrs. Truman's Social Curtain: No Comment," *Newsweek* printed the first lady's brusque responses to a series of written questions, such as this excerpt: "*Q. What is Mrs. Truman's conception of the role of first lady?* No comment. *Q. What qualities innate or acquired does she think would be the greatest as-*

set for the wife of a president? Good health and a well-developed sense of humor. *Q. If such a thing were possible, what special training would she recommend to prepare a woman for the role of first lady?* No comment. *Q. Any special professional background?* Skill in public speaking would be very helpful. *Q. Does she think there will ever be a woman president of the United States?* No. *Q. Would she want to be president?* No."[38]

Bess Truman's demure approach departed markedly from Eleanor Roosevelt's. An article entitled "Back to Normalcy" stated, "Mrs. Harry Truman, the unassuming wife of the president, has intimated that she will not follow the publicity pattern of her predecessor. There will be no press conferences, no 'my day' summaries, no radio chit-chat, no platform appearances." This had implications for social stability. "Mrs. Truman does not feel she has anything to contribute to national security, so she clings to the traditional domestic security in the house of which she is now mistress." The article argued that the great majority of Americans would approve of "this homesteading woman who leaves to her president husband the business of meeting representatives of the press." Bess Truman had restored domestic "normalcy," or separate spheres, to the White House.[39]

While Bess Truman had learned to be skeptical of publicity, this move was also strategic. Charlie Ross, White House press secretary, wanted only a narrow channel of communication between Bess Truman and women reporters. He specifically did not want her to emulate the press relations of Eleanor Roosevelt. When the *World Almanac* had erroneously printed that Bess Truman had followed the custom of Eleanor Roosevelt in holding press conferences, Ross wrote to the publisher to correct the error. He said that it pained him to read such a misrepresentation in one of his favorite guides to wisdom.[40]

In the beginning of the Truman administration, Ross met with Bess Truman's staff to figure out how to "dispose of a great many individual inquiries which are now coming from the women correspondents" and "eliminate much future annoyance." They discussed a question-and-answer session, followed by a tea, with women correspondents. All questions related to public affairs would be barred, and questions would be limited to social and personal matters. In May 1945, Bess Truman did have the women reporters to tea in the upstairs quarters to give a few details about the their home life and hopefully placate them. The meeting was off the record, and Bess Truman was ill at ease, disliking the press invasion into her private life. So, the more gregarious Margaret Truman was recruited to ensure a pleasant flow of conversation.[41]

Bess Truman's staff often deferred to Ross. On 9 August 1946, Reathel Odum, Bess Truman's personal secretary, sought Ross's opinion on two requests for written statements from the first lady. One was from a handwoven textiles group requesting Bess Truman write a forward to a booklet and another was from a public relations firm requesting a statement lauding the small-town American family. Odum told Ross that thus far the first lady had written nothing except brief greetings and congratulations to groups. In reply, Ross wrote, "I think both of these requests should be turned down."[42]

The press typically covered Bess Truman's activities, even those that expanded women's citizenship, from domestic angles, including food, family, and festivities. In the fall of 1945, a friend of Bess Truman's had convinced her to host a group of cabinet wives and prominent Washington women, including Mamie Eisenhower, to study Spanish in order to help foster international goodwill. Study groups were an old tradition in Independence. Under the tutelage of a Spanish professor, the study group convened weekly in the White House Library. Truman took the course seriously, but she complained to her husband and daughter that the other wives treated it more like a social occasion. So did the press. For example, one press report covered the courses from the food angle, detailing how after lessons they learned how to whip up Spanish-style luncheons. The report noted that the wives would "do the marketing—everybody sharing in the expenses as at a church supper—the cooking, the serving." The women would scour markets for the ingredients and then join Truman in the kitchen for the grinding of beef, pork, lamb, almonds, raisins, olives, and hot spices for picadillo. The wives also learned how to make Cuban-style black coffee by using cheesecloth and letting it simmer.[43]

Press coverage of receptions organized by India Edwards for women appointees often zoned in on fashion. At one Democratic reception, a report speculated that Bess Truman had recently shed twenty pounds and noted that she wore an understated blue-black crepe frock enhanced by a pearl necklace. "Pearls also gleamed on her off-the-face hat which consisted of a circle of white and the palest of pink flowers combined with green veiling." India Edwards wore a "street-length" gown with lace inserts, and a "black velvet ribbon accented her large black straw hat." The tea service was set atop a long table with a huge arrangement of lavender and yellow blooms. Francis Perkins, the sole female serving on the Civil Service Commission, poured tea, having "discarded her usual tri-cornered hat for a sailor type one of black straw with a matching ruffle."[44]

Bess Truman's actual days and hours as first lady were focused on her family and domestic responsibilities. At eight in the morning, the family breakfasted together. From nine until one o'clock, the first lady worked on mail and conferred with her housekeeper on menus and the details of housekeeping, as well as with her aides on plans for social affairs. At one in the afternoon, she would usually lunch with family. The rest of the afternoon was her personal time. She would write letters in longhand and visit with friends. Then there were the late afternoon official teas during the social season and finally dinner with family or an official dinner.[45]

A letter from Harry Truman to his wife on 10 June 1946 neatly summed up what she was to him and his presidency. "Well, I miss you terribly," he wrote. "No one to see whether my tie's on straight or whether my hair needs cutting, whether the dinner's good, bad or indifferent." In other words, she did what millions of other women did after the war. She focused on keeping her family well dressed, fed, and happy.[46]

MAMIE EISENHOWER

"In the White House lives a loving, happy family. Our first lady is a woman of charm and simplicity, whose only ambition is to serve her country in the way she knows best—her care and devotion to the husband we call 'President,'" Bertha Adkins said these words as the 1956 election approached. She believed that women voted for Eisenhower in 1952 because they wanted security, thrift, and integrity. Mamie Eisenhower's actions rounded out this image.[47]

While she had never been a suburban housewife, Mamie Eisenhower came to the White House equipped to model postwar living for American women, particularly middle-class white women. Throughout her career as an army wife, she lived in a range of conditions, from cockroach-infested quarters to a French mansion. As a young wife, she learned how to budget and economize. Mamie Eisenhower turned orange crates into dressing tables, covering them with thumbtacks and cretonne. She picked furniture, such as a rattan chaise and octagon-shaped table, from a dump pile. She did not have a diaper service or a dishwasher. She would go to great lengths, hauling groceries up a hill instead of taking a taxi, to save a quarter. During World War II, as her husband's profile rose, she knew she was being minded and wanted to set a good example to the other wives who had been left behind. She never went anywhere to dine, never patronized a nightclub, never was around alcohol, and never sent any subpar clothes donations to churches.[48]

When she was deciding what she wanted to do as first lady, the legacy of Eleanor Roosevelt was still fresh in Mamie Eisenhower's mind. As Bess Truman had before her, Eisenhower purposefully decided to take a different path. As Anne Wheaton would later recall, "I think she was cognizant enough of what was done during the FDR days," and she had no desire to be Eleanor Roosevelt. But her path was also not the same as Bess Truman's. Mamie Eisenhower did not hide from the press and publicity. She publicized her choices and activities in dress, dining, and domesticity and so responded to the interlocking trends of social consolidation, family stability, and consumer culture of 1950s America.[49]

As we have seen, Mamie Eisenhower's politicking inside the campaign train was tailored to wooing active party women. But outside the train, on the rear platform before the crowds, her performance was designed to portray strong marital bonds. At the conclusion of each whistle stop speech, Dwight Eisenhower would say, "And now meet my Mamie." She would emerge from a door and stand behind her husband, waving heartily to the cheering crowds. A campaign aide in the parlor just behind the platform would blast the romantic ballad *The Sunshine of Your Smile*. One journalist covering the campaign noted how, during Dwight Eisenhower's public speeches, Mamie would gaze at him "with a truly rapt and beautiful smile." If the smile was sincere, he concluded, "Mamie must still be deeply in love with her husband after 36 years—a condition which warmly draws the crowds to her." The reporter said the crowds found her presence "somehow reassuring."[50]

On the campaign train, there were cars filled with correspondents— newspaper reporters, radio and television technicians, and photographers. Mamie Eisenhower would often meet the women reporters who were on board in the dining car of the train. She would not talk public issues, but she did talk about what she liked, how she was writing to her son then stationed in Korea and "just telling about the habits of a very sweet American mother." Part of Anne Wheaton's job was to promote Mamie Eisenhower and everything relating to her, such as articles in magazines and newspapers and press interviews. Anne Wheaton recalled the story behind the iconic shot of the Eisenhowers in their pajamas. The campaign train stopped in a town at six in the morning. A large crowd had gathered, and Dwight Eisenhower, still in his pajamas, insisted on going out to speak to them. So, he and Mamie threw their robes on. Mamie tied a ribbon around her head and into a bow. When they stepped out to greet the crowd, one of the wire photographers ran out and got the shot. The picture captured the spirit of the times, portraying marital intimacy and Mamie's femininity. The pajama photo also illustrates how personalized the campaigns had become.[51]

Citizens for Eisenhower, the grassroots organization that helped draft Dwight Eisenhower to run for president in 1952, used Mamie Eisenhower's domestic life in its broadcast spots to appeal to women voters. One ad began, "Women who have both personal budgets and national budgets so much on their minds these days may be interested in what Mamie Eisenhower has to say about budgeting." The transcript recounted advice that her father gave her before her wedding, that a family's independence and the husband's pride depended on how wives managed money. Mamie Eisenhower said, "Ike has always given me his paycheck and my pride in that responsibility made me stretch it to cover our expenses. . . . So long as he had razor blades and cigarettes, he did not mind stew instead of steak at the end of every month, if it made my accounts come out even." Another spot entitled, "Mamie Eisenhower . . . Bride," targeted newly married women who were struggling to make ends meet. It told how she managed on Ike's meager salary in a two-bedroom apartment that lacked a stove and icebox. Inside the nonworking fireplace, she built shelves on which to display his books. She made curtains to conceal the pots and pans, also stored on the bookshelves. In family budgeting as in national budgeting, Mamie

Eisenhower told women voters that leaving and cleaving could best be achieved if a young couple had no debt.[52]

Dwight Eisenhower spoke often about the value of women to the 1952 campaign. In his platform and stump speeches, he argued that the country must return to spiritual values and moral standards, saying that the "comprehension of these deep values by our women, the mothers of our children, is necessary if we're going to correct the things that are wrong with us." He believed this was necessary to overcome the destruction of war and threat of communism. At his inauguration, after taking the oath of office, Eisenhower broke precedent by kissing his wife. He also broke precedent by starting his inaugural address by asking his audience to bow their heads and join him in prayer. It had also been customary for the president and vice president to ride together in the inaugural parade. But Dwight Eisenhower chose to ride with Mamie. The presidential marriage and values it embodied were front and center.[53]

In March 1953, Mamie Eisenhower held a press conference. Bess Furman of the *New York Times* threw out the first question. She asked about the most interesting thing the first lady had done at the White House. Mamie Eisenhower replied, "You mean, so far as the furnishings." She went on to describe the rooms in the living quarters that presidential families were free to personalize. For example, she told how she had her bedroom walls painted a calming green color and added pink furniture. Pink was her favorite color, and she used it liberally in her décor. The women reporters pressed her for more. What shade of green was it? Have you changed the draperies? Is President Eisenhower's furniture still Drexel French provincial? And (to laughter) do you now have enough closet space? The press women knew Mamie Eisenhower did not have enough closet space. As J. B. West commented, "Never, before or since, has a first lady had quite so many clothes!" The staff had to convert third-floor storage rooms into closets, which then overflowed with the first lady's dresses. She preferred full-skirted ones by designer Mollie Parnis and creative hats by Sally Victor. While she owned a few Paris gowns, she also ordered inexpensive dresses and hats from department stores. They also asked her about the details of her daily schedule. Eisenhower told about her morning activities, which were spent working from bed on White House domestic matters. In her pink and green bedroom, she would first peruse the morning paper. Then she would order her breakfast tray around eight, also requesting two fresh bouquets of pink rosebuds and pink carnations. She would go over the menus for the day and for any upcoming entertainments and then confer with the housekeepers, ushers, and her secretary, Mary Jane McCaffree, and take care of all household business by noon. Mamie Eisenhower believed every woman over fifty should stay in bed until noon. As we have seen, her afternoons were mainly devoted to meeting women's groups.[54]

Eisenhower received only one overtly political question at her press conference. A reporter asked, "Mrs. Eisenhower, are you following any legislation on the Hill with any degree of special interest? For instance, this bill that would exempt working mothers from paying a tax . . ." The first lady cut off the questioner, saying, "I have read, and I have listened to the comment over the television . . . and have been interested in the tax reduction—like who hasn't." In 1953, Lenore Sullivan, a congresswoman from Missouri who was elected in 1952, proposed to amend the tax code to allow working mothers to make deductions for child care. But Mamie Eisenhower went no further. The next questioner asked whether she had finished her own income tax. She had. The upcoming visit of her four grandchildren dominated the rest of the press conference.[55]

Women's magazines barraged Mamie Eisenhower for tidbits about the White House to use in their stories. Modern conveniences had been installed with the Truman renovations, such as a new white and stainless steel electric kitchen, three automatic dishwashers, a laundry, and parquet floors. Homes across 1950s America were also implementing these conveniences, so the press wanted to know about how the first lady was using them. For example, one magazine inquired, how many meals were served from the electric kitchen? How was the food kept hot or cold en route from the kitchen to the family dining room? How was the food carried to each place? Did the first lady have any auxiliary cooking equipment on the second-floor living quarters? What was the typical family dinner menu? Had Mrs. Eisenhower shopped for any food? How often were the main floor public rooms cleaned? Was there any routine for changing sheets on the beds? Had the weight of the first lady gone up or down from 138 pounds? Unlike Bess Truman's famous

Mamie Eisenhower poses beside a display of personal china of various presidents. She is holding a plate from the Taft collection. The photo was taken in the White House China Room on 9 May 1959. Courtesy Dwight D. Eisenhower Presidential Library.

"no comment" retorts, Mamie Eisenhower answered most questions in some detail.[56]

When reporter Helen Thomas wanted to do a story on the hemlines Washington women would be wearing in the fall of 1953, she sought Mamie Eisenhower's opinion on the subject. Designer Christian Dior had recently made waves by raising his hemlines several inches, to a height of seventeen inches from the floor. Women around the country were making the alterations. Eisenhower responded that she was planning to keep her hemlines at thirteen inches, as this was most suitable for her height and weight.[57]

When deadlines for the 1953 Thanksgiving magazine issues came about, a United Press reporter wanted to know Mamie Eisenhower's menu favorites. Will duck or goose be served in addition to the traditional turkey? What was the recipe for her favorite Thanksgiving dressing? The reporter said that the many people who fondly follow the doings of the Eisenhowers would be especially interested in special sweet potatoes or gravies. That Thanksgiving, Mamie Eisenhower furnished reporters with her widely circulated recipe for pumpkin chiffon pie, which incorporated gelatin, the popular postwar thickening agent.[58]

Not only did women's magazines want to know what was inside of Mamie Eisenhower's pantry, they were curious about what was inside her mailbag. How many letters did she get each week? Which were answered personally? How many controversial letters did she get? To respond to such inquiries, her office kept track of the kinds of letters she received. According to their records, many were expressions of spiritual support, to let the Eisenhowers know the writers were praying for them and how they were pleased to have a religious family in the White House. Children also wrote, including their own drawings and likenesses of the presidential couple. Aspiring songwriters and poets sent works that expressed admiration. Many also requested autographs, photographs, and memorabilia, such as buttons, handkerchiefs, salt and pepper shakers, earrings, and recipes. Some wrote about problems—old-age pensions, social security, and housing—and those were referred to the appropriate agencies. But given the postwar economic recovery, requests for assistance did not overwhelm her office, as they did for Lou Hoover and Eleanor Roosevelt. Instead, her mail substantiated a national strengthening, with the president and first lady as happy, comforting celebrity-leaders.[59]

Though Mamie Eisenhower often cooperated with press, and they treated her favorably, she also exercised discretion, especially on questions of homemaking that veered into the political. Murray Snyder, Dwight Eisenhower's assistant press secretary, for instance, asked her to avoid questions on their retirement farmhouse in Gettysburg, Pennsylvania. The Gettysburg farm was a popular topic of media inquiry. The Eisenhowers purchased the farm in 1950 for $200,000. Mamie wanted her own home after living in government housing her entire adult life. Snyder felt inquiries related to the farm impinged on the question of whether Dwight Eisenhower would run again in 1956. It was not certain that he would, and the heart attack he suffered in September 1955 only added to the speculation. As Marilyn Irvin Holt has commented, the Eisenhowers were in sync with the postwar building boom that witnessed more than 13 million new homes constructed between 1948 and 1958. As one press inquiry from *House & Garden* magazine stated, "Her home in Gettysburg is not only the fulfillment of her own dreams but it is also a symbol of the dream home of every American family."[60]

The Gettysburg farm also offered a fixed homestead for the extended Eisenhower clan, including Mamie Eisenhower's four young grandchildren. The Eisenhower grandchildren were in lockstep with the national baby boom. The birth rate for third children doubled between 1940 and 1960, and the rate for fourth children tripled. Magazine advertisements featured pictures of families with five or six people. Mamie Eisenhower was presented to the public as a doting grandmother, mirroring trends in family togetherness. The grandchildren frequently visited the White House, where they were photographed, and the press and public were enthused to have young children there after a prolonged absence. As one editor from *Women's Wear Daily* wrote to daughter-in-law Barbara Eisenhower asking for an interview on her children's play and dress-up clothing, the press was "especially interested at this time in the many children in the public eye" and the "Eisenhower children now head this public interest."[61]

Today, a first lady is identified by her project, a publicized cause around which her activities are organized. While Mamie Eisenhower did not have such a project, she did have special causes. The role of women in the Cold War influenced her mini-projects. The 1950s ushered in a new era of global awareness. It was the decade of the airplane, and television brought world events into American living rooms. By the time the Korean armistice was signed in 1953, the war against the spread of communism had claimed tens of thousands of American lives. That same year, Russia announced the development of a hydrogen bomb. Mamie Eisenhower's mini-projects encouraged national strength by urging wives and mothers to stand as a bulwark against communism and atomic warfare.[62]

Mamie Eisenhower promoted saving bonds, a project tied to the Treasury Department. Dwight Eisenhower said faith in bonds was necessary for economic and national welfare, especially "if we are going to be able confidently and permanently to counter the Soviet threat to our form of life." Bonds promoted a sound economy and fended off the communist threat.[63] Mamie Eisenhower served as honorary chair of the National Women's Advisory Committee on United States Defense Bonds and of the Women's Crusade for Security, the distaff side of the government's effort to increase the sale of savings bonds. Its Bond-A-Month program encouraged women to save systematically by purchasing bonds monthly through the bank, automatically deducted from their checking accounts. Mamie Eisenhower made public pleas through written statements, which were distributed to the women of the country. One of her first such statements directed to the women of America noted that by buying and inducing others to buy bonds American women could build a more secure future for their families. In other words, women could impact national security as bond purchasing agents, fighting communism abroad and strengthening families at home.[64]

She issued a number of public service statements during her tenure. Again, many of these linked mothers to Cold War security. She urged mothers to donate blood, funds, and volunteer time to the Red Cross because doing so would assist those wounded in the Korean conflict. As Eleanor Roosevelt did during World War II, Mamie Eisenhower mobilized women to become active in civil defense, saying in another public service message that "any housewife may be tomorrow's heroine—if war comes to America." She tried to impress upon women that they might be targets for an atomic bomb attack and should volunteer as nurses, dental technicians, or food service workers in preparedness efforts. For United Nations week, she stated, "The women of this country know how great is their stake in peace. They know too well the anxiety and the anguish that war brings. That is one reason why the United Nations is so deeply meaningful to them—for it is an instrument of peace."[65]

Marilyn Irvin Holt has argued that Mamie Eisenhower was a perfect fit for the 1950s. Ruth Montgomery, writing in *Look* magazine, captured the public affections toward the first lady when she wrote, "If the American voters ever decided to elect first ladies, they would probably find no candidate more suited to the job." Mamie Eisenhower was an effervescent grandmother to a postwar nation that was busily engaged in rebuilding and fortifying itself with homes and families at the foundation.[66]

JACQUELINE KENNEDY

"In these times of danger when world peace is threatened by communism, it is necessary to have in the White House a leader who is capable of guiding our destiny with a firm hand," said Jacqueline Kennedy in a 1960 television spot advertisement. She affirmed that her husband would "watch over the interests of all sectors of our society who are in need of the protection of a humanitarian government." Standing in front of damask wallpaper and staring straight into the camera, she addressed her broadcast audience in Spanish, asking them to vote Democratic because world peace and children's futures were at stake. JFK's major foreign policy goals were to eliminate the scourge of communism and enhance America's image and esteem in the eyes of the world. This was the Cold War backdrop against which Jacqueline Kennedy projected her famous glamour and style. Though she believed her attention to arts and culture stemmed from her obligations as the president's wife, she also prioritized mothering her two young children, a goal not at odds with the President's Commission on the Status of Women (PCSW).[67]

"This country has passed through very difficult days," said JFK in his brief appearance during Jacqueline Kennedy's televised White House tour. America's history "makes us feel we'll continue in the future. . . . I consider history—*our* history—to be a source of strength to us here in the White House and to all the American people . . . and that's why I'm glad Jackie is making the effort she's making." With these words, JFK conveyed the deeper meaning behind his wife's restoration project—to make the country feel and appear strong against the threat of communism.

"A Tour of the White House with Mrs. John F. Kennedy" aired on CBS on 14 February 1962, while the restoration was still underway. The black and white broadcast began with the first lady narrating an architectural history of the White House. She then guided correspondent Charles Collingwood around the mansion, discussing her historical findings. She had draped the Diplomatic Reception Room with scenes of America, such as Niagara Falls, New York Harbor, and West Point. In the East Room, Collingwood asked her for her opinion on the relationship between government and the arts. She demurred, stating, "That's so complicated, I don't know. I just think that everything in the White House should be the best." But in the Red Room, a painting depicting the Civil War prompted her to give a speech on the stature of the White House in the eyes of the world. "I feel so strongly that the White House should have as fine a collection of American pictures as possible," she said. "It's so important the setting in which the presidency is presented to the world, to foreign visitors. American people should be proud of it. We had such a great civilization, and so many foreign visitors don't realize it." The fortitude of the republic and its stature in the world—this was the thesis Jacqueline Kennedy delicately wove through the program.

She explained the history behind the famous Gilbert Stuart portrait of George Washington, rescued from flames by Dolley Madison, and the Monroe candelabras on the East Room mantle. In the State Dining Room, she showed off the Eisenhower gold china, gold flatware, and the gold Monroe centerpiece and candelabra. The glassware, procured from West Virginia, belonged to the Kennedys. She highlighted the reproduction of white buffalo heads that Theodore Roosevelt had designed—he wanted an American animal—that were soon to be installed on the mantel.[68]

An estimated 46 million Americans tuned in to "A Tour of the White House." Not only was it popular at home, it proved a valuable propaganda piece abroad. The United States Information Agency (USIA) was the government's main voice overseas, charged with distributing Cold War propaganda, mainly via film and television. The USIA distributed copies of the program to 106 countries, including to six behind the Iron Curtain and many in the developing world, making it the most widely watched documentary of its day. Some countries televised it. In others, the USIA made sure it was shown to opinion leaders—journalists, educators, women's groups, and government personnel. The global press praised the first lady for her knowledge of history and art, her intelligence and sophisticated taste.[69]

Jacqueline Kennedy's press releases on her restoration project were also careful to highlight national strength through history and wealth. The press release announcing the completion of the Red Room, for example, stated that the walls were "covered in scarlet silk with a gold scroll border." The west fireplace wall was flanked by an armchair with "gilded carved decoration." Other objets d'art included a pair of urns in an "unusual green patina and fire gold ormolu mounts" and an "oval green tole monteith with cast swan necked fire gold handles." Gold or some form of it was mentioned no less than thirteen times in the brief release. These intricacies were not dumbed down to appeal to pedestrian sensibilities.[70]

The Blue Room was renovated to symbolize a return to glory after destruction. According to a White House press release, the Blue Room was returned to the period of James Monroe, who ordered the furniture and bronzes for the room in 1817 after all the previous furnishings had been destroyed by the fire of 1814, when the British torched the White House, thereby exposing the young republic's vulnerabilities. Jacqueline Kennedy's office announced, "A superb set of Empire bronzes have been acquired to go with the Monroe Minerva clock and candlesticks on the mantel. These consist of a chandelier similar to the one ordered by Monroe, . . . and two large candelabra composed of female classical figures, mounted on a triangular base, holding aloft globes mounted with candles." The Fine Arts Committee also acquired a portrait of Monroe, and the first lady was delighted to report on the detective work that went into finding out the true artist behind the painting. It had been originally thought that the painting was the work of Rembrandt Peale. But through a thorough search of his letters and diaries, it was discovered to be the work of Samuel F. B. Morse, the "brush work and the warm reflected lights and shadows" being characteristic of his work. The first lady admired Monroe, whose White House restoration was bolstered by a new national confidence after the end of hostilities in the War of 1812.[71]

Jacqueline Kennedy also enhanced America's image abroad through her foreign travels. Her first international trip as first lady was a friendly one to Canada in May 1961. Two weeks later, she traveled with her husband on a high-stakes diplomatic trip to Europe, with stops in Paris, Vienna, and London. JFK hoped his European trip would further the unity of the free world to secure a lasting peace. He spoke of the desire of citizens living behind the Iron Curtain to be free and independent. Foreign policy issues on the table included nuclear testing and disarmament.

While JFK spoke of America's strength, Jacqueline Kennedy radiated prosperity, vitality, and depth. Her visit was considered a phenomenal success. One international correspondent noted, "It is difficult to understand how in only six days this woman, who is undoubtedly very beautiful but completely unknown in Europe, could have been transformed into an international celebrity and become an idol of the multitudes." She dazzled fashion-savvy Parisians, who noticed every change in costume and shade of lipstick. For the banquet in the Hall of Mirrors at the Palace of Versailles, she paid homage to French design by wearing a Givenchy gown, made of white silk with a bell-shaped skirt and embroidered all over with flowers and accented with diamond clips in her hair. She also captured the interest French president Charles de Gaulle. According to Jacqueline Kennedy, she asked de Gaulle questions about French history, betraying her own deep knowledge. An amazed de Gaulle remarked to JFK, "Mrs. Kennedy knows more French history than most Frenchwomen."[72]

In Vienna, reporters were quick to draw comparisons between Jacqueline Kennedy's chic wardrobe and Nina Khrushchev's frumpy clothes. The two wives appeared together at a luncheon in Pallavicini Palace. Kennedy wore a navy silk suit, triple strand of pearls, and pillbox hat. Khrushchev wore a gray and white loose patterned dress, her hair pulled back in a low ponytail. As one international reporter noted, "In the communist world the homeliness of the leaders is emphasized by the deliberate lack of glamour and charm of their wives. 'To be pretty' presupposes a high grade of social progress, and requires investments in creams, perfumes, lotions, and clothing which no communist country can now manage." Baggy pants and loose blouses marked the communist signature style. The contrast between capitalism and communism could not have been more apparent in the wives of the heads of state, leaving open the possibility that the feminine apparel and accouterments of the president's wife could play a role in the gradual democratization of political society.[73]

This role was made even more apparent when, in March 1962, the first lady made an unprecedented semiofficial goodwill trip to India and Pakistan. Both countries were new democracies. It was the first peacetime solo trip a first lady had made abroad as the president's representative. Letitia Baldrige said it was entirely a "working trip," as Kennedy visited children's hospitals, schools, art shows, and design centers. The USIA sent a crew to film her visit, which they made into two color documentaries: *Invitation to India* and *Invitation to Pakistan*. They were initially supposed to be distributed within India and Pakistan, but demand for them was great around the world. They were eventually released in twenty-nine languages and to seventy-eight countries. The films were soft and subtle, as the filmmakers sought to convey the stature and dignity of America, its democratic spirit, and the first lady's care for the people of smaller countries. Many of the shots reinforced her maternal role.[74]

Jacqueline Kennedy characterized herself as a beacon of apolitical femininity to Prime Minister Jawaharlal Nehru. She believed his family life lacked this. According to Jacqueline Kennedy, the prime minister's sister confided to her that his daughter, Indira Gandhi, "fills the poor man's life with politics. It's politics at lunch, politics at tea, politics at dinner. He never has any relaxation. So that visit—I mean, nothing profound was talked about or even that we were going to Pakistan next, but you know, it was a relaxation for him—the kind of thing I'd try to bring into Jack's life in our evenings at home."[75]

Yet Jacqueline Kennedy was an astute observer of international affairs and did not hesitate to make her opinion known to her husband if she felt strongly about something. Her trip to Pakistan prompted one such intervention. While there, she gleaned an unfavorable impression of American ambassador to Pakistan Walter McConaughy. She recalled, "The only time I ever wrote Jack a letter, which I wrote coming down from the Khyber Pass and gave him when I got home, was what a hopeless ambassador McConaughy was for Pakistan, and all the reasons and all the things I thought the ambassador there should be. . . . And I suggested some other people." The president was so impressed by the letter that he showed it to Dean Rusk, secretary of state, and said, "This is the kind of letter I should be getting from the inspectors of embassies." In addition to the weekly CIA summary, she at one time received all of the India-Pakistan cables because she loved to read the writings of John Kenneth Galbraith, Kennedy's ambassador to India. And for a time, she had McGeorge Bundy, national security advisor, send her all the top intelligence briefings.[76]

In Jacqueline Kennedy's mind, her public actions stemmed from her obligations as a wife, not as a mother. A line from her official White House biography is telling. "While Mrs. Kennedy places her family duties first above all other obligations, *as wife of the president* she has devoted a great part of her time and energy to the encouragement of the arts" [emphasis added]. She refused to engage in public mothering of her children. As a mother, Kennedy sought to protect her children by concealing them from the limelight, which was a constant battle because the press and public hounded her for information.[77]

When *Parents* magazine wanted to feature Jacqueline Kennedy in an article on child rearing theories, her press secretary, Pamela Turnure, turned them down, stating that the first lady felt that the subject was "an intricate and personal matter" and did not wish "to participate in any discussion of this subject." Not mincing words, she said a "general article on this subject would be misleading and confusing, and the addition of any personal touches would be violating Mrs. Kennedy's policy toward her children's privacy." She tried, somewhat in vain, to do her actual mothering in private.[78]

Jacqueline Kennedy fought a constant battle for their privacy, even against press secretary Pierre Salinger. She said, "I used to get so mad at Pierre because he did have a certain hamming-up thing that really didn't help protect my children much." She fought against women of the press. At the Women's Press Club dinner the first year of the administration, she became furious when Bonnie Angelo, a reporter for *Time*, "came out on a tricycle as Caroline and sang some awful song."

Jacqueline Kennedy refused to attend the event the following year because of that incident, saying, "I just felt so strongly about those children."[79]

To further protect her children's privacy, Jacqueline Kennedy started
a White House preschool. Her office did issue a very brief press release about the school when the 1962 academic year began. It stated the
school would include about twenty boys and girls, ages four and five,
who would come to the White House Monday through Friday morn-
ings. The program included supervised activity on the third floor, as
well as outdoor play. The school was maintained as a cooperative, with
parents of the children sharing all expenses. The release was silent on
early education theories and curriculum.[80]

Jacqueline Kennedy's prioritization of her children did not contra-
dict JFK's agenda on women. Leaders of the PCSW, though they argued
for major changes in women's legal status, affirmed the nation's commitment to motherhood and held that rearing a family was a woman's
primary responsibility. According to Cynthia Harrison, "The dichotomy between the primacy of traditional sex roles and the goal of equal
treatment for women at work produced a tension which the commission never satisfactorily explored or resolved."[81]

And although Jacqueline Kennedy advanced the first lady's role
through her restoration project and foreign travels, she also carved a
line between his sphere and hers. "How could I have any political opinions, you know? His were going to be the best. And I could never conceive of not voting for whoever my husband was voting for. . . . I mean,
it was really a rather terribly Victorian or Asiatic relationship which we
had," she remarked. Reflecting on how emotional she would get when
her husband was criticized, she stated, "I think women should never
be in politics. We're just not suited to it." She contrasted herself to her
energetic and demanding social secretary, Tish Baldrige, commenting,
"Tish is sort of a feminist, really. She used to tell me she loved to have
lunch in the White House Mess so she could argue with men. She's
great, but she was so different from me and just exhausted me so."[82]

It was not uncommon, in the early 1960s, for women to sneer at
feminists but also engage in work outside the home. In 1963, Betty Friedan published *The Feminine Mystique*, in which she argued that there
was a crisis situation brewing among college-educated homemakers.

"Politics, for women, became Mamie's clothes and the Nixons' home life," Friedan wrote. In her book, she recommended "a new life plan for women" in which they combined motherhood with creative work of their own, which required the development of their own interests and use of their own education and training. While Betty Friedan was writing about her new life plan for women, Jacqueline Kennedy was living it. She professed not to identify with feminists or political women, yet she worked heartily on her restoration project. She prioritized her children but also believed that presidents' wives should contribute something. Jacqueline Kennedy's tenure highlights the complexities that were emerging for women in society. It would be left to the first ladies of the second wave to try to tease out these tangled strands.[83]

THE SECOND WAVE

he second wave of the feminist movement challenged political and legal barriers to women's access to public life. Equality was its rallying cry, and the ERA was the paramount women's issue. Presidential administrations responded to demands for equality by creating women's outreach offices, advocating affirmative action for women in the federal government, and advancing laws that guaranteed equal protection. This chapter shows how first ladies acted to advance women's political and legal equality, as they coordinated with White House women's outreach efforts, bolstered female appointments, and worked to get the ERA ratified.

LADY BIRD JOHNSON

Though Jacqueline Kennedy liked and admired Lady Bird Johnson, she was taken aback by the Johnsons' political partnership. Kennedy recalled, how on a 1960 campaign visit, "anytime Lyndon would talk . . . Lady Bird would get out a little notebook—I've never seen a husband and wife so—she was sort of like a trained hunting dog." Lady Bird Johnson wrote down facts about people, names, and phone numbers. Jacqueline Kennedy commented, "It was a—ewww—sort of a funny kind of way of operating." Arthur Schlesinger likened them to a "hockey team." Esther Peterson attributed Lyndon Johnson's concern for women's equality to his wife. Peterson characterized Lady Bird Johnson as a woman with ability and with brains, having been a businesswoman of her own. She said, "I think he is accustomed to recognizing that there are other skills that [women can have]. . . . I've always felt that part of his basic understanding of the problems of working women was because of her and the relationship that he has with her."[1]

The first lady's office during the Johnson administration did showcase women's capabilities and contribute to advancing equality. Lady Bird Johnson's office supported the president's efforts on behalf of women's appointments. She showcased women's political and policy capabilities through her women doers luncheons and by campaigning for female candidates. The first lady also demonstrated her own mettle as a presidential campaigner.

Lady Bird Johnson was born Claudia Alta Taylor in Karnack, Texas, on 22 December 1912. Her father ran a successful cotton business and general store. Her mother, having been in and out of sanitariums, died when Lady Bird was only six. She attended St. Mary's School for Girls in Dallas before enrolling in the University of Texas, where she studied journalism. She was educated as an equal with men, demonstrated the same intellectual ability, and trained for the same career. She met Lyndon Johnson in 1934, when he was working as a congressional aide, and they were married that same year. According to Lewis Gould, it was a marriage of mutual advantage. Her family's wealth provided a means to his political aspirations, while his career was her ticket out of Karnack, which offered limited opportunities for educated Texas women in the 1930s. In 1937, Lyndon Johnson ran in a special congressional election and won.[2]

During World War II, Lyndon Johnson served in the navy in the South Pacific. While wives of other military men flocked to factories, Lady Bird Johnson ran her husband's congressional office, which she described as the ultimate political education. She dealt with local and national policy problems and found the work stimulating. The experience gave her self-confidence, and she emerged believing she could make a living for herself. In 1943, she purchased a radio station in Austin, Texas, and turned it profitable. This led to investments in broadcast stations all over Texas. And after a decade of trying to conceive, Lady Bird gave birth to her daughters Lynda in 1944 and Luci in 1947. During her child-rearing years, Lady Bird Johnson became more involved in her husband's career, helping to organize the women's branch of his Senate campaign in 1948 and his presidential bid in 1960.[3]

In many ways, Lady Bird Johnson's life before the presidency mirrored how women's spheres were shifting. She, along with other well-educated wives of the time, valued a job for the personal rewards it conferred. Economic pressures of the late 1940s pushed her into the world of paid work. Meanwhile, she worked in the family business of politics, developing her own skills and partnering with her husband.

The Johnson marriage, however, was not a model of mutual respect. Upon returning from their honeymoon, Lyndon demanded that Lady Bird serve him coffee, bring him the newspaper in bed, lay out his clothes, fill his cigarette lighter, and shine his shoes. She complied. He would often bark orders at her from across crowded rooms and criticize her appearance—her weight, her dress, and her low-heeled shoes—in front of others. Some even observed that in their relationship, her opinion did not count.[4]

The Johnsons were, however, keenly aware of the movement that was taking place in the early to mid 1960s that the editors of *Harper's* called "crypto-feminism." Privately and nonmilitantly, women were reexamining their public and private roles. The mechanized home brought millions of women more leisure hours. The average American woman was still in her twenties when she was through with childbearing, leaving her possibly forty productive years to fill. The editors concluded, "Whatever their solution, many are finding that the institutions that are supposed to serve women are not very helpful." One of these institutions was the federal government.[5]

Against the backdrop of "crypto-feminism," Lyndon Johnson was eager to capitalize on the goodwill created by the President's Commission on the Status of Women (PCSW). In January 1964, he declared he would appoint fifty women to high-ranking policy positions. Johnson's appointments were motivated by something deeper than patronage. He wanted to use the federal government as a beacon for women who were looking to put their education and talents to use.[6]

During the Johnson years, the first lady's office was the White House clearing house and command center for advancing the administration's vision for women. Liz Carpenter, Lady Bird Johnson's press secretary and one of Lyndon Johnson's closest female advisors, was instrumental in these efforts. On 24 February 1962, Liz Carpenter sent a memo directed to "anyone interested in women." She stated, "There is a wide and increasing interest by the press in the upgrading and appointment of women." In the memo, she advised that any cabinet member or agency head appointing a female should "announce it with a little more fanfare than usual—a picture of the agency head with the woman appointment, and a statement that the appointment emanates because of President Johnson's call for the federal government to make greater use of qualified women in executive appointments." If the federal government was to be a beacon, showcasing female appointments was necessary.[7]

Reporter Helen Thomas wrote to Carpenter, "Sometime ago I told President Johnson that in line with his tremendous policy of putting women in top government jobs, I had a candidate for director of the Children's Bureau. He said 'good tell Liz.'" Besides Carpenter's own connections, the first lady's office proved useful at name generation in other ways. Carpenter issued a memo to Bess Abell, the social secretary, asking, "Can you give me the names of five bright women that you would like to see put on task forces or committees . . . with a four-line evaluation of their age, capabilities, and what their principal interest is? We might score some hits if we had some new names." Lady Bird Johnson herself suggested names for consideration. For instance, she had Martha Allen, director of the Camp Fire Girls, put on an appointment list.[8]

Lady Bird Johnson bolstered female appointments in her speeches and events. In an address to the American Home Economics Association on 25 June 1964, she told her audience that in order to fill highly professional public offices with superior minds, the country needed to "tap the immense reservoir of talent that lies among American women." Responding to the dilemma facing many women about what to do with their lives once their children were grown, she said that "women are particularly suited to resume professional careers as public servants. Their presence assures a more representative approach, for the simple reason that half the American citizens are women." Lady Bird Johnson was cognizant of the challenges women federal appointees faced. She said it was not easy for them to weigh a government post against family responsibilities, especially when an appointment required them to relocate to Washington. But she did say that about 75 percent of her husband's initial 150 appointees were married, many with children.[9]

In 1964, at the same time Lyndon Johnson was heating up his drive to recruit women into government service, Lady Bird Johnson, Liz Carpenter, and Bess Abell began planning a series called women doers luncheons. According to Carpenter, the luncheons began because she

Lady Bird Johnson confers with Liz Carpenter en route to Denver, Colorado, on 17 October 1966. Courtesy Lyndon B. Johnson Presidential Library.

and Lyndon Johnson wanted to honor and showcase women in the administration and also because "Mrs. Johnson didn't want to have luncheons of people to sit around and talk about their ailments and their bridge games." In Carpenter's words, the luncheons were intended to feature "a more vital type of woman." At a typical luncheon there would be eighteen guests. The luncheons were held in the private second-floor presidential family dining room. They would try to recruit women activists in different fields to speak on their areas of expertise. Lady Bird Johnson made lists of vital women she read about or met on her travels. They would draw on those names for speakers and guests. The luncheons became prestigious. One reporter wrote that the luncheons were "the newest status symbol for career women." Equal employment opportunity was the largest legal advancement for women in first half of the 1960s, with passage of the Equal Pay Act of 1963 and Title VII of the Civil Rights Act of 1964. Lady Bird Johnson's women doers luncheons, featuring prominent women in business, public life, education, the professions, and arts highlighted these advancements, as well as created an atmosphere that placed working women, as well as their achievements and problems, in the national spotlight.[10]

The first women doers luncheon featured Barbara Solomon, director of the women's archives at Radcliffe College. The choice of Solomon was symbolic, as the Radcliffe archives had an extensive collection relating to American women's public influence from the suffrage movement to women's impact in the professions. When they were considering Solomon, Carpenter wrote in a memo to Lady Bird Johnson that she sounded "very intelligent and articulate . . . and would be a nice egg-head touch." In remarks at the luncheon, Solomon discussed how pioneer life did much to shape woman's independent character and working partnerships with her husband, and how this impacted the fight for political and legal equality.[11]

Another women doers luncheon featured Mary Bunting, a Johnson appointee to the Atomic Energy Commission. As Lady Bird Johnson told her guests, "I remember so well the great sense of pride we all had, especially the President, who had been persuading her since January to come down for at least 365 days." The first lady characterized her as "a real architect of a world where women can contribute their creative intelligence." A mother of four, Bunting was also a great example of how women could combine both career and family in service to the government.[12]

Lady Bird Johnson later extended the focus of her luncheons to women who were involved in solving local and national policy problems. In 1968, the luncheons expanded from eighteen guests to fifty. They also changed the format. In the first women doers luncheon of 1968, "What Citizens Can Do to Help Insure Safe Streets," guests heard from a panel of three women experts in the field of criminal justice.[13] Another, entitled "The Consumer Is You," focused on the greater need for consumer protection, a priority of the Johnson administration. And one entitled "What Citizens Can Do to Improve the Health of the American Child" was designed to promote Lyndon Johnson's health-care agenda.[14]

Though carefully planned and controlled, the women doers luncheons were not insulated from controversy brewing beyond the White House walls. For example, the luncheon on safe streets became entangled in Vietnam War protests. At that luncheon, singer and guest Eartha Kitt went on a tirade. She spoke as a mother who knew the feeling of having a baby boy "coming out of my guts." The main point of her meandering speech was that America's youth were rebelling, by smoking pot and other means, because of the war in Vietnam. Kitt's remarks received widespread press attention. Thousands of citizens wrote to the White House expressing indignation. Meanwhile, the organization Women Strike for Peace demonstrated in front of the executive mansion, waving signs declaring, "Eartha Kitt speaks for the women of America." Notably, just two years earlier, Carpenter wrote President Johnson to persuade him to send more women to Vietnam in military roles. She complained that of the 298 women then serving in uniform in Vietnam, only 13 were not nurses.[15]

Not only did Lady Bird Johnson's actions reflect women's increasing role in government, they also showed how women were becoming increasingly important in elections. The 1964 election was the first in which women voted in greater numbers than men. That year, Lady Bird Johnson logged a total of 76,357 campaign miles, 31,009 with the president and 45,348 alone. These solo miles were unprecedented for a first lady.[16]

Lady Bird Johnson's talents as a campaigner first caught the attention of administration officials during her tour of the American West in the summer of 1964. There, she highlighted conservation and equality. At a reception to salute women in the Grand Teton National Park, she said, "They rightly call Wyoming 'the Equality State.' There never was a time in Wyoming's history when woman wasn't man's full partner. . . . Women helped wrangle the cattle and stake out the homesteads. They sat on the juries as long ago as 1870, and pronounced sentence on cattle rustlers, horse thieves, and murderers." While echoing the emerging theme of free and equal citizenship, her words also touched delicately on problems beginning to wend their way through the courts. One of these issues was whether women could be exempted from jury service on the basis of their sex. A decade later, the Supreme Court would rule that women could not be excluded from jury venires.[17]

Upon her return, accolades poured into the West Wing. On 18 August 1964, presidential aide Douglass Cater wrote to Lyndon Johnson, "Mrs. Johnson represents a political asset for the campaign which is unique in presidential history. She is highly appealing and effective on the platform. She comes across as intelligent and knowledgeable and <u>unlike</u> Eleanor Roosevelt thoroughly feminine." He believed she could give a push in critical states. Lady Bird Johnson's mix of personal qualities—intelligence plus womanliness, wherewithal mixed with grace—made the Johnson campaign believe she could ease tensions in the South.[18]

In the 1964 campaign, amid mounting racial tensions, southern tides were flowing in the direction of Republican candidate Barry Goldwater. In this tense political environment the nineteen-car Lady Bird Special campaign train departed Union Station in Washington, D.C., for a 1,682-mile trip through Virginia, the Carolinas, Georgia, Florida, Alabama, Mississippi, and Louisiana. The first lady gave forty-seven speeches in four days. According to Liz Carpenter, her real role on the train was to say, "This President and his wife respect you and you are loved."[19]

While her message was intended to placate, behind the scenes, the whistle stop revealed developments in and tensions over women's increasing political role. According to Liz Carpenter, the whistle stop tour was female-run. Though men were aboard, the women were "calling the signals." Lyndon Johnson was highly supportive of his wife's

Lady Bird Johnson aboard the Lady Bird Special in Alexandria, Virginia, on 6 October 1964. Lyndon B. Johnson Presidential Library photo by Frank Muto.

trip and the work the women were doing. Carpenter, however, had a tougher time with members of Johnson's staff, particularly Kennedy administration holdovers, who, according to Carpenter, "had no respect for any women in politics whatsoever." Carpenter said, "The whole attitude of the Kennedy men . . . was to keep women barefooted and have them on their feet, preferably pregnant, on Election Day—but nothing beyond that." When the train trip was in the planning stages, a West Wing official even wrote, "The old-fashioned whistle stop technique is going to be very difficult for any woman. . . . She cannot, effectively, talk about labor's role in an automated economy, the gross national product, or why Barry Goldwater can't see through his empty spectacles." Yet the first lady did talk about the economy. For example, in Richmond, she said, "Virginians earn $205 per capita more now than they did in 1960. . . . I would be remiss if I did not point out that these were Democratic years." When one reporter asked her how this campaign differed from Johnson's first congressional bid in 1937, she said, "Those were rather different days. Women in general didn't participate as much as they do. I packed the bag and washed the socks and reminded him to eat. Today women take a greater part, and I'm glad." In other words, her campaign role reflected the advances women had made into the public sphere. Though women on the whistle stop still faced discriminatory attitudes, Lady Bird Johnson traveled solo, made speeches, talked policy, and stood her ground, while her female staffers did the behind-the-scenes logistics.[20]

The whistle stop did encounter strong protests over the administration's support for the 1964 Civil Rights Act. Lady Bird Johnson chose to enter into the controversy. As Liz Carpenter recounted, "We wanted to go into the towns that nobody else could get into. Anybody can get into Atlanta and out with their hide on even if you're for a civil rights bill. We took Savannah. It's tougher. We took Charleston. It's very much tougher. . . . And in some places, you know, they weren't all applauding." The first lady encountered many "ugly voices." In Columbia, South Carolina, a group of protesters heckled her during her speech. She raised her hand and silenced them. In the coming years, the second wave of the feminist movement would piggyback on the gains made during the civil rights movement for African Americans. Lyndon and Lady Bird Johnson's racial politics, therefore, raised the possibility that minority women could be included in the broader movement for women's political and legal equality that was brewing in the 1960s.[21]

During the 1964 campaign, Lady Bird Johnson made equal opportunity for women in public life a theme of her travels around the country. In Vermont, she promoted Lyndon Johnson's record on women. "My husband has increased our opportunity to make our voices heard and our contributions count," she said. In Ohio, she campaigned for Frances McGovern for Congress. There, she stated, "Women of this country have a place in public life, and in the annals of the Great Society, it will be recorded that women took on their responsibilities alongside men." In Pennsylvania, which she called a "land of super-women," she campaigned for Senate candidate Genevieve Blatt. She stated, "The federal government has truly become a showcase for equal employment opportunities for women. . . . Because of this president's determination women will no longer be the forgotten sex in labor, in business, or in government." Lady Bird Johnson clearly wanted women's equality to be part of her husband's legacy.[22]

In 1964, Lady Bird Johnson also headlined the DNC "tell a friend" women's get-out-the-vote drive. Launching the campaign on 14 September 1964, she talked with a woman in each of the fifty states, including a double amputee, a mother of thirteen children, and a retired economics professor. Each call recipient was then to phone ten more friends, asking them to call ten others. Lady Bird Johnson told one call recipient, "every time I read the statistics where there are less women to take the opportunity to vote . . . I am annoyed by it, so let's cut it down this time." Not only was 1964 the first presidential election in which women who voted outnumbered men, it was also the first in three cycles where women cast a greater percentage of votes for the Democratic ticket than men, 62 percent compared to 60 percent. This was a 13 percent shift of women from the Republican to Democratic column from the 1960 election. A new trend in women's voting patterns was taking shape.[23]

The Johnsons did not push for the ERA. Just weeks into his presidency, Lyndon Johnson, under the direction of Esther Peterson, used a letter to the Lucy Stone League to fully state his position. He chose to hold the line on the PCSW recommendation that the Constitution already guaranteed equal rights and that groups should litigate discriminatory laws and practices. But the Democratic position on the ERA, once beholden to the interests of reformers, was soon to change.[24]

PAT NIXON

In 1970, Helen Bentley, chair of the Federal Maritime Commission, was worried about groups that were pushing for women's rights and how they might hold the Nixon administration accountable. "Women are beginning to talk in terms of a 'movement,'" she warned. In the Johnson administration, the debate about women's rights and roles was shifting, but during Richard Nixon's administration, it became full-blown. One of the problems, said Bentley, was that none of Nixon's high-ranking officials had wives or daughters in executive positions. "Mrs. Johnson worked," reminded Bentley. Pat Nixon also worked, though she was not known for it. Bentley was also distressed about sexist remarks administration officials made about women, such as when Ron Ziegler, Richard Nixon's press secretary, cracked that Constance Stuart, Pat Nixon's press secretary, had a "menopause problem." She was only thirty-two.[25]

In her first year in office, Pat Nixon also did some damage to the administration's posture on women's equality. Before her White House reception for the state status of women commissions, she told reporters, "I really feel women have equal rights if they want to exercise those rights. The women I know, who are really interested in going out, pitch in and do good. I don't think there is any discrimination. I have not seen it. I know my husband doesn't feel that way." Her comment evoked an outcry from women's organizations. Mail critical of the first lady poured into the White House. The National Federation of Business and Professional Women sent a telegram asking Richard Nixon to clarify his position in light of his wife's comments, arguing that her remarks would endanger the ongoing court cases and legislative activities to eliminate barriers to equality. The National Organization for Women (NOW), founded in 1966, sent an open letter to Richard Nixon, with copies going to newspapers, governors, legislators, and women's groups, stating that Pat Nixon's comments "greatly disturbed countless women throughout the nation." The administration was forced to do damage control. They responded that the first lady's comments were misinterpreted and that both Nixons had a keen appreciation of the long and valiant struggle for women's rights. They assured the groups that they believed further progress was possible. The outcry highlights the first lady's power—real and symbolic—over women's equality. Administration officials recognized this and believed she could be a positive force as well.[26]

And she did become a positive force. Though Pat Nixon, just like the rest of the nation, underwent an education about the new women's rights movement, she eventually advocated for women's equality under law and in politics. She coordinated with the administration's new Office of Women's Programs and helped to mobilize women voters. The impact of the second wave was clearly manifested in the first lady's actions.

But upon becoming first lady, Pat Nixon was already plagued by her image as "plastic Pat"—the compliant, docile, and oblivious political wife, unerringly proud of her husband's words and deeds. Yet her background could not have been further from the synthetic persona ascribed upon her. She was born on 16 March 1912 and christened Thelma Catherine Ryan, the daughter of working-class Irish and German immigrants. She was raised in California, her upbringing characterized by hard and steady work. From the time she lost her mother at age thirteen, she had to shoulder the domestic responsibilities, caring for her father and siblings. Her father died when she was eighteen, and she took on part-time jobs to sustain the family during the Great Depression. At the same time, she took college courses and acted in dramatic productions. In 1932, she drove eastward, eventually landing a job at Seton Hospital in New York City. In 1934, she returned to California and enrolled in the University of Southern California, where she studied commerce and earned a teaching certificate, while also working part-time. She secured a teaching job at Whittier High School. During this time she met Richard Nixon at an audition for a community production, and they were married in 1940.

According to Mary C. Brennan, the young couple wanted to go places. "They might have started out in small towns with limited prospects, but they recognized in one another a kindred spirit of ambition and wanderlust." During World War II, Richard Nixon enlisted in the navy, during which time Pat got a job for the Office of Price Administration in San Francisco earning a good salary. Their first daughter, Tricia, was born in 1946, at the beginning of the baby boom, while Richard Nixon was campaigning for Congress. But Pat Nixon did not stay at home. She left Tricia to the care of others and worked for her husband because they were short on funds. That election, which Richard Nixon won, was a turning point for Pat. Up to that point, she, like many American women, had blossomed with the new doors of economic opportunity that war had opened. But as Richard Nixon climbed the political ladder, securing the vice presidential nomination in 1952, the postwar media solidified her "plastic Pat" persona. While this rendering was in sync with the times, it did not accurately represent her past. During the vice presidential years, magazines portrayed her as the perfect suburban housewife who did it all, even though she frequently left her domestic duties and young daughters, Tricia and Julie, who was born in 1948, to travel with her husband on diplomatic missions, a job she relished.[27]

Pat Nixon's image complicated her relationship with the emerging women's rights movement. Moreover, Pat Nixon, like the much of the rest of the nation, underwent a political education on women's rights during her husband's presidency. Nixon administration officials even needed to be educated. "A new social and political awareness has been developing among women," Jean Spencer, special assistant to the vice president, and Barbara Franklin, staff assistant to the president in charge of recruiting women appointments, wrote in an internal memo in October 1971. "If there is a single concept which can encompass and express the concern of women today it is *freedom of choice*," they explained. From this central concept stemmed concern about other areas of discrimination. Women were angry about unequal access to college and graduate school. They were concerned about ongoing employment discrimination, in hiring, pay, and promotion. They wanted maternity leave and support for child care. They wanted to end discrimination against middle-aged women reentering the workforce. They wanted more women in meaningful policy roles in government. And they wanted to ratify the ERA, which Spencer and Franklin characterized as the "emotional cornerstone" of the feminist cause. Moreover, Spencer and Franklin noted that the feminist movement had an emotional dimension that made it attractive to cover, and women's equality was being discussed in news magazines and women's magazines and on national talk shows.[28]

Richard Nixon supported the ERA when he ran for president in 1960 and 1968. Franklin and Spencer were concerned, however, that he did not take a strong enough public posture on the ERA while it was being debated in Congress. During deliberations, press women asked for and Pat Nixon gave statements in support of the ERA. For example, during congressional deliberations in May 1970, Constance Stuart told reporters, "I have spoken to Mrs. Nixon about this matter and Mrs. Nixon, of course, supports the amendment. As she indicated to me, every Republican convention has supported an amendment since 1940—I believe was the date she gave me—and that her husband supports it and that she supports it. Mrs. Nixon does not believe in discrimination of any kind be it on any basis—race, creed, religion, color or sex." The House passed the ERA in August 1970, but the Senate failed to ratify it during that session.[29]

Pat Nixon was aware that in the early 1970s Republicans were losing ground on women's rights. As Christina Wolbrecht has written, before 1970, Republicans were more likely than Democrats to cosponsor pro–women's rights bills. But between 1971 and 1972 Democrats became far more likely to cosponsor women's rights bills than Republicans. Democrats, because they had become linked to the peace, student, and civil rights movements of the 1960s, were more sympathetic to the changing women's rights agenda than Republicans, whose agenda did not fit with radicalism, countercultural politics, or government intervention. Furthermore, beginning in 1970, women's rights issues became highly salient. Nixon and other elected officials worried about the consequences of not supporting women's rights for the 1972 election.[30]

To lessen the Democratic edge on women's rights, Pat Nixon had Constance Stuart issue a memo to her staff and Barbara Franklin. She stated, "In response to criticism about what the Republican Party or this president has done for women's rights, we should point out that the Republican Party adopted the Equal Rights Amendment as part of the party 4 years before the Democratic Party. President Nixon as a Senator co-sponsored the Amendment on the floor of the Senate in 1951." She also prepared and attached a timeline showing Republican firsts on women's rights.[31]

One of the most significant developments in women's rights was the founding of the National Women's Political Caucus (NWPC). The group first met in Washington in July 1971. Its purpose was to advocate for the election and appointment of women to office and for women's interests in the political system. Founding members included Betty Friedan, along with noted feminists Bella Abzug, Gloria Steinem, and Shirley Chisholm. Barbara Franklin and Jean Spencer warned administration officials that because the event generated a great deal of media attention, it "may have carried the cause of feminism to a new level of political visibility." While the group aimed to be bipartisan, most members were Democrats.[32]

Following the NWPC meeting, Richard Nixon and Secretary of State William P. Rogers quipped that a photo of the conventioneers looked like a burlesque. The comment was featured on the front pages of American daily newspapers and in weekly news magazines. When Pat Nixon was asked about the NWPC founding at a press conference, she answered, "I haven't even read about that. It sounds pretty wild to be frank. It really wasn't something I wanted to read about." Though the organization had just been formed a few weeks prior, her remark was ridiculed in the media. She said she was in favor of equal rights and promised to campaign for more women in political office, but her comments about the NWPC overshadowed her other words and actions. Her education was ongoing.[33]

By April 1972, Pat Nixon had learned enough about the NWPC to write them a remarkable letter commending their work. In contrast to her previous comments, in this letter the first lady showed an astute understanding of the rapidly changing landscape on women. She also framed herself as on board with those changes. "With the rapidly changing concepts of women's challenges, privileges, and potentials, women are becoming increasingly more influential in the determination of our national destiny," stated the first lady. "Through dissemination of information, programs of education, and practical demands accompanied by constructive action, organized women's groups such as yours are setting the pace for the ever-growing and enthusiastic acceptance of women in fields heretofore traditionally exclusive to men." Affirming the right of all women to develop to their fullest potential, Pat Nixon stated, "The National Women's Political Caucus is to be applauded for vigorously implementing its recognition that this fast emerging philosophic transition is of vital importance in the political sphere." Therefore, she did actively try, on behalf of the administration, to maintain the goodwill of the NWPC.[34]

In another effort maintain positive relations with women's organizations, Richard Nixon set up a White House office focusing specifically on women. Suggestions to establish such a body came from many quarters, including the first lady's office. In August 1970, the East Wing staff wrote a memo suggesting the creation of a national council on women, headed by a woman who would bear the title special assistant to the president. They proffered a list of qualified candidates. They suggested the office could be in charge of liaising with women's interest groups and providing leadership on "women's equality, pay scales for women, day care centers, the pill, etc." Finally, in April 1971, Barbara Franklin was appointed to head the first official White House women's recruitment program, though Liz Carpenter had done this informally through the first lady's office. Then, following Nixon's reelection, Anne Armstrong was appointed to head the Office of Women's Programs, the first White House office to deal with women as a special constituency.[35]

Franklin and Armstrong coordinated work with Pat Nixon's office. The need for collaboration existed because many of the groups that in the past would have requested a simple tea or social tour were now focusing on women's rights. Franklin and Armstrong generated event proposals to highlight the Nixon administration's record on women, and Pat Nixon was often featured in those. While not every proposal moved forward, the first lady was central to their publicity strategy. Likewise, Pat Nixon's staff consulted Franklin and Armstrong about scheduling events for the first lady. For example, in May 1973, Franklin wrote a memo to Armstrong about social secretary Lucy Winchester's efforts to bring women's groups to the White House. She wrote that Winchester was "interested in having any ideas about White House social functions or entertainment which involves, includes, or highlights women. It would be good, for example, to make sure women leaders are invited to church services and other functions." Also, Franklin and Armstrong stood in for the first lady when she was unable to receive groups. For example, when Pat Nixon could not meet the National Federation of Business and Professional Women while she was traveling abroad, Armstrong visited with the group instead. Likewise, Pat Nixon stood in for Franklin and Armstrong. This role sharing illustrates how the functions of the offices of Franklin, Armstrong, and Pat Nixon overlapped.[36]

Barbara Franklin and Pat Nixon also did overlapping work in pushing for female appointments. For example, Franklin detected a strong sentiment among women in favor of the president appointing a woman to the Supreme Court. In the fall of 1971, Nixon had two vacancies to fill. Franklin said she was "literally attacked" with questions and suggestions from professional women on this issue. She believed that women of all ages and occupations, conservatives and liberals alike, favored the appointment of a woman to the Court. Pat Nixon was one of the leading voices—and certainly the one closest to the president— pressing for a female nominee. Her daughter Julie wrote that because of her mother's urging, Richard Nixon instructed John Mitchell, the attorney general, to submit a list of qualified women to him. In September 1971, Pat Nixon told reporters, "Don't you worry; I'm talking it up . . . If we can't get a woman on the Supreme Court this time, there'll be a next time." In October, however, Richard Nixon announced that he nominated Lewis Powell and William Rehnquist to fill the vacancies. According to Julie, at dinner on the evening of the announcement, Pat Nixon strongly restated her belief that one of the nominees should have been a woman. But the president, with "exaggerated weariness," cut off the conversation. The first lady was disappointed that her husband did not choose a woman and felt slighted that her advice, which she had declared in public, had gone unheeded.[37]

Pat Nixon argued for women in other high offices as well. On NBC's *Today* show in February 1972, she told Barbara Walters that more women should run for Congress. She said that women needed to be given "lessons" to support other women. She also stated, "I would support any well-qualified woman for any job, including president," though she claimed to not want the position herself. She also said she would not be surprised if a female vice presidential candidate were to be nominated at the upcoming convention. "I think if we had a well-qualified one that she'd be very popular," she stated. Pat Nixon's comments about women in appointed and elected office were even included in campaign speaker kits to use as background material to bolster Richard Nixon's record on women.[38]

In the 1972 campaign, Pat Nixon courted women voters, though the campaign's overall strategy was not clear. Franklin and Spencer initially believed that the first couple should steer clear of sex-segregated campaign events, writing, "In the past Mrs. Nixon has campaigned very effectively in women's groups while the president spoke to the men or the general public In 1972, we feel that her activities must be more oriented to mixed audiences, with speaking topics of general interest." Feminists would have frowned upon any suggestion that women's groups were second-class citizens or that the first lady was incapable of addressing general issues. In this spirit, Pat Nixon kicked off the 1972 campaign season with a press conference. She came ready to speak with substance, and she did, commenting on topics as diverse as the gross national product, Jane Fonda, and the Vietnam War.[39]

Franklin did not entirely follow through on her plan for integrated events. Her preconvention schedule proposals for the first lady focused on women's groups. These included cohosting a "salute to women" reception to cap off a proposed equal opportunity for women week, placing a bust of Susan B. Anthony in the White House for the anniversary of the first women's rights convention, and visiting with wives of prisoners of war.[40]

At the Republican convention in Miami Beach, Pat Nixon was an active participant. Far from sounding like a reluctant political wife, she told reporters that she planned to attend every session and visit every delegation. Her convention appearances were designed to highlight Republican support for women's equality and women's emergence into new public roles. She was a featured speaker at a breakfast honoring women candidates. In her remarks, she celebrated women coming out from behind the scenes and into their own history-shaping roles. More than 2,000 people attended a brunch for women of achievement in honor of Pat Nixon. A pageant depicting the advancement of women through American history was planned, as was a slide show of Pat Nixon's diplomatic travels. The brunch was designed to pay tribute to Pat Nixon's activities that have "added a new dimension" to the position of first lady—"that of a stateswoman."[41]

And following an introductory film narrated by Jimmy Stewart that focused on Pat Nixon's substantive role as a stateswoman, the first lady addressed the entire convention. After approximately eight minutes of thunderous applause, she gave very brief remarks noting, "I stay in the wings and don't come out in front too often, so this is quite unusual for me." Indeed, at the time, it was unusual for any candidate's wife. These remarks earned her the distinction of being the first Republican first lady to address a national nominating convention. Though her actual words were self-deprecating, the overall thrust of her convention appearance was symbolic of women emerging into the public spotlight.[42]

Pat Nixon also delivered a signed written message to convention delegates trumpeting the administration's record on women. She wrote that during her husband's term, America experienced "greater legal and social encouragement of equal opportunity for women." Her message reviewed the history of Republicans leading the fight for the ERA and the greater acceptance of women in the fields and professions. "The

President has given special support to this effort, setting new precedents in the hiring of women for positions in the federal government," she wrote. She told conventioneers that her husband's administration had appointed more women to high-level positions than any other in history. She attributed these achievements to the Republican ideals that were flexible enough to adjust to a continually changing society. Congress had ratified the ERA in 1972, and there was widespread support for it during most of the Nixon years. The building controversy was eclipsed by Richard Nixon's resignation in the wake of Watergate.[43]

BETTY FORD

While Pat Nixon echoed the long-time Republican support for the ERA, Betty Ford made her mark on women's legal equality by lobbying state lawmakers on behalf of the measure, even as it lost support within her own party. She continued Pat Nixon's work of vocally supporting high-level women appointees and coordinating with the Office of Women's Programs. She was also part of the administration's strategy for International Women's Year, the main global push for women's equality to emerge from the second wave. Her personal background made her more attuned to the challenges of women in politics, as well as in the home.

From an early age, Betty Ford was fixated on a career. She was born Elizabeth Ann Bloomer on 8 April 1918 and raised in Grand Rapids, Michigan, where she had a comfortable childhood. Though the Bloomers were not wealthy, there was plenty of money left over to send young Betty to dance lessons, which she began at age eight. She adored dance, and, over time, directed her career ambition toward the dance profession. Eschewing the strictures of ballet, she immersed herself in modern dance. She loved the freedom of movement modern dance pioneers preached and how it allowed her to express herself through her body. When the Great Depression hit, she started a makeshift dance studio to help contribute to her upkeep. After her high school graduation, she attended summer dance camps at Bennington College in Vermont, where she first came under the tutelage of modern dance performer Martha Graham.[44]

Eventually, she convinced her mother to allow her to move on her own to New York City, where she began work with the Martha Graham Dance Company. She lived frugally and worked as a model on Seventh Avenue—at millineries, fur houses, and dress houses—to make ends meet. Betty loved her work life. She also loved her social life, which got in the way of her dance career. Martha Graham would lecture Betty that she could not carouse and be a dancer too. She never made it into Graham's traveling troupe, and her mother persuaded her to move back home to Grand Rapids.[45]

It was there she married her first husband, Bill Warren, a diabetic exempt from war service and working in the insurance business. Betty Ford called her marriage "the five-year misunderstanding." Since factory work was abundant during the war, Betty got a job at a frozen food factory and then as the fashion coordinator at a department store. But she was not happy. She was ready to settle down, but Bill was not ready to give up the bar scene. After Bill recovered from a diabetic coma, Betty initiated divorce proceedings. She would become the first president's wife in the modern era to have been divorced.[46]

Betty met Gerald Ford when he was campaigning in the Republican primary for a congressional seat. They married and were anxious to have children. After an operation on her uterus, Betty Ford gave birth to four children—three boys and a girl—in the span of about seven years. She enjoyed her work as a housewife. As she described it, "I was a den mother. I was a Sunday-school teacher. I was an interior decorator and a peacemaker and a zoo keeper." However, her child-care responsibilities and her husband's demanding work schedule took their physical and mental toll. She suffered a neck injury, which required physical and psychiatric therapy. As she has written, "I've often said I'd lost my feeling of self-worth, and that's what sent me for help. I think a lot of women go through this. Their husbands have fascinating jobs, their children turn into independent people, and the women begin to feel useless, empty." Betty Ford eventually concluded that her mental state was linked to her physical illness. Betty Ford's activities as first lady, however, would provide an opportunity for her to find herself again.[47]

Displaying her trademark candor, Betty Ford outlined her agenda during her first press conference on 4 September 1974. She declared her support for equal rights for women, saying that she and her husband used to kid about equal rights, but "now his position is quite clear." She encouraged women to become "very active in politics." She said that she would campaign for the ERA in states that had not ratified it.[48]

Like Pat Nixon, Betty Ford publicly advocated for high-level female appointments and cajoled her husband behind the scenes. In her interview on *60 Minutes*, she confessed that she prodded her husband into putting a woman on the cabinet. She was referring to Carla Hills, secretary of housing and urban development. "I won that one," said Betty Ford, "And I'm working on another. If I can get a woman on the Supreme Court bench, then I think that I'll . . . have accomplished a great deal." Gerald Ford had his opportunity when Justice William O. Douglas retired, but he appointed John Paul Stevens instead. Betty Ford lamented, "I probably didn't do enough research, and I lost that battle." However, several women, including Carla Hills, were on his list of potential nominees. She also unsuccessfully tried to get Anne Armstrong chosen as her husband's 1976 running mate, but she did take credit for getting Armstrong appointed ambassador to Great Britain. In her memoir, Betty Ford confessed that she deployed all available tactics, "including pillow talk at the end of the day, when I figured he was most tired and vulnerable."[49]

Betty Ford's female appointment efforts were likely hampered by the unusual circumstances in which her husband took office. Ford decided to keep most of Nixon's cabinet and staff, leaving few opportunities for women to move into high-level posts. Armstrong and her staff turned their attention away from appointments and toward women's policy and programs. As with Pat Nixon, Betty Ford coordinated efforts with Armstrong, their offices serving as extensions of one another. Just one week after Ford was sworn in, Armstrong sent Betty Ford a letter along with a packet of briefing materials on women's issues. Armstrong told Ford that she stood eager and ready to help her in any way on women's matters.[50]

When Armstrong resigned, Patricia Lindh took over the Office of Women's Programs. Lindh's papers contain numerous letters, memoranda, schedule proposals, and suggestions that highlight how closely her office worked with Betty Ford. When Lindh left her position in the spring of 1976, she wrote to Betty Ford, "Probably at no time, and certainly not within recent memory, have the East Wing and the West Wing worked so closely together on issues of mutual concern. In particular your wholehearted support of the principle of true equality has been a tremendous source of morale for my office." Lindh noted that Betty Ford's dedication even improved her own quality of service to the administration. Lindh's letter shows that the first lady's office served as a wellspring of support for women's issues and materially improved the administration's work on women's equality.[51]

Richard Nixon had proclaimed the year 1975 International Women's Year (IWY) in the United States, following the lead of the United Nations General Assembly. When Gerald Ford was sworn in, Armstrong's office was in full swing planning IWY activities. In January 1975, Gerald Ford established the National Commission on the Observance of International Women's Year. Its purpose was to promote national activity in the field of women's rights and responsibilities. In the signing ceremony, Betty Ford was positioned behind her husband's chair, peering over his shoulder. After Gerald Ford made a brief statement, Betty Ford put her right hand in his left, smiled widely and said, "Congratulations, Mr. President. I'm glad to see you have come a long, long way." An internal memo indicates that administration officials had staged it this way, as they wanted to showcase the first lady as a conspicuous, vigilant presence on women's issues.[52]

Betty Ford was integral to Anne Armstrong's initial vision for the IWY program. Armstrong sent Betty Ford and all female presidential appointees briefing materials to update them on IWY planning. She also forwarded a long list of suggestions for Betty Ford's IWY participation, including both Fords serving as honorary chairs of the IWY commission in order "to envision the idea of partnership." She also suggested Betty Ford host a "massive celebration" at the National Woman's Party headquarters when "the ERA is ratified in 1975 (hopefully)." When Patricia Lindh took over, she also besought Betty Ford to chair the IWY commission. In a persuasive memo to Ford, Lindh gave seven reasons why she would be the ideal chair. Among these reasons, she argued that Betty Ford's personal commitment to women's rights was widely recognized, her stature would elevate the commission's work on the national agenda, and her unique position would generate maximum interest and response from the American people. Though Betty Ford did not take on the chairmanship, that it was considered shows how enmeshed she had become with women's equality.[53]

In 1975, Lindh continued to press for the first lady's involvement in IWY. Controversy surrounded the decision whether to send Betty Ford to the United Nations Conference of the International Women's Year held in Mexico City. Lindh argued that she should participate. Other first ladies would be heading delegations and addressing seminars. West Wing staffers thought her attendance would be good politics, since she helped the administration to maintain a positive image on women's issues. The National Security Council, however, was concerned that independent radical groups might disrupt the proceedings. A compromise was reached wherein Betty Ford sent remarks that were read before the convention. In her remarks, Betty Ford affirmed that the United States was committed to the goals of the conference. She stated that equality for women meant equality for all, freeing both sexes of restrictive stereotypes and opening up new possibilities for all individuals.[54]

Betty Ford did speak at many domestic IWY events, where she echoed feminist views on women's equality. She spoke to the Greater Cleveland Congress of IWY, the largest IWY observance in the country, with about 30,000 people in attendance. Betty Ford tailored her remarks around women's right to choose their life's work. She told her audience that barriers still blocked the paths of most women. They were not paid equally for equal work, and the contributions of wives and mothers were still undervalued. She challenged restrictions of "custom and code" that sprang from emotional ideas about what women should and should not do. She told her audience that those discriminatory attitudes had been formalized into law and used her speech to argue for the ratification of the ERA.[55]

By the time Gerald Ford took office, ERA ratification had stalled, needing five more states before becoming law. Disheartened by a string of states that failed to ratify, Betty Ford decided to get involved. While she did not make frequent public speeches on the ERA, she did lobby behind the scenes. Meanwhile, ERA opponents were arguing that it would lead to radical policies. ERA proponents and opponents both believed that the ERA would require women be drafted into military combat. The public was also skeptical of the courts, with the Supreme Court just having handed down *Roe v. Wade*, and was reluctant to put the interpretation of the ERA in its hands. The ERA pitted feminists against a budding social conservative movement, and Betty Ford found herself swimming against the undercurrents of her own party.[56]

Betty Ford's ERA lobbying was met with opposition from Phyllis Schlafly and her influential STOP ERA organization. Schlafly, a long-time Republican activist, halted the ERA's forward momentum by successfully arguing that the ERA would destroy traditional families, which galvanized Christians and homemakers. She used her newsletter "The Phyllis Schlafly Report" to promote arguments about the havoc the ERA would visit upon American society.[57]

When the first lady had announced at her press conference her intention to work for ERA ratification, Schlafly immediately issued her an invitation to attend a STOP ERA meeting of state chairs. Schlafly wrote, "We have heard your statements on television that you are opposed to discrimination against women, and noted that you have met with women's groups representing various minority points of view. We hope you will not discriminate against those of us who hold a contrary view, but will grant us our equal rights of visiting with the first lady." Schlafly was of the opinion that Betty Ford was unfairly throwing her weight behind the pro-ERA point of view. Yet, Betty Ford did not reach out to Schlafly, despite her high standing in the Republican Party. For the meeting of state chairs invitation, for example, Susan Porter, the first lady's appointments secretary, phoned to regret.[58]

On 6 February 1975, Betty Ford issued a memo inviting the entire White House staff to join her in the Family Theater for an ERA update. She wrote, "I plan to be on hand to meet you and hope you will bring co-workers for this important briefing." The upcoming year would be crucial to ERA ratification and the first lady believed it was "vital to both the men and women who work here to have a clear understanding of the legislation." While the first lady did not attend because of a sudden flare-up in her neck pain, the program went on with about 160 staffers attending. Schlafly became incensed and issued a Mailgram to the first lady, asking for equal time to present her side to the staff. She also protested holding the ERA staff meeting during working hours and requested an accounting of how much federal money had been spent in making long-distance phone calls to legislators and on staff salaries of federal employees working for ERA ratification. A group of STOP ERA protesters, all women, even picketed the White House with placards reading, "Happiness is Stopping ERA" to urge the first lady to stop her lobbying efforts. In response, Betty Ford vowed to stick to her guns and to continue to use her home to make the calls. Thus, the stage was set for an unharmonious relationship between anti-ERA forces and the Ford administration.[59]

In January 1975, Betty Ford began her state-level lobbying in earnest, when North Dakota was considering the measure. She wrote to William Kretschmar, a Republican representative who supported the ERA, to thank him for his support and urge other members to vote their consciences. Three days later, North Dakota became the thirty-fourth state to ratify the ERA. Though no more states would ratify the ERA in 1975, battles raged in many of the unratified states. The first lady targeted these battlegrounds. Early that year, she also made phone calls to lawmakers in Nevada and Arizona. She even talked by telephone to U.S. senator Barry Goldwater to express her views, even though the Arizona senator opposed the legislation. Neither state ratified the ERA.[60]

In Illinois, Schlafly's home state, the ERA debate was intense and protracted. Given Schlafly's ties, anti-ERA forces were strong. Also, at the time, Illinois required a three-fifths majority to ratify a constitutional amendment. This was a steep hurdle. Betty Ford called on Bud Washburn, a Republican state legislator, to urge him to support a rules change for a smaller majority. He said he would, and the first lady followed up on the pledge, though the supermajority requirement was not dropped until the ERA ratification deadline had passed.[61]

Betty Ford also phoned Illinois lawmaker William Harris to urge him to help keep the ERA from dying in committee. When the bill made it to the floor, Harris reported the progress to Betty Ford at the White House. Yet, the first lady's phone calls were not welcome among all lawmakers. For example, after Illinois Republican Donald Deuster heard of Betty Ford's lobbying phone calls, he wrote her a letter requesting that she immediately desist in her long-distance telephone lobbying campaign and that she refrain from using her position as first lady to promote the emotionally charged amendment. He also questioned the "propriety and wisdom" of using the "stature and respect" of her position to place taxpayer-funded phone calls to promote passage of bills in the states. In his letter, he also cited an Illinois government report that concluded the ERA would cause judicial chaos, subject women to the draft, and wipe away all statutory sex distinctions. The report and his letter echo Schlafly's arguments, showing how influential her organization had become in the state.[62]

In Oklahoma, the Republican response to Betty Ford's ERA lobbying also illustrated just how divisive the measure had become. The Republican Convention of Oklahoma passed a resolution opposing the ERA and requesting that the spouses of elected officials abstain from trying to influence legislation. Drawing upon Schlafly's arguments, the Oklahoma Republican State Committee wrote to Betty Ford urging her to reconsider her position.[63]

On the eve of the ERA vote in the Florida legislature, only two of twelve Republican senators had committed to voting for the ERA. Betty Ford placed eleventh-hour phone calls to Republican lawmakers. However, her phone calls were not universally welcomed. Senator Warren Henderson told her, "I'm still not voting for the thing." Four anti-ERA Republican senators who received calls decided not to return them. Senator Walter Sims stated, "I wrote her a letter once and told her she should mind her own business and quit spending the tax money to push her political philosophy." Another remarked, "There's nothing more she could tell me about it I haven't already heard." And yet another stated, "I have enough trouble voting on the state government without the federal government telling me what to do." Senator Lori Wilson, the only female senator, worried that Betty Ford's efforts might anger some undecided lawmakers enough to vote against it, given that anti-ERA forces had made a big issue out of Betty Ford's phone calls. The ERA failed by a vote of twenty-one to seventeen.[64]

In 1975, the ERA debate was also heated in Missouri. Betty Ford called two Missouri legislators just before the final vote in its House of Representatives, and the measure did pass. Betty Ford was excited to hear the news, and some press accounts credited her with getting the final favorable vote. The Missouri Senate, however, rejected it.[65]

During the height of Betty Ford's ERA lobbying, she received tens of thousands of letters. Her staff carefully monitored the first lady's mail. In February 1975, her office reported that the White House mail was running three to one against the ERA. They said that the first lady was unperturbed by the numbers, though many accused her lobbying efforts of being unrepresentative, unfair, and unladylike. But the tide eventually turned and supportive letters poured in. One of those supportive letters, for example, was written on behalf of the female staff members of the *Oakland Tribune*, expressing "admiration and gratitude" for her "forthright stand" on the ERA. As a sign of solidarity, they also included a clipping of their story on a mastectomy model wearing a bikini. By late March, her mail was running three to one in support of the ERA.[66]

Though Betty Ford's advocacy did not stop as the calendar turned to 1976, it was not as focused on legislation pending in the states. In March, she attended singer Helen Reddy's ERA concert in Washington, all of the proceeds going to the ERAmerica organization. Reddy won a Grammy Award for her song *I Am Woman*, which the United Nations had adopted as the theme song for International Women's Year. Liz Carpenter, who was then working with the organization, called her "part booking agent" for the concert because of her influence and rapport with Reddy. In addition, Betty Ford penned a message for *Redbook*, in which she argued that the ERA would bring tangible changes in women's lives. She wrote that it would speed progress against legal and economic discrimination and that it would change discriminatory attitudes about women's capabilities. Moreover, she wrote that the ERA would mean more choices for women and greater respect for the decisions they made at home and in the marketplace. Then in August, when pro-ERA activists held a vigil outside the White House and organizers requested a message from the first lady, she told them she stood "shoulder to shoulder" with them and was holding her own vigil inside the White House. Sounding a note of encouragement, she added that she hoped they would soon have a great rally to celebrate ERA ratification. However, no states would ratify the ERA in 1976.[67]

In the final days of the Ford administration, the first lady was bolstered by some ERA news. In January 1977, the ERA Indiana organization made an urgent request for Betty Ford to call Governor Otis Bowen to encourage him to work for Republican legislative support. Republicans were not making a strong ratification push, but ERA coordinators believed Betty Ford could make a difference. Betty Ford did call Governor Bowen and asked him to include the issue in an upcoming speech. Just two days before Jimmy Carter's inauguration, the ERA passed in Indiana, making it the thirty-fifth ratified state. It would be up to Rosalynn Carter to work for the remaining three.[68]

ROSALYNN CARTER

Rosalynn Carter did work for the remaining three. Getting the ERA ratified was one of her main priorities, and, like her predecessors, she pushed for women's equality. As a southerner and a Christian, Rosalynn Carter seemed an unlikely person to lobby for the ERA, since both were turning away from the ERA in the late 1970s. During her first ladyship, the political environment surrounding women's rights was becoming increasingly charged.

For the woman born Eleanor Rosalynn Smith on 18 August 1927, the church had been the center of her social life growing up in Plains, Georgia. Her formative years were filled with church picnics, revival meetings, and Bible school. She met Jimmy Carter during her school days. During World War II, Rosalynn commuted to Georgia Southwestern, a nearby junior college. She never did get a college degree as her father had wished. She married Jimmy Carter in 1946 soon after he graduated from the Naval Academy. His first assignment was in Norfolk, Virginia, and near their first anniversary, they welcomed their first son. Of her life as a navy wife, Rosalynn Carter has written, "I washed and ironed. I cooked and cleaned, mopped floors. . . . I bought women's magazines and clipped recipes and household tips, bought how-to books and learned to crochet and knit and make curtains." Her day-to-day living was not much different than the typical housewife's in the postwar era.

Except she did get to experience living in diverse locales. So Rosalynn Carter was devastated when her husband decided to move back to Plains and take up the family peanut-farming business after his father died. Jimmy Carter did not have enough money to hire employees. Though she was devoted to raising her three young boys at the time, Rosalynn Carter slowly started going into the office and keeping books, gradually taking on more responsibility. When Jimmy Carter won a seat in the Georgia Senate, Rosalynn eschewed the role of political wife to stay home and keep the business running. Though the civil rights movement was redrawing the lines between the political parties in the

South, the Carters bucked the shifting tide and remained Democrats. At the age of forty, after having a uterine tumor removed, Rosalynn Carter gave birth to a daughter, Amy. Soon thereafter, Jimmy Carter began campaigning for the Georgia governorship. It was during the campaign she began to hear from citizens about mental illness. When her husband was elected, she decided she did not want to spend her time on social engagements. She had her own projects lined up.[69]

During the presidential transition, Jimmy Carter issued a memo to his cabinet designees ordering them to appoint "women and minority males" to high-level positions, thus inviting the press to screen for diversity. He appointed Patricia Roberts Harris as secretary of the Department of Health, Education, and Welfare. She was the first African American woman to hold a cabinet post, an important symbolic milestone in the quest for political equality for minority women. By his delegating this responsibility to his cabinet, the role of the White House became less important. Rosalynn Carter, who sat in on cabinet and other high-level meetings, was kept in the loop about female appointments. Yet her role mimicked that of the broader White House—important but not central.[70]

Rosalynn Carter wanted the public to know, however, that she impacted the president's appointments. As she said in a speech before the New York Women in Communications, "I want to assure you that I use my influence at home on behalf of women whenever I can. . . . I have been known to, well, mention he needs—more women on the White House staff—more women in departmental jobs—and a list of distinguished women just in case he finds himself looking for a woman Supreme Court Justice."[71]

Though Jimmy Carter did not get the chance to nominate a Supreme Court justice, we do see Rosalynn's Carter influence in judicial appointments. Initially, only a handful of women and minorities were being suggested to Carter for judgeships. This concerned Paul Costello, press secretary to Rosalynn Carter. In a letter to her, Costello stated that this trend could have "grave implications" because the president would be blamed for the lack of diversity. He asked her to discuss her concern about the heavily white male judicial pool with senators, governors, and their wives, in hopes of generating some pressure. She did. For example, she told the gathering of the New York Women in Communications that one of the best things they could do was "to put the heat on your senators about nominating women to the bench." In her staff papers on judicial appointments, there is a handwritten note from Rosalynn Carter that reads, "Does Sarah Weddington have a list of women's names for possible appointments? If not she should have." She instructed Weddington to get the names to Hamilton Jordan, Jimmy Carter's chief of staff. The first lady exercised power within the nomination process by keeping the names of women appointees flowing to the president and through his inner circle. Prior to Carter's administration, only eight women had been confirmed to federal judgeships. Carter named forty women to the federal bench. Eleven were to appeals courts and twenty-nine were to district courts. Rosalynn Carter was part of the pressure system that attained these appointments.[72]

Rosalynn Carter also got women included in White House arrival ceremonies for visiting heads of state. When a group of servicewomen wrote to her asking for help, she issued a statement of support, which was followed by a Pentagon directive that added women to ceremonial units. Her office announced their first assignment. They would be lining the driveway as flag bearers and present in marching units for the arrival ceremony for Kenneth Kaunda, president of Zambia. Rosalynn Carter stated that she was gratified by the willingness of the military to "correct an imbalance in the ranks."[73]

Rosalynn Carter also intended to use her position to help get the ERA ratified. Though her ERA involvement did not match her investment in mental health reform, early in the administration she declared it would be one of her top priorities. And it was. She saw her role as a national ERA educator. She believed that if she could convince people that the ERA simply meant equal rights for all—and would not lead to the changes ERA opponents were raising—it would cease to be controversial. Just one week after Jimmy Carter's inauguration, Kathy Cade, Rosalynn Carter's projects director, wrote to her to say they had been "deluged" with requests for the first lady to intervene on behalf of the ERA in several states. Senator Birch Bayh's office and ERAmerica leaders had also been flooding her office with calls. Bayh had drafted the version of the ERA that Congress ratified in 1972. Given the torrent of requests, Cade suggested a vetting process. All requests for the first lady's help would go to Cade, and she would clear them with Bayh's office and ERAmerica. They would also be free to alert her to any situation requiring the first lady's immediate attention. Cade thought her system would keep the first lady from intervening in states where the ERA would not likely be ratified.[74]

But in January 1977, ERA supporters in North Carolina, Nevada, and Mississippi were hoping for a miracle. Cade held out little hope for passage in Mississippi and Nevada, but Bayh's office had been working in North Carolina and believed there was a good chance of passage there. Cade gave Rosalynn Carter the names of four wavering legislators to call. Perhaps recalling the negative press surrounding Betty Ford's phone calls, Cade was adamant that nothing should be said to the press or public about these calls. As she told Bayh's office, the first lady preferred to demonstrate her support "in a very private way." The North Carolina House of Representatives did narrowly vote to ratify the ERA in February 1977, but it was quickly defeated in the North Carolina Senate. And reports of the first lady's calls did leak out.[75]

The beleaguered ERA was also in need of a cash infusion, evidence of just how fraught the battle had become. The League of Women Voters was conducting a million-dollar fundraising campaign directed toward ratification efforts in Illinois, North Carolina, Florida, and Oklahoma. In a Blue Room ceremony, Rosalynn Carter presented her own personal check. In her remarks, she lamented the "shrill" voices on both sides of the issue that had obscured what she believed the ERA would and would not do. But the shrillness did not abate. Instead, it was about to climax.[76]

In November 1977, feminists and antifeminists clashed over the National Women's Conference, held in Houston, Texas. The conference was funded by the federal government, planned by a presidential commission, and chaired by ardent feminist Bella Abzug. The convention adopted a controversial platform supporting abortion and gay rights. Meanwhile, across town, Phyllis Schlafly held a pro-family rally. It was specifically designed to counter the National Women's Conference, adopting its own resolutions in support of home, family, and morality. The meetings were impassionedly opposed to each other. According to one newspaper report, the two groups "hurled epithets" over the five miles of Houston that divided them. Headlining the pro-family rally were women like missionary Elisabeth Elliot, who decried feminists

Rosalynn Carter with Betty Ford and Texas delegates Liz Carpenter and Elly Peterson at an ERA rally at the National Women's Conference in Houston, Texas, on 19 November 1977. Courtesy Jimmy Carter Presidential Library.

for putting "the final virtue on self." Meanwhile, headlining the National Women's Conference were three first ladies: Lady Bird Johnson, Betty Ford, and Rosalynn Carter.[77]

The image of the three first ladies joining hands with Bella Abzug to grasp the ERA torch, which had been lit at Seneca Falls, New York, the site of the first women's rights conference, and carried by a relay of runners to Houston, was broadcast nationally. Jimmy Carter had asked Rosalynn to be his emissary, representing the administration. She thought it was symbolically important to have three first ladies together on stage "to affirm the continuity in our government's efforts to improve life for all." Her message to the conference was intended to be conciliatory. She stated that the goal of the conference was to build toward women's equal participation in national life and create a better future for the country's children. At a reception put on by ERAmerica, she urged attendees to shorten and simplify their messages. She said that supporters should try to convince others of how the ERA would help women gain equal access to credit, insurance, health care, inheritance, pay, promotions, education, and retirement. Without the ERA, she said, "the only right the Constitution guarantees is that we women have the right to vote." Yet, no matter how concise, the pro-ERA messages had difficulty cutting through the voices of the opposition. And the opposition only gathered steam after the Houston conference.[78]

For example, Robert Grant, who had founded the American Christian Cause, one of the initial groups to organize religious conservatives into a politically active social movement, sent a mailing to his members. He used Rosalynn Carter's conference remarks to fan the flames of opposition. While the first lady had said that the conference was to improve life for all, Grant pointed out that delegates "voted to abort their children, approve homosexuality as a legitimate life style, and even approved adultery and prostitution." He wrote of the conference's exhibition hall, with booths containing obscene literature and mechanical sex aids. Grant included a pre-addressed postcard for his subscribers to send to Rosalynn Carter to voice their opposition to the Houston conference and its resolutions. His group also organized a series of counter-rallies across the nation to speak in defense of America's spiritual heritage. In total, the first lady's office reported receiving 14,647 cards concerning her participation in the Houston conference.[79]

As the calendar turned to 1978, both sides became more desperate. When Congress had ratified the ERA in 1972, it attached an expiration date of 22 March 1979. Time was running out. Rosalynn Carter offered to help in any way she could, even turning traditional ceremonial events into opportunities to promote her ERA message. At her spring luncheon for Senate wives, over mulligatawny soup, salmon, and lemon mousse, the first lady told the wives how she was "working quietly" to get the three states needed and searching for new ways to explain the ERA to those gripped by "doubt or fear."[80]

Over the next several months, she directed that quiet work toward ratification in Illinois. Pro-ERA leaders believed Illinois held the key to ratification before the expiration date. Liz Carpenter of ERAmerica asked Rosalynn Carter to get in touch with officials from the powerful Chicago political machine. In May, Rosalynn Carter flew to Chicago to attend the city's annual Polish Constitution Day festivities. John Fary, a U.S. congressman from Illinois, was invited to accompany her on the plane. Rosalynn Carter gave Fary a list of persuadable Illinois state representatives and asked him to implore them to vote favorably on the ERA. He did.[81]

In 1978, ERA activists hustled to get the U.S. Congress to extend the ERA deadline. Rosalynn Carter made some behind-the-scenes phone calls to move it forward. For example, she called Billie Lee Evans, congressman from Georgia, to argue in favor of the extension. It passed the House of Representatives on 15 August 1978. When the resolution was under consideration in the Senate, Rosalynn Carter held a meeting in the East Room to express her support. Invitees included members of Congress and female presidential appointees. The Senate passed the extension, and on 20 October 1978 Jimmy Carter signed it, with his wife looking over his shoulder. Immediately afterward, she addressed ERA postcards in the Roosevelt Room, an effort sponsored by ERAmerica to urge ratification in unratified states.[82]

In 1978, ERA mail to Rosalynn Carter peaked. She received 2,170 letters on the issue, more than in any other year. Of these, only 360 expressed support and urged the first lady to continue her activism. The other 1,810 writers were opposed and expressed concern over the ERA's far-reaching effects on society.[83]

On the ERA and other issues, Rosalynn Carter's office coordinated efforts with the West Wing staffers in charge of women's affairs. Housed in the Office of Public Liaison, women's outreach was headed by Midge Costanza and then Sarah Weddington, both holding the title special assistant to the president. Rosalynn Carter and her staff were proactive about setting up meetings with Weddington to discuss ERA strategy. However, coordination was not always seamless. For example, Rosalynn Carter became upset with Weddington after Weddington failed to notify her in May 1979 that the ERA was about to come up for a vote in Florida. In an apology note to the first lady, Weddington said, "I obviously should have kept you and your staff informed. I . . . promise to do better. I am sorry." In actuality, Weddington thought there was little hope of influencing Florida lawmakers, though Rosalynn Carter thought otherwise. The measure did not pass.[84]

In 1979, Rosalynn Carter continued her ERA advocacy. She received the Religious Committee for the ERA at the White House to pray for ratification. She held luncheon strategy sessions with George Nigh, governor of Oklahoma, and also with Oklahoma state legislators. In

June, when the Treasury Department released the Susan B. Anthony dollar, Rosalynn Carter accepted the new coin in a White House ceremony. The coin was intended to be a constant reminder of the continuing struggle for equality for all Americans. In October, the Carters hosted an ERA summit at the White House. Nearly 500 guests were invited to the East Room reception, including Lady Bird Johnson, who wore a large, pink button proclaiming, "I'm a Homemaker for ERA."[85]

Despite Rosalynn Carter's efforts, the ERA remained stalled in the states. But in 1980, activity started to pick up again in Georgia. Rosalynn Carter lobbied hard, even with the Iowa caucus looming. Weddington, who was coordinating with national and local pro-ERA groups, provided the first lady with a list of telephone calls of persuadable Georgia lawmakers. Weddington wanted the lobbying to be all-out and visible, so Rosalynn Carter spent a frantic weekend at Camp David making phone calls. The measure failed by a vote of twenty-three to thirty-two. While she did not impact the overall outcome, Rosalynn Carter's calls to Richard Green and Lee Robinson, members of the Georgia Senate, were reportedly the decisive factors in their final decisions to support the ERA.[86]

By June 1980, the ERA fight had moved back to Illinois. Before the ERA came up for a vote, Weddington's office had been working closely with the state congressional leadership, especially those who were Carter delegates to the 1980 Democratic convention. Rosalynn Carter made lobbying phone calls to Alan Dixon, Illinois secretary of state, and Marty Russo, U.S. congressman from Illinois, to see if they could have any influence on local lawmakers. But again, the ERA failed. Jimmy Carter called it a major disappointment. More than that, it was indicative of a broader cultural and political shift.[87]

ERA opposition forces predicted that the Illinois vote would mean the Republican platform would drop the ERA. It did. Ronald Reagan, the party's nominee, consistently said that he supported equal rights for women but not the ERA. He welcomed the Illinois vote, saying, "I think we're all agreed on equal rights. We just disagree on the best way to do it." Phyllis Schlafly noted that there was a national swing toward conservatism. "Reagan is gaining all the time," she stated. She was correct. Reagan resoundingly won the 1980 election, including the twenty-six Electoral College votes for Illinois. The ERA was effectively dead.[88]

CHAPTER FOUR *The Personal Is Political*

The second wave of the women's rights movement challenged the boundary between the personal and political. The personal issues of daily life became political issues susceptible to state solution. The movement challenged personal relationships and roles in the family, particularly the association of women with child care and domesticity. At the same time, a powerful countermovement began to arise, arguing for the preservation of women's traditional roles. The power dynamics of the presidential marriage came under scrutiny, including the authority first ladies were permitted to exercise. How first ladies of the second wave responded to the cry, the personal is political, is the subject of this chapter.

LADY BIRD JOHNSON

In October 1966, NOW gathered for its inaugural conference. The group wanted to wrest women's policy from the hands of the government, and from the beginning it was clear that NOW and the Johnson administration were not in accord. Esther Peterson called the group militant. The NOW statement of purpose rejected the PCSW position that a woman's most important role was to care for her family. It also cast aside the assumption that men should be the sole breadwinners and that women should be entitled to lifelong support by a man upon her marriage. NOW advocated the equitable sharing of home and child-care responsibilities and economic burdens. The new debate about women's relationship to the home compelled Lady Bird Johnson to articulate a vision of ideal womanhood, reflected in her speeches and public events, as well as in her work on behalf of early childhood education and the environment. Her public outreach did not escape without controversy, as she tried to reconcile emerging fissures between the interests of career women and housewives.[1]

Lady Bird Johnson's speech to the Texas Women's University highlighted the differences between the administration and NOW. As she received her first honorary degree, Lady Bird Johnson enthusiastically proclaimed to the graduates, "It is a good time to be a woman. It is a good time to be alive." Whereas NOW deplored conditions that prevented women from enjoying equal opportunity and freedom of choice, Lady Bird Johnson spoke of women's wide-open job opportunities and their full and equal political rights. Whereas NOW hammered away at the jobs women were not doing and the degrees they were not earning, the first lady assured the women that they were born at an opportune time. Whereas NOW said that popular culture was fostering women's self-denigration and contempt, Lady Bird Johnson infused her words with optimism.[2]

Lady Bird Johnson and NOW did share some views, however. NOW deplored women's limited participation in American society and lamented that they were not reaching their fullest potential. NOW also believed that technology had liberated women into a world where they could use their creative intelligences to a greater extent. Likewise, Lady Bird Johnson declared to an American Association of University Women conference that one of the country's most wasted resources was the idleness of the educated woman. "Some of us never survive the battle fatigue of launching a family," she said. "Others become accustomed to being homebodies and find the old rut too comfortable, or too deep, to climb out. Or we may simply lose our self-confidence about the worth of our talents." She urged women to find their hidden strengths, change their communities, and make things happen. However, NOW blamed women's limited participation on laws and unwritten social codes, whereas Lady Bird Johnson blamed women themselves.[3]

The first lady used her platform to articulate her own conception of womanhood that blended marriage and motherhood with a public role. Her Radcliffe College commencement address on 9 June 1964 was designed to be a substantial, news-making outline of her view of the role of women in America during a time when women, especially young, educated women, were wrestling with their relationships to men, marriage, and family. She began her speech by acknowledging women's internal turmoil. Nodding to the feminine mystique, she said that it was hard for women to have inner peace "with every bookstore offering up the joys of emancipation and every newsstand proffering the delights of femininity." The first lady told of a new, remarkable woman who was emerging in the United States, dubbing her the natural woman.

> She has taken from the past what is vital and discarded the irrelevant or misleading. She has taken over the right to participate fully—whether in jobs, professions, or the political life of the community. She has rejected a number of overtones of the emancipation movement as clearly unworkable. She does not want to be the long-striding feminist in low heels, engaged in a conscious war with men. But she wants to be—while being equally involved—preeminently a woman, a wife, a mother, a thinking citizen.

As society considered how to help the forty-year-old woman enter the labor market, Lady Bird Johnson urged the graduates to consider their lives from the longer perspective, after their children were grown. She also warned the graduates that their intellects could be dulled by the "unremitting domestic labor" that was ahead in their childrearing years. She urged them to get involved in their children's schools, improve the aesthetics of cities, create happy homes, get involved with the political parties, and forge into underserved communities. She ended her speech quoting from the thirty-first chapter of Proverbs, which encapsulated her view of the natural woman: "She looketh well to the ways of her household and eateth not the bread of idleness. Her husband is known in the gates where he sitteth among the elders of the land; she stretcheth out her hand to the poor."[4]

Lady Bird Johnson expanded and applied her vision of the natural woman in subsequent speeches. On 24 June 1964, she praised the delegates to the national convention of the American Home Economics Association for helping American women to master the intricacies of push-button washer-dryers, automatic ranges, and convenience foods, relieving them from the "total bondage of home chores." But rather than denigrating the work of the homemaker, she praised the group for bringing home economics know-how to girls and women and for using the home "as a springboard to citizenship." She praised the home economists for managing several lives successfully: home, professional, career, and children. They were exemplars of the natural woman.[5]

In describing the natural woman, Lady Bird Johnson was essentially describing herself and her work as first lady. Anthropologist Margaret Mead wrote that Lady Bird Johnson, who was unruffled by the feminine mystique, had "successfully woven together strands of a complicated life." These strands included maintaining a home and caring for children, while pursuing a career and civic activities. Mead said that her first lady style could be a model for all American women. While Johnson was not dogmatic about which roles women should play, Mead wrote that the first lady reached out and touched them all. Besides Lady Bird's tending to her domestic first lady duties and the needs of her own daughters, Mead cited two examples of the first lady's active involvement in civic affairs: her work with Head Start and the Committee for a More Beautiful Capital, a central component of her beautification project.[6]

Lady Bird Johnson's involvement in Head Start, the program for disadvantaged preschool children and a component of Lyndon Johnson's war on poverty, began in early 1965. On 3 February 1965, at the behest of Sargent Shriver, she invited the Advisory Council of the War on Poverty for tea, cocktails, and a meeting in the Red Room. Lady Bird Johnson was inspired by the discussion. She recounted in her diary that as the guests filed out, Shriver asked if she would sponsor Head Start through an honorary chairmanship, not intended to lead to any actual work. Shriver thought her honorary role would make women want to volunteer. The first lady wrote, "I don't like being just 'honorary' anything. If I take it on, I want to work at it."[7]

She kicked off her work with a White House volunteer drive. Four hundred women crowded into the East Room for the initial meeting. Enthusiasm for the project overflowed. She made films, arranged for children's music theater programs, wrote letters to bolster projects, videotaped public service television spots, and spotlighted project sites. For example, in August 1965 she visited two program sites in New Jersey. She witnessed classrooms of five-year-olds just learning words for ordinary kitchen things—flour, salt, meal, milk, and oatmeal. Through her trip, Americans were given a glimpse of preschoolers who, through Head Start, were fed a balanced meal, given dental care and inoculations, and taken on field trips to ordinary places many had never ventured, such as the grocery store, post office, and police station.[8]

Head Start volunteers were mainly women, and she connected the program directly to motherhood. "Every mother in every stratum of society will be thrilled to hear about the program. There is now a way all of them can help either in encouraging a child to attend or in giving volunteer time to projects," she stated. She called on mothers in every community to see that no child missed an opportunity catch up in life. Margaret Mead also viewed the first lady's involvement in Head Start as an extension of her motherly role. Reaching out beyond her own daughters' needs, Mead wrote, Lady Bird Johnson was deeply concerned with the needs of the almost 1 million five-year-olds living below the poverty line. The natural woman, after all, takes responsibility for her own home, the community, and the world at large.[9]

Lady Bird Johnson is best remembered for her work on the natural world. Her concern for beautification was born in her girlhood home of Karnack, Texas. She loved the piney woods and cypress trees, and spoke often of how they inspired her. After the 1964 election, when Lyndon Johnson was meeting with his cabinet to make ready his Great Society proposals, Stewart Udall, secretary of interior, suggested that the first lady focus her beautification efforts on Washington, D.C. President Johnson then dedicated portions of his 1965 State of the Union message to the environment.[10]

From this message grew the first lady's Committee for a More Beautiful Capital. And on 11 February 1965, she led its first organizational meeting. Later that day, she wrote in her diary, "How many things are launched under the name of a tea!" Traditional White House teas were certainly taking on a new meaning in the Johnson Administration. What had started with Jacqueline Kennedy—a sustained programmatic initiative with which a president's wife could be identified—really took shape with Lady Bird Johnson. She even acquired a staff assistant for beautification, which, according to Lewis Gould, reflected how Lady Bird Johnson shaped the institution to fit her own goals.[11]

Lady Bird Johnson's early childhood education and beautification projects allowed her to embody the natural, complete woman. To her

Radcliffe audience, she said, "while indeed the world beckons and the problems of Zanzibar are your inheritance and your challenge, it still all begins right with you, in your job or studies, in your home, in your husband's work, and in your community and the way you want it to look." This quote provides insight into how she modeled what American women could do and be in the 1960s. Her projects grew out of her home and her husband's work. She did not advocate striking out on her own, as strident feminists were doing. Yet these programs allowed her to work for the greater good of the community, and they helped her to find personal satisfaction and develop her own identity and legacy.[12]

While the natural woman was broad enough to touch on all areas of a woman's life, this model was not without controversy. For example, the women doers luncheons were intended to showcase other natural women. But after the inaugural luncheons were held, some citizens wrote accusing the first lady of being unmindful of "ordinary women." Liz Carpenter admitted that the honorees and guests were "professional career woman types . . . vital, but not always an attractive lot, and not always the kind that the average woman can identify with." The first lady's choice to highlight working professionals, rather than nonworking women, shows that fissures existed even at this early date.[13]

Meanwhile, the first lady's office struggled to strike an appropriate balance between the domestic and the civic. For example, Liz Carpenter pushed back on providing the press details of the first lady's wardrobe. She went out of her way to not announce what Lady Bird Johnson was wearing. According to Carpenter, Lady Bird Johnson did not put clothes first in her list of priorities. "And you had a previous first lady who . . . was a clothes horse," Carpenter said. In contrast, the East Wing "wanted to accent what Mrs. Johnson did rather than what she wore." But American women remained interested in what the first lady wore, and the women's press corps took issue with Johnson's fashion pushback. The reporters often resorted to detective work. If Lady Bird Johnson left her jacket draped over a chair, the newswomen would go over and inspect the label.[14]

Carpenter did, however, release the domestic fine points of the women doers luncheons, which the women's press corps devoured. For example, the luncheon on beautification included Maryland cream soup, baby squab, strawberries, and demitasse. Flowers adorning the table included yellow, white, and orange ranunculus and freesia and blue bachelor's buttons. The table was set with the Truman china and sterling flatware. Though Carpenter would release the text of the first lady's remarks at the luncheons, the press at times seemed more interested in domestic minutiae. For example, after one luncheon, syndicated columnist Vera Glaser reported that guests sat in "mahogany chairs under an Empire chandelier in the blue-and-white dining room of the presidential apartments, eating crab meat avocado prepared by the Johnson's long-time cook Zephyr Wright and served on the Lincoln and Roosevelt china." Her report detailed style, such as the Kennedy crystal, engraved matchbooks and silver ashtrays, and gold-rimmed place cards. Glaser mentioned nothing about the substantive content of the luncheon. A picture of the menu was included along with the caption, "Lady Bird still manages to keep size 10 figure."[15]

PAT NIXON

Soon after the 1968 election, the press began speculating about what Pat Nixon's project would be. Many in the West Wing staff pressured the first lady to zone in on one project. "Volunteerism" became the term used to describe Pat Nixon's efforts to recognize ordinary, private citizens who were working toward the betterment of the nation. Volunteerism was a conservative, traditionally feminine focus but also encouraged women to move outside of the home. In early 1969, her volunteer efforts generated favorable press coverage.[16]

Pat Nixon, however, resisted having volunteerism labeled her sole focus. She wanted to be known for her diplomatic work, which she began during the vice presidential years, when she traveled to fifty-three countries. While Eleanor Roosevelt and Jacqueline Kennedy had both traveled abroad, substantive international diplomacy was Pat Nixon's innovation to the first lady's role. Between 1969 and 1974, she visited thirty-two foreign countries. Moreover, as feminists increased their pressure on the administration, her foreign travels showcased the president's wife exercising agency, moving beyond the ceremonial and tackling substantive policy assignments at the president's direction. Her foreign travels, in other words, were a way for the administration to politicize the power dynamics of the presidential marriage.

Meanwhile, Pat Nixon had to address the charge that the ERA would destroy the family, as well as field questions about abortion and government-funded child care.[17]

On some trips, she traveled with her husband but was given her own diplomatic responsibilities. On other trips, she traveled solo and was designated as an official presidential representative. She traveled to Peru in June 1970 to visit areas devastated by an earthquake that killed 50,000 and left another 800,000 homeless. Pat Nixon wanted to help, and Richard Nixon suggested that she should go. She left the country on Air Force One, loaded down with relief supplies contributed by volunteer groups. Diplomatic teas did not top Pat Nixon's agenda. According to a press release, Pat Nixon's official mission was to assess firsthand what kinds of assistance could be most effectively used by the Peruvian government and relief organizations and to contribute to a better understanding of how U.S. citizens could assist the Peruvian people. She flew into high mountain areas to view damage Peruvian officials had not even seen. She walked through rubble and visited with stricken villagers. The trip was considered a diplomatic success.[18]

But it was her January 1972 trip to Africa—to Liberia, Ghana, and Ivory Coast—that caused the press to proclaim that a "new Pat Nixon" had emerged. A story in *Newsweek* reported that she "blossomed" in Africa. Africans saw "a relaxed, confident, even fun-loving public figure." The first lady, however, denied that a new woman had budded. She said, "I've been traveling on the international scene since 1953, and I did all the things I do today. But, of course, our trips then were not covered so well. Now people have a chance to know what the real Pat Nixon is like." Pat Nixon's new substantive role fit with the second-wave celebration of wives taking power. The media was looking for her to model wifely proactivity, and her diplomatic trips gave them what they were looking for.[19]

The official purpose of the Africa trip was to represent the president at the inauguration of Liberian president William Tolbert. She was honored in an official diplomatic arrival ceremony with a nineteen-gun salute usually reserved for a head of state. She rode forty miles with Tolbert in an open-air motorcade. Tolbert praised her in his inaugural address as a "testimony of strength, solidarity and permanence of this special relationship between our two countries." She offered the na-

*Pat Nixon dressed in the national costume of Liberian women on her January 1972
diplomatic trip to Africa. Courtesy Richard Nixon Presidential Library.*

tions two one-year graduate scholarships, fully financed by the State
Department, for young women to study in the United States. As *Time*
magazine stated, "Never before had an American first lady visited Africa, acted as the nation's official representative at an event of state, or
conferred with heads of state on behalf of her husband."[20]

The Africa trip was centered on foreign policy. The State Department
prepared briefing materials and talking points on African and international policies, including Rhodesia, South Africa, and the future of U.S.
foreign aid. In all three countries, Pat Nixon briefed heads of state on
her husband's upcoming trip to the People's Republic of China, telling
the leaders that the main purpose of the trip was to reduce tension, not
to establish formal diplomatic relations. Internal White House memoranda acknowledged that the first lady's trip did enhance the reputation of the United States.[21]

Her Africa trip also bought the administration political capital with
women's groups. Barbara Franklin wrote to Pat Nixon's daughter Julie,
"It is clear . . . that women were delighted with your Mother's successful trip to Africa. I believe they identify strongly with a first lady repre-

senting the country on a very substantive assignment." As her first lady role began to encompass autonomous politics and policy, her public image shifted away from plastic Pat.[22]

For the Nixons' historic visit to China in February 1972, which was intended to mend twenty years of broken diplomatic relations, Pat Nixon had little control over her schedule. Though she digested briefing papers before the trip, her itinerary was micromanaged by her official Chinese guides. But an American press contingent was allowed to travel with the delegation, and Americans saw the country through the eyes of the first lady. Americans watched her tour the Peking Zoo, sample native cuisine in the kitchens of the Peking Hotel, and witness an acupuncture treatment. Then in May and June 1972, the Nixons traveled to Moscow. While Richard Nixon talked strategic arms reduction, Pat Nixon again handled the people-to-people aspects. She could not freely mingle with the people there either. She visited children's ballet classes and Soviet classrooms. She shopped in a department store and was startled by a bear at the Moscow circus.[23]

Pat Nixon's involvement in the Russia and China trips was a public relations triumph for the administration, even though they did not showcase the first lady on substantive assignments. Her trips did, however, reflect the changing roles of women at home and abroad. Just before Richard Nixon departed for China, he announced that Pat Nixon would be handling the people-to-people aspects of the trip. In the same speech, he said, "For us in the United States to recognize that in many parts of the world women are now reaching a new state of recognition and that we on our part should demonstrate that we also have that same standard, that is a message on a people-to-people basis that is enormously important to get across." Therefore, Richard Nixon was in essence saying that his wife's job was to reflect women's new status of visibility and credibility. Pat Nixon's foreign travels also provided evidence of Richard Nixon's recognition of women's abilities in the public sphere. For example, one administration talking points memo noted that the status he accorded to women was evident in his personal life, as evidenced by "the unprecedented role of responsibility and partnership which he accorded the first lady during their visit to China, and during her earlier solo tour . . . in West Africa." Therefore, on her foreign trips, Pat Nixon's role was a way to showcase the presidential marriage, particularly the agency accorded to the first lady by her husband.[24]

As Jane Mansbridge has written, "For many conservative Americans, the personal became political for the first time when questions of family, children, sexual behavior, and women's roles became subjects of political debate." The year 1973 witnessed the beginnings of a conservative backlash to the women's movement. The backlash drew support from those Richard Nixon called the Silent Majority.[25]

The ERA personalized the political for many Americans and provided an impetus for the backlash against feminism. By late 1973, the forward momentum on the ERA had come to a near standstill, especially as Phyllis Schlafly began to argue that the ERA would damage the family. For example, her August 1973 newsletter, under the heading "The Precious Rights ERA Will Take Away from Wives," argued that ERA ratification would mean all laws that say the husband must support his wife would immediately become unconstitutional. Divorced women would lose the presumption of custody of children. Unwilling homemakers would be forced to provide half of the family's income or be subject to criminal penalties.[26]

Citizens who wrote to Pat Nixon about the ERA worried about how it would impact the family. "Not being political minded I don't understand much of Washington but the ERA is another thing," wrote one woman. "If the family goes, so goes the nation and this movement will destroy the nation via the family." Another writer stated, "The Equal Rights Amendment frightens me. As I interpret this, the laws will be changed to the effect that women are 50 percent responsible for the family income. . . . It seems to me that the right for career women, as outlined in the amendment, takes away my right to choose to stay home. . . . It literally forces the homemaker out of the house and into the working world." She pleaded, "Please, Mrs. Nixon, help us save the family units by allowing we full-time homemakers to stay home if we wish." Other writers expressed disapproval of the first lady's pro-ERA stance. As one writer lamented, "I cannot believe . . . that you won't come to the same conclusions that most God fearing women who are informed have, that this is an unnecessary and chaotic stand. What kind of a heritage will we leave our families if this form of rights is imposed on us?" By supporting the ERA, Pat Nixon stood against the groundswell of opposition that would eventually attach itself to her own party.[27]

In 1973, the Supreme Court handed down *Roe v. Wade*, ruling that the Fourteenth Amendment included the right to have an abortion. The decision further mobilized conservatives. The ERA and abortion became linked because feminists discussed both in terms of women's rights. Abortion also linked the personal to political, as it represented the ultimate rejection of motherhood and, therefore, of the entire social structure based on the family unit. By association, abortion placed a controversial frame around all women's rights issues.[28]

Richard Nixon took a public stand against abortion. Even before *Roe v. Wade* was handed down, women officials in the administration wanted him to minimize the abortion issue, although they acknowledged it would not be easy. Abortion questions were being hurled at politicians, with the first lady a prime target. At her first press conference of the 1972 campaign season, she fielded questions on abortion, stating that it was "a very personal thing." She said that she was "really not for abortion," especially "abortion on demand." At campaign appearances in Chicago that year, she was subjected to a rigorous inquisition on abortion and appeared shaken. One reporter asked her whether a woman who had an abortion should be prosecuted as a criminal. The first lady said, "Oh, no, I think it's a personal decision with the woman." When told that in some states a woman could be prosecuted as a criminal, the first lady replied, "Well, I don't know anything about state laws, but I know it is controlled by a state. I mean, I don't know which laws are which state, but I have already taken a public stand on that—and I noticed that both conventions did not take a stand for legalized abortions." In 1972, both Republican and Democratic platforms were silent on abortion, though both continued to support the ERA.[29]

Reporters also pressed Pat Nixon on government-funded child-care centers. American feminists viewed state-sponsored child care as a necessary step toward women's economic equality. To conservatives, however, government-funded child care was another assault on the family. The 1972 Republican platform acknowledged that lack of access to child care limited job opportunities for women. At the same time, the Republican platform recognized that the family was primarily responsible for a child's care. Ultimately, Republicans supported locally controlled child-care facilities that did not heavily engage the federal government. This compromise stance is indicative of the tug between feminists and social conservatives in Republican ranks at the time. Pat Nixon spoke out against child-care centers, saying that they were too costly and should be handled through private efforts. Her stance was indicative of Republican distancing from this personal-political issue.

In 1973 and 1974, the press bombarded Pat Nixon with Watergate queries. In 1974, she traveled as a presidential representative to the in-augurations of the presidents of Brazil and Venezuela. The administration hoped it would generate needed positive coverage, but the pall of Watergate followed her there. Under pressure, she appeared irritated and continued to affirm support for her husband amid mounting evidence of wrongdoing. Thus, the image of plastic Pat was resuscitated as the Nixon administration drew to a close.[30]

BETTY FORD

Betty Ford's outspokenness on marriage, abortion, infidelity, co-habitation, and women's health helped her to connect the personal to political. She became known for her candor precisely because she connected the personal to political on a regular basis, bringing into the public forum issues that had previously been considered private family matters. The public perception that she sided with the women's liberation movement compelled her to reach out to housewives, and she used her White House platform to model domesticity in an economy plagued by high inflation.

In her remarks to the Greater Cleveland IWY Congress in October 1975, Betty Ford decried social customs restricting women's roles, stating that they sprang from "emotional ideas about what women can and should do." Referencing her work to get the ERA ratified, Ford said that the criticism she received showed what happened when a definition of proper behavior collided with the right of an individual to personal opinions. Ford even decried the limitations on the first ladyship, particularly her status as a wife. "I do not believe that being first lady should prevent me from expressing my ideas," she said. "I spoke out on [the ERA] because of my deep personal convictions. Why should my husband's job, or yours, prevent us from being ourselves? Being lady-like does not require silence." In other words, marriage and femininity should not suppress a woman's voice, even that of the first lady, whose position is defined by her marriage.[31]

To many social conservatives, Betty Ford seemed to be dislodging the family from its national moorings. No first lady before or since spoke so forthrightly about abortion. In her very first press conference, a reporter asked for her opinion on the liberalization of abortion laws, inquiring whether her opinions were closer to those of vice president designate Nelson Rockefeller, who favored abortion rights, or to Senator James Buckley, who had introduced a constitutional amendment to undo *Roe v. Wade*. Betty Ford replied that her stance was definitely closer to Rockefeller's.[32]

In her *60 Minutes* interview, correspondent Morley Safer observed that the higher a man reached in politics, the less outspoken his wife became. Safer said that the opposite seemed to happen to Betty Ford, especially on abortion. Betty Ford responded, "I feel very strongly that it was the best thing in the world when the Supreme Court voted to legalize abortion, and in my words, bring it out of the backwoods and put it in the hospitals where it belonged. I thought it was a great, great decision." Betty Ford's comments raised the ire of the increasingly vocal pro-life movement, but she thought that making the personal political was more important than appeasement. The press and public also questioned the extent to which she and the president were of one mind on the abortion issue. Gerald Ford, while not altogether opposed to abortion, believed that the 1973 Supreme Court decision went too far, and he supported restrictions on the use of federal funds for abortion. Even so, both Fords were distancing themselves from the pro-life movement rising in their own party.[33]

The growth of the women's liberation movement depended upon its consciousness raising ability, whereby women told each other their personal stories and claimed them as a basis for political action. Personal issues, including housework, child rearing, and sexual relations, became political issues subject to group action and change. Family relationships were brought into question, which caused defensiveness, confusion, and alarm. One reason Betty Ford's *60 Minutes* interview became controversial was that she brought these personal matters into the public dialogue. For example, she discussed cohabitation, the trend of young people living together before marriage. When Safer asked, "Well, what if Susan Ford came to you and said, 'Mother, I'm having an affair,'" Betty Ford replied, "Well, I wouldn't be surprised. I think she's a perfectly normal human being like all young girls, if she wanted to continue and I would certainly counsel and advise her on the subject, and I'd want to know pretty much [everything] about the young man that she was planning to have the affair with." Betty Ford did not espouse sexual purity, along with some in the women's liberation movement.[34]

In October 1974, *Time* ran a cover story entitled, "The Relentless Ordeal of Political Wives," which analyzed the psychological strain on women married to politicians. Political wives' personal problems mirrored the strains on other wives, but on a larger scale. The article noted that although Betty Ford had an apparently happy family life, she also veered on the edge of her "nervous resources." Political wives were expected to manage households and raise families, often without help from their husbands. Yet, they were also advisers, secretaries, vote getters, and television personalities. As such, the political wife may lose her own identity. Betty Ford publicly admitted that the demands of being a political wife caused her develop a pinched nerve in her neck that painkillers could not cure. She even admitted to seeing a psychiatrist, saying, "I completely lost my sense of self-worth." For Betty Ford, speaking candidly was one way to liberate herself from the trappings of political wifehood.[35]

The politics of the body was also a prevailing topic in the women's liberation movement. Betty Ford added to the public dialogue about women's breast health. During a routine gynecological exam, doctors had discovered a suspicious lump in her right breast. Two days later, she was on the operating table. When she underwent a radical mastectomy in September 1974, Betty Ford could easily have chosen to remain silent. But she believed the time was right to speak out. In so doing, she became the first president's wife to take the stage on a public health issue. Intimate details of her hospital stay and procedure were covered in the papers. The night before surgery, she dined on steak and fries and in the morning awoke to three bouquets of flowers from her husband. She donned toeless white operating-room socks and joked that they would be featured in *Women's Wear Daily*. It took doctors only fifteen minutes to determine that the small nodule, two centimeters in circumference

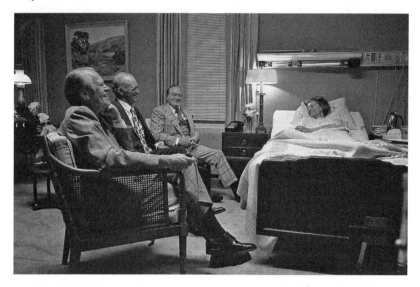

Gerald Ford, Bob Hope, and Hugh Davis visit Betty Ford at the Bethesda Naval Hospital during her recovery from breast cancer surgery on 5 October 1974. She allowed unprecedented publicity surrounding her surgery. Courtesy Gerald R. Ford Presidential Library.

and immediately fast-frozen with liquid nitrogen, was cancerous. In the two-and-one-half-hour procedure, the surgeon removed her entire right breast, its underlying pectoral muscle, and lymphoid tissue in the adjacent armpit. This was remarkable information to pass on in an age when breast cancer surgery was little understood by the public. Mammograms were a new technology, and few women performed breast self-exams. After the surgery, in national magazines, Betty Ford gave instructions on how to perform those self-exams. At public appearances, she talked about her physical disfigurement and how she began to wear low-cut dresses as soon as her scar healed. Her impact on public awareness was measurable. During her hospitalization, 45,000 letters and cards poured into the White House, and NBC reported that six times as many women were seeking breast cancer screenings.[36]

Though sympathetic to women's liberation, Betty Ford tried to reconcile her supporters and critics. "A housewife deserves to be honored as much as a woman who earns her living in the marketplace," Betty Ford wrote. "I consider bringing up children a responsible job. In fact, being a good housewife seems to me a much tougher job than going to the office and getting paid for it." In an interview with *Good Housekeeping*, she told readers that her definition of a liberated woman is one who feels confident in herself and is happy in what she is doing—whether in the home or working outside.[37]

In her public remarks, she consistently elevated the role of the housewife and tried to explain how the ERA would help them. At the Cleveland IWY conference, she said she was distressed that one outgrowth of the ERA debate had been a lack of appreciation of the role of wives and mothers. She told her audience that she was proud to have played both the roles of a career woman and a stay-at-home mother. "We have to take that 'just' out of 'just a housewife.' We have to show our pride in having the home and family as our life's work. Downgrading this work has been part of the pattern in our society that has undervalued women's talents in all areas." She told *Good Housekeeping* that homemakers were the backbone of society. A recent study had placed the housewife's average monetary value at $5,750. Betty Ford, however, said that they were worth at least $30,000 because that is what it would cost to hire a cook, nursemaid, cleaning woman, doctor, and chauffeur. And as Americans were considering the economic value of housework, Betty Ford said that the first lady deserved to earn a salary. She reasoned, "It has long hours and a lot of responsibilities. But I would have it so that a first lady can't collect unless she works."[38]

Because of her ERA activism, Betty Ford was placed on the defensive in regard to homemaking. When she was considering an invitation to speak at a seminar on women in the home sponsored by Georgetown University, Susan Porter reasoned that she should attend because it would have the "positive effect of focusing her interest in women in the home and diluting some of what has been characterized as her 'radical' stand in support of the Equal Rights Amendment." The purpose of the seminar was twofold: to give recognition to homemakers and to highlight the problems of homemakers. As the value of homemaking was being called into question, Betty Ford urged homemakers to find their identities through their "profession in the home." She spoke about her previous dancing career, saying that appearing onstage at Carnegie Hall was equally as challenging as homemaking and characterized homemaking as the more rewarding of the two professions. She was presented with an outstanding homemaker award, an honor for keeping her identity as a person while still functioning as a wife and mother.[39]

Betty Ford also used her White House platform to model for American women how to keep home during the worrisome economic climate. In the mid-1970s, inflation ran wild. In August 1974, the month Gerald Ford took office, the Consumer Price Index had risen more than 1 percent from the previous month. The Wholesale Price Index had risen over 3 percent from the previous month, the second largest increase since 1946. In his first address to Congress, Gerald Ford deemed inflation "domestic enemy number one," and he formed an organization called WIN, which stood for Whip Inflation Now, to help stabilize prices. In a Cabinet Room ceremony that fall, the first couple signed the WIN consumer pledge—to buy wisely, increase productivity, and save energy. Betty Ford lived out this pledge, exemplifying purchasing shrewdness for both her own family and White House social events.[40]

At her first press conference, Betty Ford discussed her plans for belt tightening in the White House kitchen. "You have to have a certain balance of budget if you are a housewife, and keep a checkbook. At least my checkbook has to balance," she said of her own spending. "We don't eat as much steak as they would like to have or roast beef or some of those things that the boys like," she also said.[41]

In November 1974, Betty Ford spoke at a White House economic briefing for women's organizations. Here again, she affirmed the importance of housewives during the time of high inflation. "It is important that we, as women, take a lead in this fight because we are the consumers, we are the people who decide how our families spend their money. We feel the pinch more acutely than any other member of our family, and we need to be as knowledgeable of every respect of the economy as possible." She schooled the women on the importance of children cleaning their plates and revealed that the president cleaned his plate, saying, to laughter, "if they didn't take it away, I am afraid he would eat the plate also."[42]

Magazines featured tips from Betty Ford on fighting inflation. For example, *U.S. News & World Report* told of how she held regular meetings with the chef and housekeeping staff to strategize about how to limit buying. She ordered them to shop as carefully as they would for their own families and to buy economy-sized products. She frequently served rice-, noodle-, or tuna-based casseroles. Stuffed peppers were a White House staple. Desserts were limited because the president felt strongly about the high price of sugar. Both Fords agreed to abstain from ice cream and Jell-O. Betty Ford said that she could do without designer clothes, varying her wardrobe instead of expanding it by strategically switching scarves and swapping garments with her daughter. Betty Ford would buy evening shoes in white fabric, and then dye and redye them, also opting to have old shoes resoled and reheeled by a cobbler.[43]

Betty Ford shared low-budget recipes as examples of everyday fare whipped up by the White House chef. Each could be prepared at a total cost of two to three dollars for four to six servings. These included curry of lamb with rice, baked ham, potatoes, and onions, as well as tuna fish and noodles. Newspapers around the country reprinted them and reviewed them.[44]

Betty Ford also keyed official entertaining to the problems on inflation. The blue and silver gown she wore to the White House dinner honoring Bruno Kreisky, chancellor of Austria, for example, was recycled. The first lady's social secretary related how her predecessors had White House cars at their disposal. "We take taxicabs now," she said. And even though Betty Ford served a seemingly fancy dinner consisting of turtle soup with sherry, supreme of royal squab, wild rice, zucchini sautéed, hearts of palm salad, brie cheese, and praline mousse for the official visit of Harold Wilson, British prime minister, she found ways to cut corners. She substituted soup for the traditional fish course. She also instructed the chef to cut the squab in halves, so that those who wanted less could take less. For state dinners, Betty Ford set rules for the kitchen staff. She told them to use fresh vegetables that were in season and American rather than imported wines, also instructing them to make portions small and use all leftovers.[45]

When she hosted the Republican congressional wives for an outdoor party, Betty Ford's invitations read, "Bring your brown-bag lunch." All of the details were tailored to cost saving. The tablecloths were made out of red bandana sheets, and the napkins were fashioned from coordinating blue sheets. The centerpiece pots holding red geraniums and blue bachelor buttons were set into a large brown bag and tied with ribbons. Newspapers around the country advised women to transfer this economical way of entertaining to their own bridge parties and sewing bees.[46]

Though her tips were intended to help housewives, they sometimes backfired. In a speech to the Washington, D.C., Mayor's Food Dollar Conference, Betty Ford told the 375 attendees that she was buying less beef and more fish, spurring the Ford administration into damage control mode. Congressman Paul Findley of Illinois wrote to President Ford that his wife's comment had "started a stampede of livestock producers who phoned their beef to me." He noted, "If the eat-less-meat theme catches on, financial disaster for livestock producers will stretch . . . to a headlong gallop." He asked Gerald Ford to pass the word along to his wife that beef was still a good buy. A group of Texas ranchers also sent the first lady a fattened calf purchased through a local auction ring and butchered, at a total cost of sixty-three cents per pound. They wanted to illustrate the point that beef was still a bargain once the supermarket middlemen were cut out. "Since you are the first lady of the United States, we must assume that you are also the first housewife. . . . If we can sell you on our product, then we may have a chance with the other housewives of the United States," the ranchers wrote. The White House tried to downplay the story, but the press nevertheless picked up the details of the ranchers' beef delivery. While illustrating the power first ladies can have over household buying habits, the eat-less-beef example also shows how they must exercise caution when their cooking advice delves into the politics of agriculture.[47]

Despite her actions to help homemakers, Betty Ford's outspokenness on personal issues caused problems for the Ford campaign moving into the 1976 primary season. Though Gerald Ford won in convention balloting, Republican feminists like Betty Ford were on the defensive. They fought to maintain the pro-ERA plank in the platform, which had been inserted without question in 1972. They failed to block an antiabortion plank. Instead, the platform supported a constitutional amendment to restore the right to life for unborn citizens. The Democratic platform supported the ERA and said nothing of abortion, suggesting a deepening division between the parties on women's rights. Republican feminists supported Gerald Ford, but Ronald Reagan, the preferred choice of conservative women, was able to mount a serious convention challenge. Reagan's wife, Nancy, was framed as a counter-

Gerald Ford, the Republican nominee, shakes hands with Ronald Reagan on the closing night of the Republican convention on 19 August 1976 as Betty Ford and Nancy Reagan stand at their sides. The candidates' wives sparred over women's issues during the primary, highlighting the divide that was emerging in the Republican Party. Courtesy Gerald R. Ford Presidential Library.

point to Betty Ford on women's issues, mirroring internal party divisions.[48]

In her very first prepared political speech, delivered in the wake of Betty Ford's *60 Minutes* interview, Nancy Reagan attacked the breakdown of traditional moral standards emerging among young people. To a Republican women's club in Michigan, she said, "The young people on college campuses and elsewhere are told that to be 'cool' and 'with it,' they should have no 'hang-ups' about sex and premarital living arrangements." She lamented that under the new morality, young people were eschewing committed relationships, "the most enriching human experience." Though she did not attack Betty Ford directly, follow-up questioners dealt with the contrast between their views on personal relationships. The speech garnered the headline, "Nancy Reagan Disagrees with Betty Ford on Sex." It was clear that Nancy Reagan would stand for traditional morality in opposition to feminists.[49]

On the primary campaign trail, the press further highlighted the wives' conflicting views. On the ERA, Nancy Reagan said that she supported her husband's view that the proposed amendment could "lead to a lot of mischief," while Betty Ford maintained that equal rights could not be achieved without it. Betty Ford criticized Nancy Reagan's marriage, saying, "I just think when Nancy met Ronnie that was it as far as her own life was concerned. She just fell apart at the seams." While Betty Ford continued to lament that she did not get her husband to appoint a woman to the Supreme Court, Nancy Reagan said of her influence over women's appointments, "I am sure my husband knows much better than I do who is qualified and who is not qualified." As the women's liberation movement questioned submission in marriage, the competing wife-styles frame became common in coverage of first lady candidates.[50]

The landscape for candidates' wives had certainly changed from eight years earlier. An article in the *New York Times* said that all anybody wanted to know about back in 1968 were the wives' favorite recipes, hobbies, and children's ages. With household questions gone "the way of the butter churn," candidates' wives were fair game for intimate questions about their personal lives. When asked what brought about the change, political wives mentioned three reasons: the women's rights movement, Watergate, and Betty Ford's frankness. The press and public now expected the candidates' wives to link the personal to the political.[51]

ROSALYNN CARTER

Rosalynn Carter set out to display partnership and full participation in marriage through her role as first lady. Through her initiatives, especially mental health and foreign diplomacy, she emphasized the power and agency the president accorded her. In other words, her political roles were a manifestation of the couple's personal relationship. As early as the 1976 campaign, strategists encouraged her to emphasize her independence. "This is a good woman's issue," they noted. "You cannot overstress that you are independent, yet, of course, plugged into the whole campaign at the highest level . . . the decision makers include you and your own staff." In the late 1970s, the personal lives of candidates, particularly their family relationships, were under careful scrutiny.[52]

In the closing days of the 1976 election, Jimmy Carter confessed to *Playboy* magazine, "I've looked on a lot of women with lust. I've committed adultery in my heart many times." Carter apparently made these remarks to assure *Playboy* readers that he was not puritanical. His remarks sparked uncertainty about his character, and Rosalynn Carter was dogged everywhere with questions. She said that his remarks were taken out of context and that he was trying to explain Christian forgiveness. As the candidate's wife, Rosalynn Carter was the only one who could reassure Americans about her husband's private character, now on display for the American public.[53]

During the campaign, Rosalynn Carter also had to deal with criticism of her child-care choices. While some heralded her for keeping a demanding campaign schedule, others criticized her for spending eighteen months on the road, leaving her eight-year-old daughter at home. While Rosalynn Carter assured her critics that Amy was happy and surrounded by cousins and under the loving care of her grandmother, the issue of child care and working women continued to polarize. Now that women had a choice, Rosalynn Carter had to answer for her prioritization of work over family.[54]

Women's liberation also peppered reporters' questions, as they zeroed in on the contradictions inherent in being both liberated and a political wife. In an interview with *U.S. News & World Report*, she said that she did not feel her life was submerged in her husband's. "I've been able to do so many things. . . . I feel that I have always had my own identity. I never have felt submerged. Jimmy has never considered me as submerged." She wanted to get the point across that she was able to pursue her own goals even while identifying as a politician's wife.[55]

Rather than serve as the traditional helpmeet, Rosalynn Carter framed the first ladyship as a vehicle for accomplishing her own goals, with mental health her major project. Her work on mental health allowed her to showcase the themes of women's liberation, while also bringing a previously personal issue into the political realm. Her work officially began on 17 February 1977, when Jimmy Carter signed an executive order establishing the President's Commission on Mental Health, with his wife taking on the title of active honorary chair. She got upset when she was told that, because of federal nepotism laws, she could not serve as the official chairperson. At the signing ceremony,

Jimmy Carter described his wife as "one of my partners, an expert advisor on mental health problems . . . whose judgment I trust implicitly." When he gave the microphone over to her, she said that establishing the mental health commission was her idea and a fulfillment of her own campaign promise. There was nary a hint of wifely deference.[56]

For an honorary chair, Rosalynn Carter was indeed active. Along with overseeing the twenty-member commission, she coordinated efforts with 450 individuals from around the country—professionals, local officials, and laypersons—and thirty task panels. The commission held a series of public hearings around the country, in which 400 individuals—from psychiatrists to parents of the mentally ill—testified. She attended approximately forty meetings, briefings, conferences, and seminars on mental health. In addition, she participated in about twenty-five mental health receptions and facility tours. After months of study and deliberation, the commission issued its final report to the president, containing a series of 117 recommendations. These were turned into the proposed Mental Health Systems Act, and the first lady testified on its behalf before the Senate Subcommittee on Health. Rosalynn Carter lobbied hard for it, and the bill became law in October 1980. At the signing ceremony, she described her work as extraordinary and fulfilling and clearly framed herself as the administration point person responsible for getting the bill through.[57]

The press, however, questioned her spousal authority. They speculated about Rosalynn Carter's weekly working lunches with the president, her presence at cabinet meetings, and her participation in national security briefings. "Who elected her?" questions also percolated in June 1977, when Rosalynn Carter embarked on a two-week, 12,000-mile diplomatic trip to Jamaica, Costa Rica, Ecuador, Peru, Brazil, Colombia, and Venezuela.

Rosalynn Carter's talks with heads of state were substantive. In Jamaica, she got the prime minister to promise to sign the 1969 American Convention on Human Rights. In Costa Rica, she talked trade restrictions. In Ecuador, she tried to smooth over her husband's veto of the sale of military jets to the nation. In Peru, she discussed arms control. In Brazil, she defended her husband's decision not to sell the country $50 million in arms.[58]

Judy Woodruff on NBC's *Today* show questioned Rosalynn Carter about what right she had to conduct foreign policy since she was not an elected official. She told Woodruff that her husband wanted her to go. "I thought I could represent him well. Because I'm close to him. And these leaders know that I can come back and tell him their feelings too," she said. When Woodruff insinuated that foreign officials would not take her seriously because she did not have an official position, she replied, "I think that I have a pretty important position. . . . I am close to Jimmy and I think that that makes it easier for me to be able to . . . convey that information to Jimmy." Woodruff went on to ask whether her foreign diplomacy was actually a setback to the women's movement. "You were handed an assignment simply because you're the wife of a president," she said. Rosalynn Carter disagreed. "Without exception, in every country I went to there was a remark about me being a woman and being able to do this." But Woodruff wanted to highlight the traditional trappings of the first ladyship that would prevent any of its occupants from claiming an accomplishment as her own.[59]

Though Rosalynn Carter believed she was using her marital partnership to advance women's opportunities, her actions representing the president in foreign affairs conflicted with the women's liberation movement's goal of wifely independence. As Meg Greenfield editorialized in *Newsweek*, the liberated political wife would be allowed to have "a separate set of views and purposes and a First Amendment right to air them—never mind that they may cost the old boy his job." Betty Ford, admired for her outspokenness even when her views were at cross-purposes with her husband's, was a good example, Greenfield said. But Rosalynn Carter rooting her foreign policy authority in her marriage showed that she was not liberated from the role of political wife.[60]

As Rosalynn Carter took on more responsibility in an effort to showcase her partnership, the issue of a political wife's democratic accountability also arose. Some Americans were uncomfortable with the idea of a manipulative woman being the power behind the throne. As a result, public reaction to the first lady's Latin American trip was not overwhelmingly positive. A Roper poll found that, while most believed she performed well, only 55 percent responded that a first lady should officially represent the United States in talks with foreign countries. Employed women were the group most likely to approve of her diplomatic role.[61]

Some also wondered whether Rosalynn Carter influenced her husband's opinion on abortion. As both Christians and Democrats, the Carters had to tread lightly. Rosalynn Carter was not as outspoken on abortion as Betty Ford. She opposed it for herself. In the late 1970s, the country was debating whether the federal government should fund abortions. On this issue, Rosalynn Carter stood squarely with her husband. In 1976, Congress passed the Hyde Amendment, which denied the use of Medicaid funds for abortions except when the life of the pregnant mother was in danger. Jimmy Carter was not in favor of federal funding for abortion, and Rosalynn Carter told Barbara Walters in an interview that she was not for it either. She explained to Barbara Walters that in Georgia they established family planning clinics in every county. She believed in funding alternatives to abortion, rather than perpetuating the cycle of abortions with federal funding.[62]

The partisan differences that had sprouted in the mid-1970s fully materialized in 1980. The Democratic Party was firmly pro-choice, and its platform favored federal funding for abortions. Republicans, on the other hand, advocated a pro-life constitutional amendment and the appointment of pro-life judges. Republicans supported the continued restriction on federal funding for abortion. While Reagan's 1980 victory caused the ERA to effectively disappear, the abortion controversy did not go away. Instead, abortion would polarize and inform fundamental worldviews more than ever, which would, in turn, impact the first lady's role moving into the 1980s.[63]

AFTER 1980

CHAPTER FIVE *Women's Rights and Human Rights*

hrough the actions of first ladies serving after 1980, we see the legacy of the second wave in three main areas. Though we do not see each first lady acting in every one of these areas, each one did have a role in linking together women's rights and human rights.

First, the debate over women's political and legal equality continued in the United States, though organized feminism lost its political clout. The ERA faded from debate, and journalists, academics, and even feminists themselves declared that the movement was dead. However, abortion and family politics continued to polarize, and these topics will be considered in the next chapter. Public officials also had to grapple with the gender gap in voting behavior. First ladies expounded the evolving worldviews and policy commitments of their respective parties and ideologies with regard to American women's rights and roles.[1]

Second, just as the women's rights movement had piggybacked on the civil rights movement for African Americans in the United States, other groups piggybacked on the women's rights movement. Minority groups, the disabled, and older Americans sought to end discriminatory treatment and further extend the promises of liberal democracy. Given that first ladies have historically stood for a politically underrepresented group—women—after 1980 we see some of them advocating for the rights of other such groups, an extension of their previous work.

Third, the women's rights movement spread around the globe. This occurred alongside the overthrow of communist and authoritarian regimes and an international surge toward democracy. Global activists pushed to get women's rights placed on the human rights agenda in Africa, Asia, Europe, and Latin America. Women-focused nongovernmental organizations flourished. The scope of the international women's rights movement was broad, encompassing employment opportunity, sex trafficking, parity in public office, education for women and girls, subsistence, and protection against rape and mutilation. During this era, we see some first ladies bolstering the work of global women's rights.[2]

NANCY REAGAN

Nancy Reagan was the first lady of the New Right. As Rebecca Klatch has written, the women of the new right were divided into two camps: social conservatives and laissez-faire conservatives. Both worldviews are evident in Nancy Reagan's activities, and this chapter covers her actions that touch on the laissez-faire worldview, which impacted the administration's response to the gender gap. Laissez-faire conservative women were primarily concerned about the economy and national defense, believing that human liberty was under attack at home and abroad. For example, when asked in 1980 to name the top issues American women cared about, she mentioned inflation, unemployment, and foreign policy. Laissez-faire conservative women also believed that men and women were capable and autonomous actors, possessing the right to self-determination. During the 1980 campaign, for example, Nancy Reagan said that while more women in the labor force may make the recession harder on men, "I think you have to cling to the principle that whoever does the job best, deserves the job." She was not going to advance affirmative action for women or men.[3]

Though laissez-faire conservative women were not as put off by the ERA as social conservatives, Nancy Reagan took the same position as her husband. She was for the E and the R but not the A. "I am for equal rights for everyone, not just women," she said in a campaign interview. "I'm for equal opportunity *and* equal pay *if* both men and women are equally qualified." Reflecting on the 1970s, she believed the women's movement gave women a stronger role in society and counted that as progress. However, she predicted the women's movement would settle down in the 1980s. She said, "I'm not for marches or placard waving. I think if we stopped giving all movements a 'stage' on TV, there would be fewer performances." In other words, she would not use her position to play into the feminist or antifeminist theatrics of Gloria Steinem or Phyllis Schlafly.[4]

Nancy Reagan, born Anne Francis Robbins in New York, New York, on 6 July 1923, was well acquainted with theatrics and the power of the stage. She was born the daughter of a stage actress and a used car salesman. Her parents divorced when she was a child. Nancy was left under the care of an aunt, while her mother pursued an acting career. Her mother soon married wealthy Chicago physician Loyal Davis, who was a strong conservative and impacted the views of Nancy and later her husband. She followed a typical path for a well-to-do woman in the prewar years, studying drama at Smith College and graduating in 1943. During the war years, she worked at Marshall Field's department store and as a nurse. After the war, she pursued her acting aspirations, signing on with Metro-Goldwyn-Mayer. She appeared in eleven movies, but she never became a big Hollywood star. She quit the movie industry when she married Ronald Reagan. While Ronald Reagan became increasingly involved in the conservative movement, Nancy stayed at home and raised her children. She supported him when he cochaired California Republicans for Barry Goldwater and then when he decided to run for the California governorship. She campaigned for him, choosing to make her public appearances question-and-answer sessions rather than speeches. Negative attention from the press began during Reagan's governorship. Some referred to her as "Queen Nancy" for her standards of elegance and criticized her for how she gazed at her husband when he spoke.[5]

Nancy Reagan's first year as first lady was marked by unfavorable press coverage. During the campaign, she said one of her main roles would be to bring style back to the White House. "Why shouldn't the White House be on a hill in the people's minds—both here in the U.S. and abroad?" she questioned. A stylish White House was tied to the laissez-faire conservative worldview. With the specter of communism still hanging over America, laissez-faire conservatives embraced a market economy that yielded the greatest goods and guaranteed individuals the right to the fruit of their labor.[6]

Stories about Nancy Reagan's expensive taste flared during the transition and inauguration. The press focused on her favorite designers (Adolfo, James Galanos, Bill Blass), her friends (West Coast entrepre-

neurs, Betsy Bloomingdale, Elizabeth Taylor), and her wine (chardon-
nays of Chateau Montelena and cabernets by Robert Mondavi). The
New York Times noted that Nancy Reagan represented laissez-faire ideals, founded on "buying power and an unabashed appreciation of lux-
ury" as well as "the American ethic of hard work." As the newspaper
characterized the prevailing attitude the Reagans brought to inaugural
week, what have we worked for if we can't enjoy it?[7]

Nancy Reagan's representation of the laissez-faire conservative
woman was also apparent when the Reagans asked the White House
Historical Association to establish a fund for restoring the residence.
It was the first major renovation since Jacqueline Kennedy. Private
foundations and individuals made the donations, and over $800,000
was raised. Nancy Reagan took heat when it was discovered that over
$200,000 of those funds was used to purchase 220 place settings of
Lenox china, with nineteen pieces each, including fish plates, bouillon
cups, and berry bowls. The china featured a scarlet border with gold
trim and a gold presidential seal.[8]

Nancy Reagan's laissez-faire conservatism was also highlighted
when, in August 1981, she flew to London to represent her husband at
the wedding of Prince Charles and Lady Diana. She kept a full and official itinerary, including luncheon with Margaret Thatcher, the British
prime minister, a wreath laying at the American Memorial Chapel at
St. Paul's Cathedral, and a visit to Fitzroy Square Day Care Center, a facility for handicapped children. The American press, however, focused
on how she took hundreds of thousands of dollars worth of diamonds,
rubies, and sapphires loaned to her by international jewelry firm Bulgari. British journalists critiqued her twelve-person Secret Service detail, writing about her five hatboxes, trunk of dresses, and hairdresser.[9]

Fred Fielding, counsel to the president, subsequently recommended
against accepting expensive jewelry, citing "serious appearance problems." He was concerned that they would be perceived as the "crown
jewels" and would be used to portray the first lady in a bad light. He
wrote, "Recent media coverage has, unfortunately, highlighted this
problem. It is evident that many persons in media are anxious, particularly in light of . . . budget cuts, to use any pretext to suggest that
the President and Mrs. Reagan are 'indifferent' and 'insensitive' to the
poor." Fielding characterized the coverage as less than fair.[10]

Fielding also warned Nancy Reagan against accepting loans of clothing, which she had done and the press had picked up on. To diffuse the criticism, the East Wing summoned Letitia Baldrige, former social secretary to Jacqueline Kennedy, to help with long-range planning for Nancy Reagan. Baldrige developed a plan whereby the first lady would announce to the Council of Fashion Designers of America that she would donate some clothes to museum costume collections for display and study. However, it would take a bigger effort to soften her laissez-faire conservative image.[11]

Nancy Reagan's less-publicized official activities also illustrate how she represented the laissez-faire conservative worldview. For example, on 3 February 1981, she hosted a bipartisan luncheon for the wives of eight members of the Senate Finance Committee. Her purpose was to become socially acquainted with the women whose husbands would be instrumental in passing Ronald Reagan's economic agenda. At the luncheon, she discussed the debt ceiling increase, part of Reagan's plan to cut taxes at home while increasing defense spending.[12]

Meanwhile, the Reagan administration came under fire by feminist groups. NOW publicized a gender gap in voting patterns that had appeared in the 1980 election. They seized upon it as evidence that Reagan did not have women's support because he refused to support feminist policies, such as the ERA and abortion. The Reagan administration believed that NOW's allegations were misleading. Internal polling showed that on the ERA and abortion, the opinions of men and women were not notably different. They concluded that the gender gap came from "generic" issues, particularly war and peace, the economy, and government spending for social services. Polling data also suggested that his relative unpopularity among women was driven by their perception that he lacked compassion—caring little for the elderly and poor while favoring business interests. Since the Reagans' elitist image was fostered in part by Nancy Reagan, she likely fueled the gender gap as well.[13]

Based on the conclusion that generic rather than feminist issues drove the gender gap, the administration believed it futile to "win small-scale brownie points" on what they had done for women. Instead, their strategy to win over women was to do so quietly by executing successful economic, social, and foreign policies. But they would not try to curry favor with women's groups. They purposefully stayed above the fray of feminist and antifeminist sparring. For example, Reagan's advisers did not want him to become the "third ring in the circus" in events surrounding the expiration of the ERA extension deadline, so they advised him to keep a low profile and to appear like "the magnanimous gentleman he is." This is perhaps why we also see Nancy Reagan staying out of feminist and antifeminist wrangling. It would have been a departure from the administration's overall strategy on women.[14]

The Reagan administration did have a defensive strategy on women. For example, they developed a briefing book and talking points for spokespersons on women's issues, in case they were ever asked. Nancy Reagan was one of those spokespeople. When she was pressed by an interviewer about feminist accusations that her husband had not appointed enough women to important posts, Nancy Reagan replied, "I thought you might ask that, so I have the figures right here." She also used the question to argue that women should get an appointment only if they were qualified. "They just want to have an equal shot. . . . In the final analysis your decision should be based on who best can do the job," she said.[15]

Therefore, by the end of her first year, it was clear to administration officials that Nancy Reagan had an image problem. Media coverage drove public perceptions. On 3 November 1981, social secretary Muffie Brandon wrote to Michael Deaver, Ronald Reagan's deputy chief of staff, recounting a conversation she had with a style editor at the *Washington Post*. She wrote, "I reiterated . . . our concerns were with TONE and SELECTION of material. The *New York Times* treats Mrs. Reagan as a news story; the *Post* always treats her as a style story." They believed the newspapers were not portraying her in a "fair-minded manner." A *Newsweek* poll found that 61 percent of the public believed she was less sympathetic to the problems of the underprivileged than other first ladies. Sixty-eight percent believed she was mainly concerned with style and fashion. Internal White House polling confirmed these impressions. The public cited wealth and snobbishness, the White House redecoration, and excessive expenditures as the reasons behind their negative impressions.[16]

Orchestrated by the East Wing and West Wing staffs, Nancy Reagan's project to decrease drug use among young people was the cen-

Nancy Reagan makes remarks in the East Room during the White House Conference on Drug Abuse and Families on 22 March 1982. Courtesy Ronald Reagan Presidential Library.

terpiece of her image turnaround strategy. Her focus on drugs also complemented the Reagan administration's belief that focusing on general issues would ease the gender gap. Nancy Reagan believed that the drug issue was one of the main pressures facing women and their families in the early 1980s, not the ERA, abortion, or how many women were appointed to bureaucratic posts. If she could ease the drug abuse epidemic, she believed she could improve life for all American women.[17]

In February 1982, she kicked off her antidrug campaign with a highly publicized trip through Florida and Texas. She got glowing reviews for demonstrating social sensitivity. From that point on, she fixated her work as first lady on the drug issue. As Fred Barnes later wrote, "Mrs. Reagan's crusade against drugs is a crucial part of one of the greatest political turnarounds in modern times. . . . [She has] transformed from a frivolous clotheshorse and chum of the idle-rich . . . into a compassionate friend of the troubled young." Internal polling from June 1982 showed that two-thirds of the public had positive impressions of Nancy Reagan. Older women were more likely to cite positive personal characteristics than any other group.[18]

Though liaising with organized women's interest groups was not a major part of Nancy Reagan's portfolio, as it had been for previous first ladies, many of the women's groups she did address were linked to the GOP. To these groups, her remarks were often partisan and patriotic. For example, to the National Federation of Republican Women gathered at the 1984 Republican convention, she proclaimed, "Today is a great day to be a woman and a great day to be a Republican." She told her audience that Republican women were having the greatest impact on national life. "Republican women are being heard because when they speak, it's about their values, not about themselves." She proclaimed a new era for women, one where women were free to follow "whatever path their talents and natures point to." She believed every woman had a right to feel comfortable as a chemist, executive, mother, teacher, or all of those.[19]

When Nancy Reagan did discuss women's roles, she was careful to emphasize choice and acceptance. She said, "During the seventies, the fact that the women's movement seemed to be growing so rapidly and more and more choices became available to women and also created a certain amount of pressure to make the right choices." She did not condemn the new paths opened to women by the second wave and believed the eighties brought about greater acceptance and understanding of the options available to women. She believed that one of the biggest challenges would be to find a healthy balance between one's career and one's home life. She acknowledged that children made the work-life balance issue more complicated and believed the citizens needed to find a way to ensure the country did not suffer as a result.[20]

BARBARA BUSH

Like Nancy Reagan, Barbara Bush did not condemn new paths open to women. As the wife of a conservative politician, she did not directly address many of the issues raised by the second wave, even though she was known to be sympathetic to some of its causes. She chose instead to make her mark on civil rights for other groups, particularly minorities, the disabled, and those affected by AIDS, prioritizing equality for all.

She was born Barbara Pierce in New York, New York, on 8 June 1925. Her father was an executive with the McCall Corporation, and her mother deeply influenced her love of reading. Barbara Pierce met George Bush at a dance in Greenwich, Connecticut, while he was a senior at Phillips Academy Andover and she was enrolled in Ashley Hall boarding school in Charleston, South Carolina. They became engaged while he was serving in the navy during World War II and she was a freshman at Smith College. With marriage on her mind, she did not put much effort into her studies and earned poor grades. They were married in January 1945. Barbara left Smith College behind, choosing instead to have a big family. Her first of six babies, George Walker Bush, was born while her husband was studying at Yale. Her second died of leukemia when they were settled in Texas and her husband was working in the oil industry.[21]

Even as a political wife, Barbara Bush remained somewhat aloof from the early rumblings of the second wave. The Bush family moved to Washington in 1967 after George Bush was elected to Congress. She spent her days carpooling the children to school, taking care of home and garden, attending luncheons, and entertaining. Once, she was mistakenly invited to Lady Bird Johnson's women doers luncheon for women working in the medical field. They erroneously thought she had worked as a nurse. She continued to be the prototypical political wife when George Bush served as ambassador to the United Nations and chair of the RNC under Nixon and head of the United States Liaison Office in Beijing, China, under Ford.[22]

In the late 1970s, issues of the women's movement hit closer to home for Barbara Bush. When Gerald Ford appointed George Bush CIA director, Barbara Bush plunged into a depression. She said that she was menopausal and felt depressed with her empty nest and isolated from her husband's job. She felt purposeless while women were out achieving their goals. Her depression lasted about six months. The experience motivated her to strike out on her own. She traveled the country lecturing about China to civic groups, which was the closest she came to having an occupation of her own.[23]

When George Bush ran in the presidential primary in 1980, eventually becoming the vice presidential nominee, Barbara Bush was hounded about abortion and the ERA. She believed that abortion should be allowed in the first trimester and had once been an ERA supporter. Given that her opinions did not align with social conservatives, her strategy was to deflect. To questions about her beliefs on controversial women's issues, her typical response was, "I'm not going to tell you. I'm not running for public office. George Bush is."[24]

During the vice presidential years, Barbara Bush began her literacy campaign, which would become her first lady project. Her most highly publicized moment during the vice presidency, however, occurred in 1984. Feminists succeeded in demanding that Democrats nominate a woman, Geraldine Ferraro, as the vice presidential candidate. Barbara Bush made headlines when she called Ferraro "something that rhymes with witch." With the gender gap on the minds of political strategists, Ferraro's advisors spun the comment as evidence of Republican discomfort with women candidates.[25]

While such comments earned Barbara Bush a reputation as sharptongued and honest, when she became first lady, feminists took her to task on her decision to stay mum on women's rights issues. Liz Carpenter, for example, in a book review, wrote that she could not understand why the first lady would leave the "president alone with West Wing advisers who have a long history of ignoring women's issues." Carpenter noted that Barbara Bush was uncharacteristically inarticulate on women's rights, often floundering for safe ground. Carpenter believed it was incumbent on all first ladies to discuss women's rights, calling her deflections "deeply disappointing to millions of American women." However, feminist pressures were not so strong as to compel Barbara Bush to act on her personal opinions.[26]

Carpenter's review upset the first lady, prompting Barbara Bush to draft a response, which she later reprinted in her memoir. "Long ago I decided in life that I had to have priorities," she wrote. "I put my children and my husband at the top of my list." After her children were grown, she prioritized literacy, believing it would help to solve problems ranging from teenage pregnancy to women trapped in poverty. "Abortion, pro or con, is not a priority for me. ERA is not a priority for me. . . . Teaching that all people are equal is a priority for me." Incidentally, she never sent Carpenter the letter.[27]

Nevertheless, her response illuminates her relationship to women's rights. She would not speak out directly on women's rights, a position in line with Republicans. The 1988 Republican platform was silent on the ERA and opposed comparable worth. As feminism became more and more aligned with Democrats, Republicans came to view women's rights organizations and their priorities as the adversary.[28]

Barbara Bush's letter to Carpenter, however, does reveal her intent to prioritize equality for all. She did this by advocating for rights movements that grew out of the second wave. She used her platform to advocate for Americans with disabilities and AIDS, while also forging ties with African Americans.

The 1988 Republican platform paid much more attention to Americans with disabilities than it did to women. The movement to extend rights to the disabled was likewise founded on classical liberal ideas of removing barriers to full opportunity and participation. Disabilities included learning disabilities, and this subfocus dovetailed nicely with Barbara Bush's broader literacy pet project. Early in the administration, Barbara Bush published an article in *Their World*, the annual publication of the National Center for Learning Disabilities. Titled "L.D.: The Other 'L' in Literacy," the article detailed her son Neil's struggle with dyslexia and assured readers that specialized instruction and diagnostic services were spreading throughout the country.[29]

Barbara Bush delved only lightly into actual disability policy. Instead, she used her platform to focus on the problem, which had the potential to help the administration enhance its image as sympathetic to the disabled. For example, accompanying her husband on an official visit to Belgium, Barbara Bush visited a state-funded, self-sufficient village for the handicapped to highlight her concern for the issue.[30]

In May 1989, however, Barbara Bush did hold a White House briefing on learning disabilities. No press correspondents were invited, as this was one of her more substantive activities. Six experts, mainly directors of disability-related organizations, attended, along with the first lady's top staff. The experts updated the first lady on laws related to learning disabilities, provided statistics on the learning disabled, and told her of the needs of the learning disabled, such as improved training for teachers and volunteers. They also discussed the social and emotional issues that impacted families of the disabled.[31]

The Bush administration connected the rights of the disabled to those suffering from AIDS. George Bush called on Congress "to get on with the job of passing a law—as embodied in the Americans with Disabilities Act—that prohibits discrimination against those with HIV and

AIDS." The 1988 Republican platform pledged billions of increases in federal dollars for AIDS research. It said that AIDS victims deserved compassion and that AIDS education should emphasize abstinence from drug use and sexual activity outside of marriage. Though the Bush administration increased funding for AIDS research by over $4 billion, George Bush was not necessarily viewed as compassionate to AIDS victims. Barbara Bush helped to highlight the compassionate side of her husband's administration by making AIDS one of her priorities. Barbara Bush tailored some of the first lady's traditional ceremonial activities—from visiting hospitals to attending funerals to traveling abroad—to AIDS.[32]

In the first 100 days, Barbara Bush highlighted the AIDS epidemic with a visit to Grandma's House, a Washington home for babies with AIDS. At the time, many believed that AIDS could be transmitted through innocuous personal contact. While there, Barbara Bush hugged an AIDS baby to demonstrate that those infected could and should be touched and held. The snapshot of this moment made big news.[33]

In April 1990, Barbara Bush, along with celebrities Elton John and Michael Jackson, attended the funeral of Ryan White, an eighteen-year-old AIDS patient. White had contracted AIDS through his treatments for hemophilia. His court battles waged over AIDS-related discrimination made him famous. He fought the Indiana public school system, which had forbade him from attending classes. In his quest to live a normal life, he emerged as a voice of understanding and sought to educate the nation about AIDS, a mission he shared with Barbara Bush.[34]

Over her years in office, Barbara Bush highlighted AIDS in a variety of ways. When she accompanied her husband to an economic summit in London in the summer of 1991, she and Princess Diana visited the AIDS ward at Middlesex Hospital. The patients there expressed concern over the U.S. policy not to issue visas to those who tested positive for HIV. Each year, she placed candles in the White House windows during the worldwide AIDS Candlelight Memorial and Mobilization. She posed for a photo to promote the AIDS Memorial Quilt, which was made of panels crafted in memory of loved ones who had died of AIDS. And she attended the dedication of Washington's largest AIDS clinic, the Bill Austin Center.[35]

Barbara Bush did not make a specific link between AIDS and the gay community. Others made the link for her. When Paulette Good-man, president of the Federation of Parents and Friends of Lesbians and Gays, asked the first lady to speak kind words to families with gay members, Barbara Bush replied, "I firmly believe that we cannot toler-ate discrimination against any individuals or groups in our country." At the 1992 Republican convention, Barbara Bush wore a red AIDS ribbon while her husband delivered his acceptance speech, a move the *New York Times* interpreted as a sign that the battle over gay politics had entered the mainstream.[36]

Barbara Bush was also an administration liaison to the African American community. Her effectiveness was first noticed during the vice presidential years, when Louis Sullivan, who would become her husband's secretary of health and human services, was impressed by a speech she gave to a group of African women in an adult literacy class in a university in Zimbabwe. Afterward, Sullivan convinced her to join the board of the Morehouse School of Medicine. She spent hundreds of hours traveling and raising money to better the profile of the histor-ically black school.

For her inaugural commencement address as first lady, Barbara Bush chose Bennett College, a historically black school in Greensboro, North Carolina, where a famous sit-in helped set off the civil rights movement. Bennett College was small, with only 615 total students and eighty-four graduates that year. Eleanor Roosevelt had visited in 1945 to address an integrated audience of school children, sparking compar-isons between the two first ladies and their concern for the oppressed. She preached that literacy was a path out of "slavery," citing the exam-ples of slave-turned-statesman Frederick Douglass and writer Dorothy Brown. According to *Ebony* magazine, it meant a great deal to the Afri-can American community that she would turn down invitations from an undisclosed number of "White" colleges. "She is politically and per-sonally committed to equal rights for Black Americans and she will not hesitate to use her highly visible role . . . to prove it," wrote *Ebony*.[37]

Barbara Bush also visited frequently with Washington's minority school children. For her first Black History Month as first lady, she attended an assembly of 350 pupils from an economically depressed Washington elementary school, where she sang all six verses of "We Shall Overcome" by memory. At another event, she took four school children on a tour of the home of abolitionist Frederick Douglass and attended a wreath-laying ceremony marking his birthday.[38]

Barbara Bush's appointment of Anna Perez, her press secretary and an African American woman, was also a symbol of her battle against racial injustice. Barbara Bush said that she picked Perez not because she was a minority, but because she was the most qualified. Yet she also said that she hoped that the appointment would send a message. Though Barbara Bush said nothing of affirmative action, she did tell *Ebony* magazine, "I won't say that I wasn't looking for a minority, because I was." She picked the most visible position on her staff to be filled by a black person, and Perez was the first African American to hold that position.[39]

While previous administrations customarily used the first lady to bolster female presidential appointments, Barbara Bush was brought in to celebrate African American appointees. For example, she was the featured speaker at a reception given by the Joint Center for Political and Economic Studies in honor of George Bush's African American appointees. While the broader political world buzzed about quotas, Barbara Bush carried the message that the honorees were "our brightest and best," attaining their positions through "hard work and determination."[40]

The most controversial women's issue of the Bush administration—sexual harassment—intersected with race. The accusations made by attorney Anita Hill against Clarence Thomas, George Bush's nominee to replace Thurgood Marshall on the Supreme Court, greatly increased public awareness about sexual harassment. Barbara Bush took the side of Thomas, stating, "I know Clarence Thomas, and I have the utmost respect for him. I don't believe the allegations against him. I know him to be a superb, superior individual." Though she privately recorded in her diary that she hoped some good would come of the hearings and that women would truthfully testify if they were being harassed, Barbara Bush's support for Thomas positioned her in opposition to the organized women's groups that were up in arms. Reaction to the Clarence Thomas confirmation hearings would, however, highlight the importance of women in elective office in the 1992 election.[41]

HILLARY CLINTON

The 1992 Republican and Democratic conventions witnessed the culmination of trends that had been building for over twenty years. The worldviews espoused by the parties presented polarized positions on women's relationships to the state and home. Democrats celebrated the public woman at their convention, while Republicans celebrated the stay-at-home mom. Marilyn Quayle, wife of Dan Quayle, the vice president, told the Republican convention that most women did not wish to be liberated from their essential natures. Many interpreted her words to be an implicit criticism of Hillary Clinton. Because of the spike in the number of women who ran for and were elected to public office, 1992 became known as the year of the woman. Grassroots support for women candidates soared, and contributions to the National Women's Political Caucus, Women's Campaign Fund, and EMILY's List doubled and tripled. Hillary Clinton, who promised to be an activist first lady, complemented these Democratic trends. During her husband's administration, she acted from an independent power base to attempt to reform the U.S. health-care system. She also shaped the global women's rights agenda by recognizing women's rights as human rights.[42]

Hillary Clinton was not the first feminist first lady, but she was the first to come of age during the second wave, taking full advantage of the burgeoning opportunities in education and employment the movement had opened. She was born Hillary Rodham on 26 October 1947 in Park Ridge, Illinois during the baby boom. From a young age, Hillary Clinton was raised to believe that the world offered abounding opportunities to girls and women. When her high school friends were not planning to attend college so that they could get married, Hillary could not fathom the same choice. Her mother was a Democrat and her father a Republican, and she has observed that the gender gap started in families like hers. Hillary initially sided with her father, even campaigning for Barry Goldwater in 1964.[43]

Wellesley College, in the activist student era of the 1960s, would undo Hillary's germinating conservatism. Wellesley's nurturing, male-free atmosphere allowed Hillary to excel at academics and pursue extracurricular leadership. Her Wellesley cohort was focused on worldly achievement, not marriage, further affirming Hillary's expectation that she would work for a living.[44]

After her 1969 Wellesley graduation, Hillary matriculated into Yale Law School. She was one of only twenty-seven female students. She decided to concentrate her studies on how the law affected children, researching child abuse at the Yale Child Study Center. At Yale, Hillary met her future husband, who had aspirations to return to Arkansas and run for public office. As one of the most highly credentialed young female lawyers in the country, she had an array of options. She could have signed on at a prestigious New York law firm or at an influential Washington nonprofit. After working for the Children's Defense Fund, she did join the legal team of the House Judiciary Committee that was investigating the possible impeachment of Richard Nixon. After Nixon resigned, she moved to Arkansas and married Bill Clinton. Friends told her she was crazy, but Hillary said she was following her heart.[45]

From her Yale years through her first ladyship, Hillary's work and home lives mixed the trailblazing with traditional. She kept her maiden name, a signal that she rebuffed a new identity in marriage. It was a move that was still uncommon even among women with postgraduate degrees. She joined the faculty of the University of Arkansas School of Law as one of only two female professors. While the country was embroiled in the ERA controversy, she helped prepare her friend Diane Blair to debate Phyllis Schlafly before the Arkansas legislature, where it was defeated. When her husband was elected Arkansas attorney general, a post that came with a meager salary, she switched to private practice. At the prestigious Rose Law Firm, she was the first female associate and was eventually made partner, shattering a major glass ceiling. After Bill Clinton was elected Arkansas governor, she continued in her law practice, played the role of social hostess, and chaired the Arkansas Rural Health Committee, a position her husband gave her. After the couple experienced infertility, the birth of daughter Chelsea was a high point in their lives. And it gave Hillary a personal lens into the problems facing American mothers.[46]

To help Bill Clinton in his reelection bid for the governorship following a crushing loss, Hillary took her husband's name. At the time, Arkansas ranked near the bottom of the country on a variety of education measures. Bill Clinton appointed his wife to chair the Education

Standards Committee to overhaul the system. As Bill Clinton increased his visibility through his work with the National Governors Association, a presidential run seemed increasingly possible. On the national stage, the complexities of Hillary Clinton's trailblazing and traditionalism would soon be called into question.[47]

 In the highly charged electoral environment over women's public and private roles, Hillary Clinton became a lightening rod for public criticism. She would later observe that she was controversial because she was outspoken and embodied a fundamental change in women's roles. Yet women's roles had been changing for over twenty years. Betty Ford was outspoken and pursued her own interests despite the strictures of her office, and Rosalynn Carter unabashedly presented herself as an equal partner. The year 1992 was a different environment, with the opposing sides of the culture war openly sparring. If Hillary Clinton was a public woman, she could not be for family values. The choices women faced seemed to be contradictory and irreconcilable.[48]

 During the primary season, when Bill and Hillary Clinton were campaigning in New Hampshire, he joked to an audience that their new campaign slogan should be, "Buy one, get one free." It was a way to say that his wife would be taking an active role in the administration. The press ran away with the comment, and allegations of a copresidency soon arose. After Gennifer Flowers announced that she had a twelve-year affair with Bill Clinton, the Clintons were interviewed together on *60 Minutes*. During the interview, Hillary Clinton remarked, "You know, I'm not sitting here, some little woman standing by my man like Tammy Wynette." Since a traditional wife would stand by her man, this comment further reinforced her image as anti–family values. Then, during a campaign stop in Chicago, a reporter asked her about conflicts of interest while she practiced law and her husband served as governor. She replied, "You know, I suppose I could have stayed home and baked cookies and had teas, but what I decided to do was fulfill my profession, which I entered before my husband was in public life." This comment made her sound opposed to stay-at-home mothers.[49]

 On 26 January 1993, Bill Clinton announced that his wife would chair the President's Task Force on National Health Reform. The mission of the task force was ambitious: to prepare legislation to be submitted to Congress within the first 100 days. A reporter asked if he intended to pay her for her public service efforts. Bill Clinton replied, "No. No. I never have paid her for her public service efforts. I don't want to start now." Yet, touting her previous pseudo-official roles in Arkansas, Bill Clinton also joked that he was grateful she would be sharing some of the political heat with him.[50]

Hillary Clinton's role as a presidential advisor raised questions about the first lady's legal status. Meetings were held in secret. The Association of American Physicians and Surgeons sued for access to the committee meetings, claiming that the task force proceedings must be open according to the rules of the Federal Advisory Committee Act. The administration argued it was exempt because the first lady was a government officer. Ultimately, the D.C. Circuit Court of Appeals agreed with the government. It ruled that the president's spouse is a de facto officer who performed a similar function to the president's White House aides. The decision marked an important stage in the development of the first lady's position. For the first time, a president's wife was identified as a political actor in her own right, a formally defined post in the White House. It was an affirmation of the first lady's increasingly public role performed throughout the previous decades.[51]

Health-care reform would soon unravel. The Republican sweep in the 1994 midterm election left Hillary Clinton wondering whether her public role was to blame. In 1995, she redirected her work to global women's rights. Tied to the toppling of oppressive regimes abroad, international women's rights were less controversial than domestic feminism in the United States. She believed that U.S. foreign policy had ignored issues such as global women's health, the education of girls, and absence of women's legal and political rights. At the time of the United Nations Fourth World Conference on Women in Beijing, China, in September 1995, Hillary Clinton felt that nobody who could attract media attention was speaking out on these issues.[52]

The first United Nations conference to deal with women's global problems was held in Mexico City in 1975 to coincide with International Woman's Year. It was the one Betty Ford did not attend because of security concerns. The second was held in Copenhagen, Denmark, in 1980. The third convened in Nairobi, Kenya, in 1985. Some have argued that this third conference marked the birth of global feminism. There, delegates were confronted with reports that showed efforts to

Hillary Clinton delivers remarks to the United Nations Fourth World Conference on Women in Beijing, China. Courtesy William J. Clinton Presidential Library.

reduce discrimination had benefited only a small slice of the planet's female population, leaving out the developing world almost entirely. The Beijing gathering, however, began a brand new chapter of visibility and prominence for global women's rights, and Hillary Clinton was credited with taking the cause to a whole new level.[53]

Boutros Boutros-Ghali, United Nations secretary general, knew that the American first lady could uniquely elevate the cause. When extending to her the invitation to speak, he wrote, "I believe that the Conference would benefit greatly not only from your experience, knowledge and commitment, but also from the prestige and respect which you command." Hillary Clinton delivered a plenary speech containing some of her most influential remarks as first lady. She cited horrific women's rights abuses mostly unassociated with American women's problems: babies murdered because they were born girls, girls sold into sexual slavery, women burned to death because of small marriage dowries, women raped as a tactic of war, young girls brutalized by genital mutilation, and women forced into abortion and sterilization. "If there is one message that echoes forth from this conference, let it be that human rights are women's rights and women's rights are human rights once and for all," she said. She ended her speech with a call to action, to create a world in which every woman was treated with respect and dignity and every girl was loved and cared for equally. Her call to action framed the rest of her tenure as first lady.[54]

The U.S. delegation reported to Bill Clinton upon its return that the Beijing conference was a rousing success and that Hillary Clinton contributed greatly to it. "By force of her superb speech before the Plenary Session and her powerful presence throughout her two-day visit, she brought the Conference and its purpose into focus. . . . Her presence and words have helped make [women's rights are human rights] the message. She caught the world's attention."[55]

Her message that women's rights are human rights provided the unifying theme for the resulting Platform for Action, which provided a detailed list of goals to reach by the year 2000. Its major priorities included prohibiting violence against women, valuing girls and boys equally, giving women access to education and health care, and ensuring their share in economic and political power. The Platform for Action also gave the Clinton administration a roadmap for its actions on women, and Hillary Clinton was responsible for carrying it out.[56]

After Beijing, expectations were high. Bill Clinton established the President's Interagency Council on Women, which was to implement the Platform for Action. He named Hillary Clinton its honorary chair. Immediately after the conference, Hillary Clinton's office reached out to Americans through press interviews, speeches, and conferences. For example, Maggie Williams, chief of staff to Hillary Clinton, put together a radio actuality targeting both "blue collar" and national media markets. The goal was to connect ordinary women to the Beijing conference and to combat the impression that the conference was mainly about lesbianism and abortion rights.[57]

The Beijing platform included a plank on microcredit for women. Hillary Clinton believed in microcredit, and she championed it all over the world. She first heard about microcredit while researching rural development in Arkansas. There, she was introduced to the microcredit lending program of the Grameen Bank of Bangladesh and became convinced that it had paradigm-shifting potential. She saw connections between microcredit and global women's empowerment in

March 1995, when she took a solo diplomatic trip to India and Pakistan at the behest of the State Department. She often cited her meeting with the Self-Employed Women's Association (SEWA) in India as one her most poignant experiences as first lady. One thousand women came to meet her, some walking twelve or fifteen hours through sweltering heat and rough terrain, she said. The women told her about the microcredit loans SEWA gave them to start their own businesses, and she toured their one-room office stacked with large books that kept track of loans and repayments. She believed microcredit gave the women a new sense of self-worth. Hillary Clinton wanted to turn microcredit into a global movement. By the year 2000, in part because of her efforts, microcredit was reaching more than 20 million people.[58]

Hillary Clinton directed her second-term travels to showcasing successful microcredit programs supported by U.S. foreign aid. In Chile, she met with a seamstress who bought a high-speed sewing machine with a microcredit loan to start a clothing business. The woman told Hillary Clinton that she could not stop kissing the machine, and it made her feel like a caged bird set free. In Nicaragua, she was impressed by women who received small loans to make mosquito netting, start neighborhood bakeries, and sell auto parts door-to-door. Furthermore, she educated her husband and other heads of state about the power of microcredit. For example, after Bill Clinton witnessed a Ugandan village bank program, he began penciling in visits to microcredit projects in his own travels. She got Bill Clinton to invite experts on microcredit to the White House Conference on the New Economy. She also hosted the first global summit on microcredit to draw attention to its successes in developing countries.[59]

An overarching goal of the Beijing Platform for Action was to integrate women into political and economic decision making around the world. The Vital Voices Democracy Initiative, a public-private partnership, was the main avenue through which Hillary Clinton helped move this goal forward. She launched the U.S. government's Vital Voices initiative in Vienna, Austria, in 1997. She announced that USAID was committing $3 million in new funding to help women enter and advance in the realms of politics, law, and business. Hillary Clinton wanted to make it clear that advancing women was inseparable from advancing democracy. As she stated in her Vienna speech, for democracy to succeed, women's vital voices must be heard. The Vienna conference targeted countries formerly behind the Iron Curtain, such as Hungary, Russia, and Ukraine, where women were beginning to find their voices in politics and the professions.[60]

Regional Vital Voices initiatives were launched around the globe, and roundtables were convened from Italy to Iceland, Turkey to Washington. Hillary Clinton participated in many of these. She believed they were important because they gave women the opportunity to spend time talking to each other, which generated energy and ideas. For example, the Vital Voices conference in Belfast, Northern Ireland, which was held to further the peace process, was one of the first opportunities for Protestant and Catholic women to talk together about a united democratic future. Here again, Hillary Clinton echoed the thesis that just as human rights were women's rights, economic progress depended upon women's progress. At the Vital Voices conference in Montevideo, Uruguay, she urged women to open the doors of political leadership. She told women politicians to overcome ideological boundaries on issues related to women and children. She preached that parties must treat women fairly and include them on electoral lists and that the legal system must be opened to more women judges and prosecutors. She also announced that the United States was increasing its loans to microenterprises across the Americas to over $100 million and committing two-thirds of those funds to women.[61]

In June 2000, the United Nations hosted the Beijing Plus Five conference. Its purpose was to review progress on the Platform for Action. Hillary Clinton delivered the keynote address. She talked about the voices of progress she heard as first lady. For example, she said that she heard from South African women who were homeless squatters but began using microcredit loans to build more than 100 homes, a day care center, a store, and a community. "When I asked how many planned to own their own home someday, every single hand of the hundreds went up," she said. She also noted that international atrocities remained, including killing girl babies, keeping girls out of school, forcing women into abortion and sterilization, and abducting girls to use as child soldiers and human shields. Foreshadowing Laura Bush's work, she also noted that the global AIDS epidemic had become increasingly female over the previous decade.[62]

In the spring of 1999, after Bill Clinton was acquitted in the impeachment proceedings stemming from the Monica Lewinsky scandal, Hillary Clinton began to consider a run for the U.S. Senate from New York. She vacillated at first. She believed that a Senate race would compromise her role as a representative of women's rights abroad. She had accumulated broad experience during her eight years as first lady and wanted to continue her advocacy work. Eventually, she was persuaded to run, realizing that she had been afraid to do that which she had encouraged so many other women to do, which was run for office. She won her Senate race, and eight years later ran in but lost the Democratic presidential primary and was later appointed Barack Obama's secretary of state.[63]

The first lady's office had come full circle. First ladies since Lou Hoover had encouraged women in public life. Their own credibility also grew as they gained experience in the public sphere. It was inevitable that a first lady would actualize her own message and capitalize on her experience. With Hillary Clinton, the first lady's office, historically a wellspring of support for political women, became a potential springboard into public office.

LAURA BUSH

The next first lady, however, said she did not harbor ambitions for public office, though she was asked about this repeatedly. Her work as first lady, however, did resemble Hillary Clinton's. In particular, her work on behalf of global women's rights, particularly in the Middle East and Africa, helped the Bush administration further its foreign policy agenda.

She was born Laura Welch on 4 November 1946. Like Hillary Clinton, her formative years also spanned 1950s and 1960s America. Though Laura grew up in the isolated desert town of Midland, Texas, a similar ethos about women's expanding opportunities swirled around her upbringing. She was the only child of Harold and Jenna Welch, and her mother stimulated her passion for literature as a young girl. Like other girls in Midland, she grew up listening to the Beatles, watching Ed Sullivan, and smoking cigarettes. All the while she was constantly and widely reading.

Desiring to enter the teaching profession, Laura Welch arrived at Southern Methodist University in 1964. Her parents valued education, as neither had finished college. She was also deeply impacted by the civil rights movement in college, and she felt compelled to work with disadvantaged children. She spent much of her postcollege, premarried years teaching in inner city schools. She also earned a master's degree from the University of Texas in library science. After Hillary Clinton, she would become the second first lady with a graduate degree. After graduate school, she worked for a neighborhood library in an African American section of Houston. While there, she joined a women's consciousness-raising group and read Betty Friedan, while simultaneously longing to have a husband.

After a six-week courtship, George W. Bush proposed. She then gave her two weeks' notice at the library and went wedding dress shopping. They were married in November 1977, the same month the National Women's Conference was held in Houston. She supported him in his first congressional bid, which he lost. George and Laura Bush wanted a baby but experienced infertility. She became pregnant with twins after beginning hormone treatments. Like her mother-in-law, Laura Bush stayed at home and raised her children, while her husband worked in the oil business and then as general manager for the Texas Rangers baseball team.

In 1994, George W. Bush was elected governor of Texas. As the governor's wife, Laura Bush chose to focus on education, which dovetailed with her professional background as a teacher. Perhaps her most well known legacy, however, was the Texas Book Festival, which was fueled by her love of reading. The event gathered authors in Austin, the first one attracting over 15,000 people.[64]

The gender gap was central to the campaign strategies in the 2000 election, which was predicted to be very close. The women closest to George W. Bush were deployed in campaign efforts to bridge the gender gap. Laura Bush, Barbara Bush, Lynne Cheney, and Condoleezza Rice were featured in a "W. Stands for Women" outreach effort, which included a bus tour through three battleground states. The women spoke of George W. Bush's commitment to education, women's health, and elder care. In the end, however, it was Al Gore who benefited from the women's vote. That election featured a twelve-point gender gap.

The plight of women in Afghanistan was not salient to most Americans before 11 September 2001. In the mid-1990s, the Taliban had seized power in Afghanistan. Before the Taliban, Afghan women were freer to work, be educated, and wear contemporary clothes. Organizations such as the Feminist Majority Foundation and individuals such as Mavis Leno, wife of comedian Jay Leno, began working to expose the Taliban's abuses late in the decade.

Laura Bush used her first-lady microphone to make the connection between women's rights and the war on terrorism. On 17 November 2001, she became the first president's wife to deliver the weekly presidential radio address in its entirety. Her address kicked off a worldwide effort to focus on the brutality against women and children by the Taliban, after military action against Afghanistan was already underway. "The brutal oppression of women is a central goal of the terrorists," she told her audience. As Hillary Clinton had done in Beijing, Laura Bush vividly detailed specific human rights abuses. Women were denied access to doctors. Mothers faced beatings for laughing out loud. Women could not work outside the home or even leave home by themselves. The Taliban pulled out women's fingernails because they wore nail polish. "The fight against terrorism is also a fight for the rights and dignity of women," she said. The point of her speech was to raise consciousness, as well as justify military action by linking it to women's liberation from an oppressive, undemocratic regime.[65]

The positive public reaction to her speech helped her realize the power of her platform. "At that moment, it was not that I had found my voice. Instead, it was as if my voice had found me," she wrote of her speech.[66]

Later that month, she brought eleven Afghan women exiles to the White House through the Vital Voices initiative. The women said they were amazed that they had gained admission to the American head of state's house, because in Afghanistan they were banished from all government buildings. Laura Bush wanted to make sure that Afghan women were included in the country's reconstruction. A primary goal, Laura Bush said to the women, was to make sure that all Afghan girls and women received an education. "The stability of Afghanistan . . . is very dependent on making sure that human rights includes the rights of women and children." A reporter for *Newsweek* commented, "If I had closed my eyes, I could have sworn it was Hillary Clinton talking."[67]

On 8 March 2002, Laura Bush led a delegation to the United Nations to commemorate International Woman's Day. Her message drew attention to how the United States was helping Afghan women return to the lives they once knew. She told how the United States committed over $1 million to help get Afghan women back to work and supporting their families. USAID was sending textbooks. The women's dormitory at the University of Kabul was being refurbished. "Prosperity cannot follow peace without educated women and children. When people are educated, all the indexes of a society improve," she said. Quoting a female Afghan activist, she stated, "Society is like a bird. It has two wings. And a bird cannot fly if one wing is broken." This was the theme that she wove into her work on international women's rights: society will fail if it leaves out the women, especially in education.[68]

On 23 March 2002, Afghan girls returned to school, and the Afghan government reached out to Laura Bush for material help. She worked with Vital Voices to coordinate the project. They sent several thousand manual sewing machines and enough fabric to dress 3 million children in uniforms. They also got companies to send supplies. L.L. Bean provided jackets and blankets. New Balance and Timberland provided shoes. Sarah Lee Corporation provided socks. Wal-Mart and General Motors provided financial support. In announcing the donations from the White House, Laura Bush noted that educating Afghanistan's daughters would help them imagine a future of opportunity, equality, and justice.[69]

Over her husband's first term, Laura Bush held numerous meetings on domestic soil with Afghan women leaders: teachers, lawmakers, attorneys, and judges. She also worked with the United States–Afghan Women's Council, a public-private partnership George W. Bush and Afghan president Hamid Karzai established in 2002, and served as its honorary chair. The council allowed American women to come alongside Afghan women to share leadership strategies in education, law, politics, and health. And at the dawn of the second term, she was able to see Afghanistan for herself. Under a veil of secrecy, she traveled to the war-torn country, where not even her husband had set foot.

In March 2005, she arrived for the meeting of the United States–Afghan Women's Council, held at the Women's Teacher Training Institute, which she helped found, at Kabul University. Her work as a teacher

Laura Bush talks with female students at the new women's dormitory at Kabul University in Afghanistan on 30 March 2005. Courtesy George W. Bush Presidential Library.

and librarian stimulated her commitment to the project, which trained teachers to go into the remote communities in Afghanistan. While there, she announced two education initiatives. First, the United States was committing $15 million for the establishment of the American University of Afghanistan. Laura Bush assured that the school would aggressively reach out to young Afghan women and ensure that they became vital components of the new school. Second, she announced that the United States was committing over $3 million to establish the International School of Afghanistan, which would provide classical education from kindergarten through high school. She said that the two schools were part of a bigger dream of an Afghanistan "where both men and women stand upright in equality." While there, she also met with Hamid Karzai and his wife, Zeenat Karzai, an obstetrician-gynecologist Afghanistan had the world's second-highest mortality rates for women in childbirth. The Afghan first lady begged Laura Bush to help fund a maternity hospital. Army officers also briefed Laura Bush on reconstruction projects. And before her departure, she dined on chicken fingers and broccoli while seated next to a female service officer in combat fatigues. The first lady was struck by the contrast between two worlds—one where women could wear combat fatigues and another where burkas were the required fashion. Her trip, which lasted a brief six hours, focused international attention on the continuing needs of women in the country.[70]

In her role as UNESCO's honorary ambassador for its Decade of Literacy, Laura Bush traveled to Amman, Jordan, in May 2005 to deliver a speech at the World Economic Forum. She billed it as a substantive trip, initiated by her own office. Her central message was that the education of women and children was essential to the spread of democracy in the Middle East and, echoing Hillary Clinton's Beijing message, "human rights require the rights of women." She called upon delegates to educate all of their citizens, especially women and girls. Mothers, she noted, are children's first teachers, and their literacy is closely linked to that of their offspring. She urged delegates to extend women the right to vote, reminding them that her own country did not extend women this right until more than a century after its founding. She charged them to allow women to become full participants in economic and political life. Though unreported in the press, the Saudi delegation, clad in white robes and red-checkered head coverings, walked out in protest.[71]

In total, Laura Bush made three trips to Afghanistan. On her trip in June 2008, she visited Bamiyan Province, where Habiba Sarabi had been elected its first female governor, the only one in Afghanistan. She visited fully veiled and covered women who were enrolled in the police academy. She met with women participating in the United States–Afghan Women's Council's ARZU project, which gave women access to education and health care and allowed them to earn money by selling handcrafted rugs. Laura Bush purchased two rugs for the White House and one for her Crawford ranch.

Laura Bush's global women's rights agenda extended beyond the Middle East and into Africa. George W. Bush gave more attention and funding to Africa than any other president. Laura Bush's role in African development was to extend the promises of her husband's programs to women living on the continent. In January 2006, she led a delegation to Liberia, Ghana, and Nigeria. The theme of her trip was women's empowerment. In Liberia, she attended the inauguration of the first woman president of an African country, Ellen Johnson Sirleaf of Liberia. Laura Bush wanted to show American support for Johnson Sirleaf, as well as spotlight her as a role model for little girls on the continent, since women in many African cultures were excluded from the public sphere. In Nigeria, she discussed the role of education in nurturing the development of African women leaders. A major goal of George W. Bush's Africa education initiative was to enroll more girls in schools. In Ghana, Laura Bush announced the Textbooks and Learning Materials Program, a $600 million commitment to provide books, uniforms, and teacher training in six African nations.

George W. Bush also initiated the President's Emergency Plan for AIDS Relief (PEPFAR), which attempted to alleviate the effects of the epidemic, which had taken over 10 million African lives. Laura Bush spotlighted how PEPFAR programs helped African women combat the disease. PEPFAR allowed her to discuss issues of rape, sexual abuse, and domestic violence openly, and she hoped the dialogue would help remove the stigma attached to women with AIDS.

Laura Bush made five trips to Africa during her tenure. On her first solo trip in July 2005—to South Africa, Tanzania, Zanzibar, and Rwanda—she witnessed PEPFAR's early results. In South Africa, she visited a PEPFAR-funded Mothers2Mothers program. The program required women to reveal that they were HIV positive, an important step because many women were suffering in secret. The women called her Grand Mama Laura and told her how their own mothers had disowned them when they revealed they were HIV positive. In Tanzania, she met with organizations encouraging law enforcement to protect women from sexual violence. In Rwanda, which she described as a society of women by necessity, given the numbers of men killed in the genocide, she dined with the country's prominent women, from government ministers to parliamentarians. While there, in an interview with NBC's Ann Curry, she said that she hoped her husband would nominate a woman to replace retiring Justice Sandra Day O'Connor on the Supreme Court.[72]

An extension of her human rights activism, Laura Bush worked against the Burmese junta and its treatment and imprisonment of Nobel Peace Prize–winner Aung San Suu Kyi. In September 2006, Laura Bush convened a United Nations roundtable, hearing tales of women ages eight to eighty being raped as a weapon of war. She joined the Senate Women's Caucus, first by attending their meetings where they decided to ratchet up awareness about the Burmese situation, and then in issuing a public appeal for Aung San Suu Kyi's release, holding a press conference in the White House briefing room, the first president's wife to do so. After Cyclone Nargis killed more than 100,000 Burmese, she called on Burma's military leaders to accept U.S. aid and to postpone a constitutional referendum that would prohibit pro-democracy activists, including Aung San Suu Kyi, from taking office. Reporters noted that she had been taking on a more assertive role than she had in the past. Laura Bush pointed out, "I think I just know more. . . . I'm more educated about the situation in Burma and the situation in Afghanistan, just after having lived here in the White House for seven years." Her words reveal how the first ladyship can educate and politicize its occupants, spurring them further into public activism.[73]

Through the first ladyship, Laura Bush also became an advocate for women's health. The 2000 Republican platform had lengthy sections on women's health, affirming that women had historically been underrepresented in medical research and lacked equal access to medical attention. The GOP committed itself to reversing that trend. The platform took credit for large increases in NIH funding that made possible research into diseases that disproportionately affected women and the elderly. Republicans advocated for equality for women in the delivery of health-care services.[74]

In 2003, Laura Bush partnered with the National Heart, Lung, and Blood Institute as the ambassador for the Heart Truth campaign to educate women about heart disease, which was the number-one killer of women. In television appearances, magazine articles, and numerous domestic trips and speeches, she told audiences about how the signs and symptoms of a heart attack were different for men and women. By the end of her tenure, more people were aware that heart disease was the most common cause of death among women. Her first ladyship also saw the first decreases in the number of heart disease deaths among women.[75]

Decades after Betty Ford's breast cancer surgery and the groundbreaking publicity surrounding it, breast cancer was on the global women's rights agenda. The Beijing Platform for Action asserted that women had the right to the enjoyment of the highest attainable standard of physical health, this being vital to their full participation in public and private life. Framing women's health as a human rights issue, the platform noted that deaths from cancers of the breast and reproductive system were preventable if detected early and called for strengthened programs, services, and media campaigns that addressed prevention, early detection, and treatment. Laura Bush's work furthered this objective. She traveled to nine countries in the Middle East, the Americas, and Europe to launch partnerships. Worldwide, breast cancer was the leading cancer-related cause of death among women. She urged international women to break the silence about breast cancer, as women in the United States had, with Betty Ford leading the way. For Breast Cancer Awareness Month in October 2008, as the Bush administration drew to a close, she had the White House lit pink to symbolize the country's commitment to women's access to breast cancer treatment.[76]

MICHELLE OBAMA

On 28 April 2009, Michelle Obama unveiled a bronze bust of Sojourner Truth, the abolitionist and deliverer of the 1851 speech, "Ain't I a Woman?" The bust was displayed at the U.S. Capitol, and Truth was the first African American woman to be honored there. "I hope that Sojourner Truth would be proud to see me, a descendant of slaves, serving as the First Lady of the United States of America," Michelle Obama said. She said she was proud that boys and girls could come to Emancipation Hall and see the face of a woman who looked like them. The moment was symbolic. Nobody who looked like Michelle Obama had occupied the East Wing or had shared her unique connection to the country's struggle to extend the promises of human rights. This awareness would fundamentally shape her first lady agenda, as she sought to advance educational opportunities for young minorities at home and for girls abroad.[77]

In 2013, *Politico Magazine* dubbed Michelle Obama a "feminist nightmare." Feminists who hoped for substantive policy engagement on issues such as the Affordable Care Act, Common Core, and abortion had been disappointed in the first lady's public image as a mom, fashion icon, and health guru. The article questioned whether the first lady's activities signaled that feminism was dead in the Democratic Party.[78]

The Democratic platforms in 2008 and 2012 supported enacting the ERA, enforcing Title IX, passing the Paycheck Fairness Act, ensuring abortion rights, and ending violence against women. Echoing Hillary Clinton's line that women's rights are human rights, Democrats continued to support women's access to political and economic opportunity abroad.

As the first African American first lady, Michelle Obama stood at the crosscurrents of human rights and women's rights. She, however, chose not to put many of the Democrats' domestic feminist priorities at the top of her first lady agenda. Instead, her personal story, particularly how she was able to seize equal access to education as an African American female, directed her path. At home and abroad, she stood for how education, a paramount human right, could elevate underrepresented, underserved groups, especially girls.

She was born Michelle Robinson on 17 January 1964 in Chicago. Her father, Fraser Robinson, was a precinct captain in Mayor Richard Daley's political machine, which enabled him to make a decent living as a pump operator at the city water plant, allowing her mother Marian to stay home. Michelle and her older brother Craig were raised in a small apartment on Chicago's South Side. Her parents had high standards of achievement and preached that hard work would be rewarded. Fraser Robinson was determined to give his children an excellent education, and Michelle excelled in school. She skipped the second grade and was admitted to the first magnet high school in Chicago. She often arose before dawn so that she could do schoolwork in peace. Wanting to follow her brother, Michelle set her sights on Princeton. Her school counselors, however, discouraged her, which both angered and motivated her. As first lady, she would often tell this story to disadvantaged youth.

But she did go to Princeton, where she majored in sociology and graduated with honors. For her senior thesis, she wrote about the obligation elite African Americans had to lower-class minorities, a theme that would also mark her first ladyship. She arrived at Harvard Law School in 1985, where she served as an editor for the *Harvard BlackLetter Law Journal*, joined the Black Law Student Association, and volunteered at Harvard's Legal Aid Bureau. Race and gender preoccupied her thinking and writing during these years.

Then returning to her Chicago roots, she signed on at corporate law firm Sidley & Austin. There, she met Barack Obama when he was working as a summer associate. Feeling a call to public service, Michelle left the firm for the mayor's office. Barack and Michelle were married on 3 October 1992.

Michelle Obama then took a job as director of the Chicago branch of Public Allies, where she successfully raised funds and created a mentoring and internship program. With an ever-expanding skill set, she then moved into administration at the University of Chicago. Her job was to direct the student community service program and to bridge gaps between the white campus and its urban surroundings. While working this job, she gave birth to daughters Malia in 1998 and Sasha in 2001. Barack Obama, recently elected to the Illinois Senate, was commuting to Springfield, and life as a working mom with an absentee husband was hard on Michelle. In 2002, when she interviewed for her next job at the University of Chicago Hospitals, she took along her nursing baby. Like many educated women who desired to keep their careers while nurturing a young family, she struggled to juggle it all.

Michelle Obama did opt out of the paid workforce in 2008 to support her husband's presidential run. It was then the American public was first introduced to Michelle Obama. To some, she came across as an angry black woman. "For the first time in my adult life, I am proud of my country," she told a Wisconsin audience in February 2008. Those fourteen words were replayed and reprinted. She seemed unpatriotic, unappreciative, and self-absorbed. To control the damage, the campaign refocused on Michelle's roots—her growing up on the South Side of Chicago, her family and community, and especially her father. Still, the cover of a summer 2008 *New Yorker* magazine featured an illustration of Michelle Obama, sporting an Afro and military gear while fist-bumping her husband, who was dressed like a Muslim.[79]

To avoid alienating white voters, candidate Barack Obama deemphasized race, continuing to do so into his presidency. He downplayed race-specific agendas, such as affirmative action and slavery reparations, in favor of issues affecting all races, such as health care. His inner circle of advisors consisted of white Democratic Party insiders, and he insisted that blacks and whites had unified interests. Michelle Obama likewise had to negotiate how to at once further her husband's agenda that downplayed race while also capitalizing on her unique position as the first African American first lady. Michelle Obama attempted to do this by targeting minority youths with a conservative message. Invoking her personal story, she told young minorities that they could climb the socioeconomic ladder using hard work and determination. A hand up from the government was mostly absent from her civil rights rhetoric.[80]

As her husband moved closer to the Oval Office, mentoring young girls was one of several projects Michelle Obama had envisioned. For her first Women's History Month as first lady, she gathered twenty-one female celebrities, including Sheryl Crow, Phylicia Rashad, and Alicia Keys, to share their stories to disadvantaged schoolgirls in Washington, D.C. She wanted girls to understand that it was possible for them to turn out like the celebrities. She told the students, "I worked really hard. I did focus on school. I wanted an A. I wanted to be smart. Kids would say: 'You talk funny.' 'You talk like a white girl.' I didn't know what that meant." She did not discuss access to education in terms of rights and legislation. Instead, mentoring was her means.[81]

Soon after she set up her East Wing operations, she directed her staff to establish a quiet mentoring program that paired disadvantaged teenage girls with senior female leaders in the Obama administration. Exposing girls to high-achieving women and making them feel like White House insiders, the first lady believed, was essential to their future success. "She wanted young women with no connections or clout to use hers, to walk the marbled halls not with a sense of awe but with a sense of yearning and entitlement," according to one report. About her own access to Princeton, Michelle Obama commented, "I sort of thought, what's the mystery here? What is it about this place that makes some people—even myself—think that some people should have access to it and others shouldn't? And that's where I discovered that there is no mystery in this stuff. It is hard work. It's access; it's being able to envision it." Here again, she emphasized determination and imagination, not affirmative action.[82]

Along with her message of individual responsibility, she believed that education was the single most important civil rights issue. It was the umbrella problem under which other race-related problems could be solved, from mass incarceration to racial profiling, voting rights, and poverty. After numerous discussions with and speeches to students around the country about education, in May 2014 she gave her initiative a name: Reach Higher. The goal of this initiative was to inspire young people, particularly first-generation college students like herself, to continue their education beyond high school. Her initiative lined up with her husband's goal that by 2020, the United States would have the highest college graduation rate in the world. Reach Higher had four components: exposing students to college and career opportunities, making college affordable, inspiring academic and summer planning, and supporting high school counselors and mentors.[83]

To promote Reach Higher, Michelle Obama convened professional events and conferences around the country. For example, she hosted a fashion education workshop at the White House for 150 students from twelve high schools and two colleges. Anna Wintour, editor of *Vogue*, addressed them, as did fashion designers including Diane von Furstenberg. Michelle Obama sponsored College Signing Days, celebrations designed to spotlight the achievements of seniors going on to college and to seal their commitments. For the 2015 College Signing Day celebrations, she asked Instagram users to share a photo of themselves in their college gear. She posted a picture of herself and her husband in their respective Princeton and Columbia T-shirts.[84]

In all of her initiatives, Michelle Obama harnessed the power of social media. She used Instagram for sharing photos, posting as @MichelleObama. On Twitter, she tweeted as @FLOTUS. Her posts could be used to connect with young Americans. By sharing bits of her initiatives, she could stir up the educational ambitions of American youth. Her posts also exposed her wide social media audience to the lack of access that girls in some parts of the world had to educational opportunities.

Michelle Obama's interest in global girls' education was sparked during her very first international trip as first lady in April 2009 when she visited the Elizabeth Garrett Anderson Language School, an inner-city school for girls in London, England. Most of the students were minorities, and about 20 percent were refugees. While she spoke of her own humble beginnings and how she worked hard at her education, all she could think about was the promise, intelligence, and passion of each girl in her audience. Afterward, she told her press aide, "I want to do those everywhere we go."[85]

Michelle Obama continued to feature girls' right to education in speeches, events, and international trips. And the more time she spent with the girls abroad, the more she realized their stories were like her own. For example, in 2013 she joined her husband on his Africa trip specifically so that she could highlight girls' education. In Senegal, she visited an all-girls middle school named after Martin Luther King. In Tanzania, she participated in a summit for African first ladies called "Investing in Women: Strengthening Africa," sponsored by the Bush Institute. With Laura Bush, she discussed education for women and girls and the social and economic good it could bring to a country. In September 2014, she spoke on girls' education at the United Nations Global Education First Initiative. She described the issue as deeply personal to her and preached on the need to change global cultural attitudes toward girls. She told her audience that men needed to value daughters as much as sons. "It's about whether communities value young women for their minds, or only for the reproductive and labor capacities of their bodies," she said, condemning forced marriage, genital cutting, and sex trafficking. She asked her audience, "Who among us would accept our precious girls being married off to grown men at the age of twelve, becoming pregnant at thirteen, being unable to support themselves financially, confined to a life of dependence, fear and abuse?" At the end of her speech, she announced that in the years ahead, she wanted to engage international leaders on this issue until every young woman on the planet had the opportunity to learn.[86]

Making good on this promise, Michelle Obama launched her Let Girls Learn initiative in March 2015. "Everywhere I go, I meet these girls, and they are so fiercely intelligent, and hungry to make something of themselves," she said in announcing the new initiative. "I want to use my time and my platform as first lady and beyond to make a real impact on this issue," she declared. Let Girls Learn was set up to be community-based and engage 7,000 Peace Corps volunteers in sixty countries. After-school mentoring programs, girls' leadership camps, and entrepreneurial projects were planned.[87]

She followed up her announcement with a trip to Japan and Cambo-

Michelle Obama confers with Prime Minister David Cameron and his wife, Samantha Cameron, at 10 Downing Street, London, England, on her trip to promote Let Girls Learn, 16 June 2015. Official White House Photo by Amanda Lucidon.

dia and the new social media hashtag #LetGirlsLearn. She announced a new partnership with Japan, writing in her online travel journal that the two countries planned to invest in programs that would help girls around the world get an education. On Instagram, she posted a photo of herself in a discussion with Japanese students. In Cambodia, she visited with Peace Corps volunteers receiving Let Girls Learn training. And on Instagram, she posted a picture of herself bowing to a Cambodian schoolgirl with a caption describing how the girl was committed to studying for a better life despite having to arise at four o'clock to cook for her whole household.

In June 2015, she promoted Let Girls Learn in London, where she addressed the Bangladeshi-dominated Mulberry School for Girls. She told the girls about how she often woke up at four o'clock in the morning to finish her schoolwork and how she saw herself in them. She announced $200 million in funding to partner with the United Kingdom to work together for girls' education in developing countries. Michelle Obama's Instagram feed featured photos of her conferring with Prime Minister David Cameron and Prince Harry about Let Girls Learn. Her Instagram feed also featured photos of the schoolgirls, maroon scarves wrapped around their heads, waving British and American flags.

Michelle Obama also launched a social media campaign when the Boko Haram terrorist group kidnapped over 200 Nigerian schoolgirls from their dormitory. On 7 May 2014, she took to Instagram, posting a picture of herself frowning and holding up a sign with the hashtag, #BringBackOurGirls. On Mother's Day weekend, she delivered the presidential radio address in its entirety. She urged Americans to pray for the girls' safe return. She also used the opportunity to preach about the 65 million girls worldwide who were not in school and all the others who pursued an education under the threat of violence. "Let us show just a fraction of their courage in fighting to give every girl on this planet the education that is her birthright," she said. That girls' rights were human rights was the spin Michelle Obama gave to Hillary Clinton's Beijing message.[88]

Parallels between Hillary Clinton and Michelle Obama were also evident when Obama paid a goodwill visit to China. While she, like Pat Nixon, mainly did people-to-people activities—practicing tai chi with high school students, writing in Chinese calligraphy, feeding apples to pandas—she also interwove rights rhetoric. She told a student audience that in America everyone was equal and possessed the freedom to speak, think, and worship. She talked about discrimination and the peaceful protests and marches that helped to do away with unjust laws. Woven through her tour was the idea that an excellent education should be for all, not just the rich. Though her speech did not go as far as Hillary Clinton's Beijing address, it nonetheless touched on the theme of equality of rights that had marked the first lady's office since after suffrage.[89]

CHAPTER SIX *Motherhood and Family Politics*

*I*n 1980, the major political parties provided Americans with a choice between two opposing worldviews on the meaning of motherhood in America. As Kristin Luker has written, abortion solidified these distinctions. The pro-life worldview stemmed from the belief that men and women were different. It elevated motherhood to a noble calling. On the other hand, those who were pro-choice believed that men and women were essentially the same and, therefore, should have the same roles. This worldview gave motherhood a comparatively low status, while valuing sex intended for self-fulfillment rather than procreation.[1]

Republicans began to fold women's issues into family issues. Advocating the right to life, Republicans elevated the well-being of the family above self-focused interests of women. Democrats, on the other hand, became the party of choice and individualism and regarded abortion as a necessary tool for women to achieve their own goals. Therefore, on women's rights, the parties had effectively switched sides from the positions they held from the 1920s through the 1960s.[2]

As we have seen, by the 1980s, presidents' wives were expected to shoulder projects and personas. Their personal lives within the presidential marriage had been cracked open for public scrutiny. They were expected to articulate issue positions on women's roles and responsibilities in relation to the family and to model domesticity from their White House posts. And so the stage was already set for first ladies to act in the reshaped and reinvigorated public debate about motherhood and family politics in America. First ladies after 1980 rooted their actions in their roles as mothers. How they did so amid shifting partisan tides is the subject of this chapter.

NANCY REAGAN

Women of the New Right, besides those who adopted a laissez-faire conservative worldview, saw the world through the social conservative lens. To social conservatives, the family was the bedrock of society. Social conservatives decried the moral decay of the country, which was evidenced by the belittling of marriage and motherhood and the glorification of decadence and sexual liberation. A woman's role was to be a helpmeet to her husband and a support to others. These themes—motherhood, moral decay, and wifely support—pervade Nancy Reagan's tenure, from her public persona to her signature program.[3]

Nancy Reagan's family-focused worldview was evident from the 1980 campaign. As one campaign profile noted, "Nancy Reagan, a former actress, knows something about playing a supporting role. The one she is playing today—that of the absolutely devoted wife—is for real." Reporters frequently noted the closeness of the Reagan marriage, how they operated as one, how she defended him. Nancy Reagan said that her life began when she married her husband. While the Reagans preferred to be together on the campaign trail, when Nancy did stump solo, she echoed the social conservative worldview, especially returning to the values of an earlier time. "We can make this country the way it always has been," she told her audiences.[4]

Yet the second wave of feminism and the backlash against it had left an indelible impact. It was during the Reagan administration that the country began a protracted debate over the proper role of first ladies. Nancy Reagan was praised or condemned depending upon how her role was defined. The power dynamics of the Reagan marriage and Nancy Reagan's wifely persona were extensively chronicled, questioned, and deliberated. *Ms.* magazine criticized her for devoting her time to supporting her husband rather than sitting in on cabinet meetings. Gloria Steinem called her the rare woman who could "perform the miracle of having no interests at all." Nancy Reagan gladly affirmed that she would help her husband do whatever he was interested in. "Marriage certainly isn't easy and it takes a lot of effort to make it work," she said. "Whoever said it was 50-50 was crazy. Many times it's 75-25 or 90-10, but each side has to be willing to bend a little when it's necessary."

She spoke up for marital fidelity. She lamented that people no longer worked at marriage and how it was easy to walk away.[5]

Though Nancy Reagan was in many ways the traditional wife, she did not draw a sharp boundary between East Wing and West Wing. The press was quick to point out where Nancy Reagan exercised power. White House staff recognized her as a power in the administration, especially in presidential personnel, public relations, and scheduling. She told West Wing staffers when she did not want her husband to travel or do an appearance. She believed that she was more attuned to people who might try to take advantage of him. She tried to protect him by lobbying for the firing of many top-level staffers, such as Alexander Haig and Don Regan.[6]

Nancy Reagan engaged in the politics of motherhood through her antidrug crusade. "Using the office of the first lady to inform and educate opinion makers, parents and students to the epidemic use of drugs and alcohol among children and adolescents" was a primary goal of the project, according to a briefing memo circulated during its germination. While she set out to be an opinion leader and use the power of her position to spur the public to action, the administration took care to ensure that she did not present herself as an independent actor. Carlton Turner, a senior drug policy adviser, in initial planning meetings with the East Wing staff, voiced strong concern that the first lady not be allowed to take the drug issue and promote it independent of her husband. He did not want her to set her own policy priorities and issue her own policy statements, as Rosalynn Carter had with mental health.[7]

While the gender gap and public image improvement provide part of the explanation as to why Nancy Reagan took up the antidrug crusade, the social conservative worldview with its focus on morality, motherhood, and family is important for understanding her approach to the issue. Nancy Reagan linked the drug abuse epidemic to the moral decay of the country, a prominent theme of social conservatism. She tracked the problem of drug abuse to the 1960s. "Trying to raise children in the 60s was a terrifying experience," she said in remarks to the World Affairs Council. "It seemed everything was against you—mainly your children." She acknowledged that there was a stigma in trying to eradicate drug abuse. "It was unfashionable," she acknowledged. "It was illiberal in our live-and-let-live society." Nancy Reagan believed that drug abuse was fundamentally a "moral issue" and that every American had a "moral obligation" to engage in the fight.[8]

She condemned Hollywood, another target of social conservatives, for portraying drugs as glamorous and cool. She asked a gathering of Hollywood executives to "not collaborate in the illusion that drugs are fun; that drugs are merely a casual, socially acceptable part of living," especially given that children in the 1980s were averaging twenty-seven hours of television watching per week. She even called out specific movies and pop culture figures. For example, she said that kids who went to see the movie *Desperately Seeking Susan* to watch Madonna also got a strong dose of the star smoking marijuana. Drug use embodied the humanistic values and self-gratification that lured Americans away from purity and family.[9]

To social conservatives, moral decay, drug use, family decline, and feminist narcissism were all intertwined in a secular humanistic bundle. Nancy Reagan, therefore, wove appeals to strengthen the family into her rhetoric against drug abuse. As she told a gathering of governors' spouses, "The American family is a strong family that works together to create a healthy home . . . a home which is drug free. . . . I'm convinced that the ultimate prevention of drug abuse goes hand in hand with strengthening the American family—a sustained effort to find ways of supporting the family and of bringing whole families together to provide a drug-free nation." Rehabilitating young users led to rehabilitating families, which led to rehabilitating the nation.[10]

Mending and strengthening the parent-child relationship was Nancy Reagan's formula for solving the drug abuse epidemic—not government, not police, not schools. This was in line with pro-family groups that believed the state should stay out of family relations. She wrote that family involvement gave "strength back to the family unit, which has somehow become so weak. It will strengthen the family and, in turn, the country." Parent groups, she believed, were essential to saving young people from drugs. She heavily promoted these groups and hoped that her involvement would cause parent groups to spread to every community. She believed her primary role in the battle was to draw attention to such groups.[11]

In her antidrug crusade, Nancy Reagan acted as a mother. In a memo about media appearances surrounding her antidrug campaign kick-off, her advisor Ann Wrobleski noted, "Mrs. Reagan's posture . . . should be one of a concerned mother. She is not an expert in drug abuse, drug treatment, or prevention. She is, however, a woman who, because of her position, has a marvelous opportunity to effect change." In many of her antidrug speeches, Nancy Reagan vested her interest in and authority over the issue within her motherhood. For example, in their joint September 1986 nationally televised back-to-school address on drug abuse, Ronald Reagan noted that the couple was speaking as fellow parents and grandparents. Nancy Reagan began her portion of the address, "As a mother, I've always thought of September as a special month, a time when we bundled our children off to school. . . . But so much has happened over these last years, so much to shake the foundations of all that we know and all that we believe in. Today there's a drug abuse epidemic in this country, and no one is safe from it." She went on to describe the harm drugs brought to young mothers and their newborn babies. She said there was no moral middle ground on the issue and that drug abuse concerned "all the American family."[12]

Nancy Reagan's antidrug project also stretched abroad. In April 1985, she hosted over forty international first ladies for a White House conference on youth drug abuse. She hosted a second gathering at the United Nations in October of that year. Though in official settings, these events were framed as "mother to mother" initiatives. Nancy Reagan remarked:

Throughout history, in times of crisis, women have united as mothers concerned for their children. This is a mother-to-mother forum, with concern for a crisis threatening children of the world—drug abuse. But history also shows that mothers working together can solve some of the toughest problems. It's like a saying I have often used—a woman is like a tea bag—you never know her strength until she's in hot water, and as mothers, grandmothers, and concerned citizens, we're all in hot water.

And when Javier Pérez de Cuéllar, United Nations secretary general, wrote to invite her to an antidrug conference in Vienna, she replied, "As a concerned mother and not as a government representative, I would like to accept your invitation." She carried the "mother to mother" theme on diplomatic trips to Thailand, Malaysia, Sweden, and Italy. By downplaying her official capacity and highlighting her maternal role, she distinguished herself from first ladies of the second wave, a strategy both continued and epitomized by Barbara Bush.[13]

BARBARA BUSH

Barbara Bush made it known that she wore a size fourteen and fake pearls to cover her wrinkles. She was forthright about wearing sweats on the weekends without any aspirations of actually jogging. The American public saw her happily surrounded by her grandchildren. Her favorite pastime, gardening, was something real mothers did. Her unspoken message was that motherhood was honorable, and her first lady persona reflected family values, the preeminent issue for social conservatives during her tenure. She devoted much of her first ladyship to promoting family literacy. But her focus on motherhood and the family complicated her relationship with third wave feminists. And these differing valuations of motherhood were brought to a head through her Wellesley College commencement address.[14]

As with Nancy Reagan, the press speculated about how Barbara Bush deviated from the traditional first lady script. During the campaign and transition, they wondered whether she sat in on meetings. "You'll never see me in a cabinet meeting," she said. She said she rarely disagreed with her husband and, therefore, had few opportunities to influence his opinions. She recalled a time when Richard Nixon invited all of the cabinet wives to a meeting. "We felt like dolts," she remembered. She said that she did actually sit in on campaign strategy meetings and found them fascinating and educational. "I sat and did my needlepoint and listened," she said, so that "I can learn, not so that I can have influence." She said that while she yawned her way through meetings on economics, she was very interested in meetings on child care.[15]

The 1988 Republican platform devoted a good deal of attention to child care. This was a departure from the past. In 1988, Republicans stated that it was no longer possible for all mothers to stay home with children all the time and expressed concern about latchkey children. The Republican platform argued that public policy should "acknowledge the full range of family situations." It encouraged states to promote child-care programs to support teenage mothers. At the same time, Republicans reaffirmed the unborn child's fundamental right to life and their commitment to restoring this right through a constitutional amendment. Republicans also denounced public funding for abortions.[16]

Barbara Bush continued to deflect questions on abortion. She was, however, more sympathetic to the range of family situations mentioned in the Republican platform. For Barbara Bush, family issues were bound up with literacy, and her literacy platform was honed toward problems in the family. As she told an interviewer, "I have gotten very interested in literacy and the family," specifically the "problems of the young or not-so-young woman with children—the single woman." When she traveled around the country visiting Head Start programs, she saw many single mothers who were functionally illiterate. Her goal was to ensure Americans could read and write at the fifth-grade level. She believed that only then could the country go on to solve the rest of its big problems, such as crime, poverty, and homelessness. Yet her literacy solutions were rooted in the private sphere of family and charity. This allowed her to maintain both fiscal conservatism and family values.[17]

One of her first steps in her literacy project was to launch the Barbara Bush Foundation for Family Literacy, which she did at a White House luncheon in March 1989. In her announcement, she described her family approach to the problem, which focused on breaking the cycle of illiteracy from generation to generation. Adults with reading problems raised children with reading problems, she said. She also noted that her definition of the family included "the big and bouncing kind, the single parent, extended families, divorced, homeless and migrant." She wanted to be clear that she would not discriminate against nontraditional mothers.[18]

In the fall of 1989, the National Governor's Association held its Education Summit in Charlottesville, Virginia. While George Bush conferred with the governors, Barbara Bush held her own summit with the spouses. She wanted to hear what was going on with literacy programs in their states, hoping for a free exchange of ideas. About her role, her press secretary was careful to note that Barbara Bush did not get involved in policy but did enjoy the "cross-pollination" of idea sharing. Hillary Clinton, wife of the governor of Arkansas, participated, sharing ideas about her own program.[19]

Barbara Bush wove parenting advice into literacy lessons. For example, in an article for *Reader's Digest*, she stated, "Reading aloud is one of the best-kept secrets of good parenting." She said she read to all her children and reads to her grandchildren. Reading promoted family bonding, making children feel loved, she said. She gave readers tips for starting family reading programs at home. The tips included "get started now," "make reading aloud a habit," and "involve the whole family."[20]

Some working in the field of literacy and public policy wanted her to go deeper. The American Literacy Council, for example, reportedly was not able to get past the White House operator to tell the first lady about their organization. Its director told the *Washington Post*, "Mrs. Bush says, 'Teach your children to read,' but she doesn't say how to do it." When the National Literacy Act was before Congress, Barbara Bush was asked if she would lobby for it. "I don't get into anything in front of the Congress," she said. While Barbara Bush attended the signing ceremony, George Bush did not acknowledge her in his remarks, as other presidents such as Jimmy Carter and Gerald Ford had when signing legislation related to their wives' projects. The National Literacy Act even reflected Barbara Bush's family literacy focus. It doubled authorizations for programs for adults with young children, as well as provided new funding for family literacy shows on public television.[21]

Barbara Bush used traditional first lady roles to promote literacy. For example, the White House Christmas tree in 1989 promoted literacy. It was decorated with eighty storybook character dolls. Of the tree, Barbara Bush said, "It's a celebration of reading to children. It's a celebration of children." She also hosted *Mrs. Bush's Story Time*, a program broadcast on Sundays over the ABC radio network. Barbara Bush read from notable children's books over the airwaves. The program attracted numerous celebrities. For example, during a Thanksgiving episode, Oprah Winfrey read *Aunt Flossie's Hats*.

Barbara Bush also wrote a children's book. *Millie's Book* featured the Bush family dog dictating her memoirs to Barbara Bush. The book contained photographs and snippets of Bush family life. It showed Millie playing with the grandchildren in Kennebunkport, Maine, and Barbara Bush giving Millie a surprise puppy shower when she was pregnant with her pups. Almost $1 million in grants awarded by the Barbara Bush Foundation for Family Literacy were from *Millie's Book* royalties.[22]

Despite the preeminence of family values in the early 1990s, a new assertiveness among younger women had been germinating during the previous decade. Women's colleges became bastions of solidarity and multiculturalism, aided by the development of women's studies programs that had taken root in the 1980s. The emerging generation began to label itself the third wave, and, emulating cultural icon Madonna, manifested an "in-your-face" attitude. *The Beauty Myth* by Naomi Wolf became an international best seller and resurrected conversations about the manipulation of the female body that had been commonplace in 1970s consciousness-raising groups. Meanwhile, conservatives decried academia.[23]

It was amid the debates of the third wave that Barbara Bush received an invitation from Wellesley College to deliver their 1990 commencement address. Wellesley students had voted, and Barbara Bush came in second behind Alice Walker, author of *The Color Purple*, a story chronicling a young African American woman's struggle against racism and patriarchy and a book that corresponded with third wave ideals. But Walker had declined the invitation. Wellesley students signed a petition saying they were opposed to Barbara Bush's selection. "Wellesley teaches us that we will be rewarded on the basis of our merit, not on that of a spouse," they wrote. To honor Barbara Bush would acknowledge "a woman who has gained recognition through the achievements of her husband, which contradicts what we have been taught over the last four years at Wellesley." The petition sparked a renewed nationwide debate about the relationship of marriage and motherhood to women's rights and roles.[24]

It is notable that Barbara Bush did narrowly come in second in the student poll. Feminists both young and old celebrated Barbara Bush for how she embraced her age. Naomi Wolf criticized the cultural perception that aging in women was unbeautiful. An article in *Working Women* magazine, for example, extolled Barbara Bush for waving her bare arms at the 1988 Republican convention. "There was flesh under your upper arms. And you waved them anyway! And the flesh waved too!" Perhaps the Wellesley undergraduates who voted for her believed that Barbara Bush did reflect some of their third wave values.[25]

In their protest petition, the Wellesley students requested an additional speaker who more aptly reflected the "self-affirming qualities" of a Wellesley graduate. Barbara Bush invited the Soviet first lady equivalent, Raisa Gorbachev, who happened to be a university lecturer and mother of one, to go with her. Raisa Gorbachev had already planned to accompany her husband to Washington on a diplomatic visit over Wellesley's commencement. In contrast to American first ladies, wives of Soviet officials were not pressured to make public appearances or discuss their domestic arrangements.

Barbara Bush began her speech by addressing her place within the third wave. She told the graduates, "Now I know your first choice today was Alice Walker . . . known for *The Color Purple*. Instead you got me—known for the color of my hair." While Barbara Bush's reference to her dye-free hair may have been a subtle nod to *The Beauty Myth*, she was juxtaposing her reputation for upholding family values with Alice Walker's feminist legacy. Barbara Bush noted, "Alice Walker's book has a special resonance here." Walker inspired that generation with her story of a young woman who learned to find her voice.[26]

In her commencement speech, Barbara Bush preached diversity and tolerance and used humor to bridge the cultural divide. For example, she gave an anecdote about her friend whose husband griped about "babysitting" his children. She quipped, "When it's your own kids, it's *not* called babysitting." And her most famous line, "Somewhere out in this audience may even be someone who will one day follow in my footsteps, and preside over the White House as the president's spouse—and I wish him well," referenced the groundswell of support for women candidates that was building in the early 1990s. Yet, she remained true to her family-first message. She told the women to invest in human relationships with family and friends and prioritize them above careers and work. "Fathers and mothers, if you have children, they must come first," she said.[27]

Television networks carried her speech live. It was dubbed an overwhelming success. An East Wing staffer who was tracking the tone of phone calls reported a positive response. "As of 4:00, we'd received 103 positive calls, and 2 negative!" read the memorandum. Many callers

Barbara Bush and Raisa Gorbachev deliver commencement addresses at Wellesley College on 1 June 1990. Courtesy George Bush Presidential Library and Museum.

said they were in tears listening to her speech. A woman from California said, "I have very liberal views and I'm a Democrat, but she transcends politics." A woman from Virginia said, "For what it is worth—I am a Democrat, but I think Mrs. Bush is a credit to women and to humanity." The two negative responses came from unmarried women. One noted, "I don't like marriage being pushed by Mrs. Bush and others. Republican administration seems to be pushing marriage."[28]

Republicans were pushing marriage. By the 1992 election, the phrase "family values" came to encapsulate the two-parent family with the dad as the breadwinner and mom as homemaker, with the pro-life position on abortion predominating. With abortion the preeminent issue, Schlafly had revived and refocused her STOP ERA organization into the Republican National Coalition for Life and worked closely with the Bush campaign to ensure a unified and consistent pro-life stance. The Christian Coalition had also become powerful within Republican ranks and influenced the GOP to organize around the family values mantra.[29]

The 1992 Republican platform plank on uniting the family was placed ahead of all other issues. The candidates for first lady were even referenced. It quoted Barbara Bush's Wellesley speech to anchor its message: "At the end of your life you will never regret not having passed one more test, not winning one more verdict, or not closing one more deal. You will regret time not spent with a husband, a child, a friend, or a parent." The platform declared that every child deserved to be raised in a loving home, stating, "We applaud the fine example of family values and family virtue as lived by the President and First Lady." The platform denounced Democrats for proposing children should be able to sue their parents, which was a reference to Hillary Clinton's writings, causing economic conditions that forced women into the workplace, and promoting tax structures that discouraged marriage.[30]

Given this family values frame of reference and Barbara Bush's association with it, she was featured prominently at the convention, also an attempt to leverage her high approval ratings on behalf of her husband. She gave a prime time speech on an evening referred to as family values night. Her speech, however, did not sound entirely like the Republican platform. She stated, "However you define family, that's what we mean by family values." She lauded single mothers and fathers, calling their efforts "heroic." She told of families who comforted crack babies and AIDS babies. She praised families where "the father and, indeed, the mother" were serving in the Persian Gulf and the neighbors had assumed parental duties. In so doing, Barbara Bush echoed the themes of diversity and tolerance as she always had in both her human rights and family politics. With her husband fighting off the label of a wimp, Barbara Bush also affirmed his breadwinning and leadership roles within the family. She discussed his long hours and hard work in the oil fields of Midland and his wise hand that guided and disciplined his children. She noted the myriad roles she performed: car pooler, den mother, and Little League booster. Her paternal and maternal messages were reinforced by the potent image of her twenty-two grandchildren parading onstage after the speech.[31]

HILLARY CLINTON

In 1990, while chairing the board of the Children's Defense Fund, Hillary Clinton wrote an editorial in the *New York Times* lauding the superiority of the French child-care system. She argued that France better reflected family values because of their mandated paid parental leave, preventative health services, and trained, well-paid teachers. Family values in the United States, she wrote, assumed parents alone could determine and provide what is best for children. The editorial foreshadowed her tenure. Hillary Clinton, particularly in the second term when the Democratic Party became more oriented around the family, focused on children and also advocated a greater role for the state in raising them. But in the culture wars of the early 1990s, being both pro-family and pro-state seemed contradictory.[32]

During the 1992 campaign, Republicans used Hillary Clinton as evidence the Democrats did not value the traditional family. As Pat Buchanan remarked to the Republican convention, "There is a religious war going on in our country for the soul of America. It is a cultural war. . . . Radical feminism [is] the agenda Clinton & Clinton would impose on America—abortion on demand, a litmus test for the Supreme Court, homosexual rights, discrimination against religious schools, women in combat." Buchanan also said that Hillary Clinton believed that children should have a right to sue their parents and that the institutions of marriage and the family were comparable to slavery. Buchanan's words were based on a 1973 article she published in the *Harvard Educational Review*, in which she argued that children should be entitled to constitutional guarantees on an equal basis with their parents and that children who suffered harm under the custody of parents should be protected with state intervention. State authority could outweigh parental authority, she wrote. This conflicted with the conservative view that parents should have complete control over family matters.[33]

Following her primary zingers about tea and cookies and Tammy Wynette, the press noted Hillary Clinton's attempts to soften her image. When asked what her future role would be, she would reply, "I want to be a voice for children in the White House." Her image as a strident feminist, however, had already taken root. Many Americans believed she was childless. Given the antagonistic worldviews about motherhood, one could not both advocate for children and devalue them by pursuing an independent career. Hillary Clinton would struggle to overcome this dichotomy. For example, to show that one could have both a career and a fruitful home life, she joined a cookie bake-off promoted by *Family Circle* magazine, besting Barbara Bush with her chocolate chip cookies by over 55 percent of the vote.[34]

In accordance with the worldview of those in the pro-choice movement that men and women were essentially the same and should have the same roles, Hillary Clinton blended her sphere of influence into her husband's. Before the inauguration, Bill Clinton was asked by an interviewer, "John Kennedy said that after he was elected, he began to think in terms of who it was he had to have in the room when he made the really big decisions. For him, that was Robert Kennedy. Who is it for you?" He unequivocally answered, "Hillary." Hillary Clinton physically broke down the wall separating male and female domains when she moved her office into the West Wing. She wanted to be nearer to the domestic policy staff. The office arrangement indicated that the Clintons, by sharing space, would also be sharing power.[35]

Then Bill Clinton announced that his wife would head health-care reform. As Meg Greenfield editorialized after Hillary Clinton's congressional testimony on health care, "She is a strong, separate source of power inside the administration with a mandate of authority from the president and an operational base from which to carry it out." According to William H. Chafe, dissent arose among the president's staffers, many of whom worried about the costs of the overhaul and favored a more incremental approach. And a chasm between his team and her team developed, with the resulting 1,342-page bill highlighting that Hillary Clinton dismissed those who raised questions about her plans. The health care debacle was wrapped up in the first lady's mandate of authority. Hillary Clinton even confessed to Laura Bush, during the customary White House tour for the first lady designate, that if she had to do it over again, she would not have had an office in the West Wing and that she rarely used it after the health-care debate.[36]

Hillary Clinton's feminine focus after the failure of health care and the Republican sweep in the 1994 midterm elections cannot be understood apart from the parties' moderation on family values. In 1992, both parties were polarized around women's relationship to the family. In 1996, they tried to mask those differences. In 1992, the Republican convention featured traditional wives. In 1996, it profiled political women, such as first lady candidate Elizabeth Dole, who maintained a political career after marriage. The 1996 Republican platform proclaimed that public policy must respect and accommodate women whether they were full-time homemakers or pursued a career. In 1992, the Republican platform subsumed women under family values. In 1996, the Democrats did the same thing. The phrases "women and their families" and "women and children" were frequently used in Democratic public relations. Jo Freeman commented that the Democratic linking of women with children and families undermined thirty years of feminist education, since one of the goals of the second wave was to unlink women from families and children so that women could assert their individual rights. Hillary Clinton seems to have influenced the feminization of the 1996 Democratic platform. Leading up to the election, she began to discuss family issues as "kitchen table issues," also linking them to women's issues, such as family leave, extended mammogram coverage, and adequate postnatal hospital stays.[37]

Hillary Clinton discussed these kitchen table issues in her 1996 book, *It Takes a Village*. She described the book as a statement of her continuing meditation on children based on her experience as "a mother, daughter, sister, and wife," as well as an "advocate and a citizen." While her book, especially her arguments for more state funding for prekindergarten and day care, drew criticism from conservatives, including Bob Dole in his 1996 Republican convention speech, the contents were grounded in a worldview that linked women's roles with families and children. She did not write favorably about easy divorce and out-of-wedlock births, arguing that the instability of American households posed great risks to the healthy development of children. The traditional, nuclear family was the best option, she said. She discussed the importance of establishing a baby's attachment to the new mother immediately after birth. She suggested activities promoting brain development in toddlers. "Waiting for the cookies to come out of the oven is great motivation for learning to read the clock," she wrote. She said society must do everything possible to encourage abstinence in young people.[38]

In June 1996, she sat down with *Time* magazine to talk about her child advocacy. The interviewer mentioned Hillary Clinton's difficulty conceiving and asked if she would consider adoption. Hillary Clinton replied, "I must say we're hoping that we have another child." She said that she and her husband were in continuing discussions about adoption. However, some thought the comment was politically motivated, intended to play up her feminine qualities and portray Elizabeth Dole as a childless careerist. She also said that divorce should be made more difficult, given the trauma it inflicted upon mothers and children.[39]

Looking ahead to her husband's second term, Hillary Clinton planned to speak out on issues affecting women, children, and families. This focus allowed her to exercise her expertise while also tempering her antifamily image and avoiding major controversy. Her first year of the second Clinton term was markedly different from her first year of the first Clinton term. She kicked off the second term with an appearance at Georgetown Medical Center. At an event hosted by the Association of Booksellers for Children, her central message was that reading to children should start at birth and continue during the first three years of life. She honored Maurice Sendak, author of *Where the Wild Things Are*, and talked about how she and her husband used to take turns reading to Chelsea. She then penned an article in *Time* under the subheading, "The First Mom suggests reading as an easy way to help a baby's brain grow." In the article, she reviewed the results of neurobiology studies showing that reading stimulates the growth of a baby's brain and that reading while hugging and holding a child was important to building relationships.[40]

In April 1997, Hillary Clinton hosted the White House Conference on Early Childhood Development and Learning, focusing on the practical applications of the latest scientific research on the brain. Panelists included leading researchers and childhood development experts. Hillary Clinton gave her own tips for brain stimulation: singing and reading, playing old-fashioned games like peek-a-boo and the itsy bitsy spider, taking children outdoors, pointing out items in the supermarket. A questioner asked whether the research meant that a parent should decide to stay at home with a baby rather than return to the working world. Hillary Clinton said, "Yes, I think a person could draw that conclusion," though she said she did not want to prescribe a cookie cutter approach. While she did mention that there could be a federal role to play in child development, she did not delve into policy specifics.[41]

Hillary Clinton's Prescription for Reading Partnership was one outcome of the White House Conference on Early Childhood Development and Learning. She announced that, through the partnership, pediatricians, hospitals, publishers, and libraries pledged to encourage parents to read to their children regularly. Doctors and health professionals would prescribe daily reading to young patients and even provide books. She garnered commitments from private and professional organizations. The American Academy of Pediatrics provided members with specialty reading prescription pads. Random House contributed 5,000 books a month for twelve months.[42]

Then in the fall of 1997, Hillary Clinton convened the White House Conference on Child Care. Nixon's veto of the Child Development Act in 1971 effectively tabled policy discussion of the issue for two decades. In the 1990s, the government once again began to discuss the problem, and Hillary Clinton was a participant in the debate. The child-care debate was not as charged as it had been in the 1970s. In their 1996 platform, Republicans supported flextime for working parents and, rather than denouncing child care outright, included a statement about supporting family choice in care against the Democrats' attempts to control it. At the time, 13 million children were being cared for by someone other than a parent, but many argued that care centers provided poor to mediocre care at a very high cost. Hillary Clinton wanted the conference to start a conversation and renew efforts to improve child care in America. To laughter, Bill Clinton told the audience that it was a happy day for him because he had been listening to his wife talk about the issue for more than twenty-five years. "I will finally be able to participate in at least a small fraction of what I have been told for a long time I should be doing," he said.[43]

The child-care advocacy community hoped that the conference would be the spark that lit the United States down the path toward a French-style child-care system. In January 1998, the Clinton administration presented its proposal to increase spending for child care by $21 billion. The proposal included tax credits for employers who provided child-care assistance, an expansion of before- and after- school programs, and funding for increased quality and safety. Hillary Clinton's staff worked with domestic policy advisors to develop the proposals. But her policy goals would not be realized. The child-care proposals were soon eclipsed by the Monica Lewinsky scandal.[44]

Hillary Clinton's family values were put to the test when Bill Clinton admitted to having an extramarital affair with White House intern Monica Lewinsky. For months, Hillary Clinton wrestled with whether she and her husband should stay married. The couple sought counseling, and Hillary Clinton eventually concluded she wanted to save the marriage. Given the feminist image she had cultivated, many were surprised she did not immediately file for divorce. Yet, as she wrote in *It Takes a Village*, "My strong feelings about divorce and its effects on children have caused me to bite my tongue more than a few times during my own marriage and to think instead about what I could do to be a better wife and partner."[45]

After the impeachment proceedings, in the midst of her Senate campaign, Hillary Clinton published a lavishly illustrated, glossy entertaining book, *An Invitation to the White House*. She wrote about the French Empire–style fabric she selected and told how she installed a family kitchen in the living quarters. Her West Wing office having fallen into disuse, she discussed how she conducted her day-to-day business in the West Sitting Hall of the family quarters. It was there she assembled care packages for Chelsea, who was studying at Stanford University. She elaborated on how she selected floral arrangements, detailed her workflow with the social staff, and highlighted invitations and menus for state affairs. In the section on Christmas in the White House, she detailed how she oversaw all the preparations, from selecting the theme to menus, decorations, parties, and music. The final section excerpted recipes from the White House kitchen, such as herbed tomato frittata, smoked salmon on potato pancakes, puree of butternut squash and granny smith apples, and cherry Yule log. As Hillary Clinton's entertaining book illustrates, when motherhood and family politics are prominent, even so-called activist first ladies have blended domestic duties with political and policy work.[46]

LAURA BUSH

In the wake of the Monica Lewinsky scandal, the wives in the 2000 election tried to affirm that their husbands were good, moral family men. The *Family Circle* cookie contest pitted Tipper Gore's Ginger Snaps against Laura Bush's Texas Governor's Mansion Cowboy Cookies. The

Democratic convention featured Al Gore giving Tipper a lengthy kiss before taking the stage. Laura Bush told the Republican convention, "George spends every night with a teacher." Concluding her remarks with a reference to the Monica Lewinsky scandal, she related how voters would tell her that they wanted their sons and daughters to respect the president of the United States again. The themes of fidelity, fatherhood, and family were woven throughout her speech.[47]

Laura Bush also devoted much of her convention speech to touting her husband's record on education. Laura Bush wanted to make education, literacy, and early childhood development her priorities, rooting them in her experience as both a mother and a teacher. She knew these subjects. They were her life's work up to that point. From her first lady post, she also zeroed in on delinquent fatherhood and at-risk boys in America.

One of Laura Bush's very first public events as first lady was launching her husband's Ready to Read, Ready to Learn initiative. Phrasing the goals of the program as her own priorities, she told her audience at Cesar Chavez Elementary School that she wanted to spotlight teacher recruitment, early childhood education, and research on learning and development. And though her early platform may have seemed akin to her mother-in-law's, she actually sounded more like Hillary Clinton in Hillary's second term. Laura Bush convened the White House Summit on Early Childhood Cognitive Development in July 2001. "If you have children, then like President Bush and me, you were probably not surprised to learn that science now confirms . . . the years from the crib to the classroom represent a period of intense language and cognitive growth," she said. The conference also featured the nation's foremost researchers and policy makers discussing childhood brain research. Most importantly, the conference was background prep for her upcoming testimony before the Senate Education Committee, which is where she was headed the morning of 11 September 2001.[48]

Not only did the terrorist attacks on the World Trade Center and Pentagon shift Laura Bush's focus to international women's rights, it also established her reputation as "Comforter in Chief," a term ascribed to her by *Newsweek* reporter Martha Brant to highlight how she had become, in the wake of the attacks, a voice of calm and reason for the nation. The morning following the attacks, she wrote letters to the nation's schoolchildren, reassuring them that their families and teachers loved and cared about them and were looking out for their safety. She encouraged them to write down their thoughts or draw pictures of how they were feeling. "Be kind to each other, take care of each other, and show your love for each other," she wrote. In the weeks and months after the attacks, she earned praise for how she mourned with victims' families, toured schools, and listened to children. Her role in the Bush family became a topic of interest. She reportedly chided her husband for his "macho" and "hot-tempered" cowboy talk aimed at Osama bin Laden and became "fiercely protective" of her family after the attacks. As Martha Brant wrote, "In public she'll often stand close to him, holding his hand tightly. If he seems jittery, she'll brush his arm or touch the back of his neck, a simple act of reassurance that lets him know he's not alone."[49]

Laura Bush did eventually give her testimony before the Senate Education Committee. Unlike Hillary Clinton's health-care testimony, she did not speak on behalf of a specific policy. But Laura Bush did classify early reading as a national issue in which the federal government had a role to play. Laura Bush's overall goal was to relate the findings from her White House Summit on Early Childhood Cognitive Development in order to raise congressional awareness. In her remarks, she vested her authority and interest in the education of preschool children in her roles as a mother and an experienced professional. "My emphasis on making sure that preschool children are provided stimulating activities . . . stems from my own experiences as a mother, a public school teacher and a school librarian," she said. "As a mother, I learned quickly that reading to our daughters and playing language games . . . brought joy and laughter to our home. . . . During my career as an elementary school teacher . . . I observed that some children were having difficulty learning to read . . . because they had not developed the basic building blocks of language during their preschool years." Though Laura Bush and Hillary Clinton worked on traditionally feminine projects, it is significant that they also rooted their authority, in part, in a mix of their motherhood and professional experience. This, in turn, opened more opportunities for acting in the public sphere, such as holding White House conferences, testifying before Congress, and working on policy.[50]

By George W. Bush's administration, the backlash against feminism was moving beyond women's issues. A new focus on boys and father-hood had been gathering steam throughout the 1990s. In the May 2000 issue of the *Atlantic Monthly*, conservative writer Christina Hoff Sommers authored a controversial article titled, "The War against Boys," charging that the alleged crisis in girls' education raised by books and reports in the 1990s was misleading. Feminists objected, but the article helped give rise to a new boy-centered public policy. A new fatherhood movement was also burgeoning. In 1995, Bill Clinton, cracking down on deadbeat dads, called father absence one of the most important social issues of the day. In 1997, the House and Senate formed bipartisan task forces to examine fatherlessness and policy. In 2000, the National Fatherhood Initiative held its third national summit. Though the fatherhood movement has been multiracial and bipartisan, feminist groups—distrusting traditional marriage, concerned about domestic violence and joint custody, and wanting options for family composition—were skeptical.[51]

While Laura Bush focused intently on girls' education abroad, at home she zeroed in on at-risk boys. She wrote, "For years I had known that, as a nation, we are not focusing on boys the way we should. . . . In the last forty years, the nation has entirely rethought how we raise girls, fostering their belief that they have every opportunity. But we have not given that same thought to boys; they are still locked in traditions as much as our daughters were two generations ago." Boys were more likely to drop out of school and have a learning disability and were less likely to attend college. They were more likely to be incarcerated and abuse alcohol and drugs.[52]

George W. Bush announced the Helping America's Youth initiative in his 2005 State of the Union message. He asked Laura Bush to head the effort. That fall, she convened the White House Conference on Helping America's Youth at Howard University. With over 500 civic and religious leaders, educators, and researchers in attendance, the conference encouraged families, schools, and faith-based organizations to partner together to help children, especially boys, avoid risky behavior and become responsible adults. The initiative emphasized the importance of family and promoted healthy marriages and responsible fatherhood. The first lady told attendees, "Young people who grow up without their dads suffer a profound loss. . . . Being a good dad doesn't always come naturally. Young men who become fathers need help in learning how to stay involved in their children's lives." Laura Bush headlined about fifty Helping America's Youth events around the country, though the first lady believed that the press did not give these events much attention, and the project eventually lost its focus on boys that Laura Bush had wanted.[53]

MICHELLE OBAMA

In 2008, Michelle Obama told *Ebony* what her first lady priorities would be. "My first job in all honesty is going to continue to be mom-in-chief," she said, "making sure that in this transition, which will be even more of a transition for the girls . . . that they are settled and that they know they will continue to be the center of our universe." In 2012, reflecting on her activities over the past four years, she explained to the Democratic convention, "You see, at the end of the day, my most important title is still 'mom-in-chief.' My daughters are still the heart of my heart and the center of my world." She went on, "these issues aren't political—they're personal." Michelle Obama reversed the meaning of the old feminist slogan. What used to be a rallying cry to drum up discussion about women's liberation from traditional roles, Michelle Obama used to set apart and consecrate her role as a wife and mother. As first lady, she acted as a mother through her project on kids and healthy eating, as well as through her support for military families.[54]

For Michelle Obama, stepping into the role of first lady meant stepping out of the workforce. In 2008, her daughters Sasha and Malia were ages ten and seven. They were little, and their schedules were packed with soccer and dance. As *Ebony* recorded, "Michelle knows the details of her girls' busy schedules and can map out their movement moment by moment. Barack can rest easy on that front." Following the inauguration, she limited her official work to two days per week, later upping it to three as her girls grew older. She tried not to do events after five in the afternoon, which was family time.[55]

Michelle Obama also received favorable style coverage and made appearances on numerous women's magazine covers. She wore shoulder-baring sheaths that showed off her sculpted arms. Her wardrobe featured Jacqueline Kennedy–style classics, made by Oscar de la Renta and Carolina Herrera. She also wore trendy, modern designs by Alexander McQueen and Narciso Rodriguez and sported labels worn by the masses, such as H&M, J.Crew, and White House | Black Market. It was a style many middle-aged mothers could identify with and aspire to.[56]

Like other first ladies after 1980, Michelle Obama rooted her first lady projects in her motherhood. On a chilly first day of spring in 2009, she broke ground on the first White House garden since Eleanor Roosevelt's World War II victory garden. Though a gardening novice, she wanted to start the kitchen garden because, she said, "As both a mother and first lady," she was "alarmed by reports of skyrocketing childhood obesity rates and the dire consequences for our children's health." She hoped the garden would start a conversation about organic, local food and healthful eating and how they impacted American children. Fifth graders from Bancroft Elementary School in Washington helped to plant seeds and harvest crops, including arugula, tomatillos, cilantro, and berries. The garden was in line with national trends. With the country mired in recession, many Americans were cultivating gardens to ease their food budgets. It also helped cultivate her image as a down-to-earth mother concerned about how to get kids to eat more greens. Though Michelle Obama did address urban food deserts through her healthy eating campaign, organic greens and gardening are not typically thought of as civil rights issues. By deemphasizing race, her healthy eating campaign could have broader appeal.[57]

Michelle Obama also turned her garden project into a book, *American Grown: The Story of the White House Kitchen Garden and Gardens across America*. It was similar in size and glossiness to Hillary Clinton's entertaining book. It is notable that the two Democratic first ladies of this era had such books, while the Republican wives did not, further confirming the pull of domesticity on the first ladyship. Michelle Obama's book mapped out the garden plot for each season, noting where the butterhead lettuce and fennel were planted in the spring and the collards and radicchio in the winter. The gardening book provided seasonal recipes, such as green beans with almonds for summer and sweet potato quick bread for fall. Besides the recipe section, it was part food biography, part manifesto about eating locally, and part policy review of the programs the garden eventually sprouted.[58]

One of those was her *Let's Move!* campaign. Again, her motherhood justified the program. At its launch, Michelle Obama said that child-hood obesity is "an issue that's of great concern to me not just as a first lady, but as a mom." Though shrouded in *Sesame Street* characters, it was rooted in public policy. The problem was that one in three American children was overweight or obese, with obesity rates having tripled over the past three decades, while more and more kids had diabetes and high blood pressure. Its goal was to eradicate childhood obesity within a generation. Moreover, she described her interest in obesity as "absolutely personal." She frequently retold the story of the personal origins of the program in her speeches and remarks. When she was a "regular mom" on the South Side of Chicago, fast food provided sustenance amid the family's busy schedule. Her pediatrician gave her a wake-up call when he told her that her family needed to look at how they were eating. While she was struggling to juggle it all, Michelle Obama realized that obesity was an "epidemic that showed up on our back door unexpectedly." The Obama family eliminated sugary drinks and added more fruits and vegetables, and Michelle Obama cooked a couple more times a week—and got a pleasing follow-up report from the pediatrician. She thought that if she could bring change in her own family, she could do so for the entire nation.[59]

Let's Move! set out to empower parents to make better choices. She set up the MyPlate initiative, which replaced the old food pyramid. Divided into five sections—fruits, vegetables, grains, protein, and dairy—the new icon was designed to take the guesswork out of meal planning. Again, her motherhood drove the initiative. "As a mom, I can already tell you how much this is going to help parents across the country," she said. "The last thing we need to do is be the nutritionist in our family," she said, noting the myriad roles women play—from chef to referee to cleaning crew.[60]

President Obama credited his wife with helping to get the Healthy, Hunger-Free Kids Act passed, quipping, "Had I not been able to get this passed, I would be sleeping on the couch." The act set healthier standards for the food sold in school cafeterias and vending machines. While her other initiatives could be seen as models or suggestions for families and communities, this was a federal mandate. About school food choices, the first lady said, "We can't just leave it up to the parents. . . . I think that our parents have a right to expect that their kids will be served fresh, healthy food that meets high nutritional standards." While most of Michelle Obama's campaign emphasized personal responsibility, reforming eating habits at the individual level, this cafeteria-level intrusion sniffed of the nanny state and received criticism from conservatives.[61]

While *Let's Move!* was glossed in lighthearted public relations, it was, at the same time, partisan and ideological. It served as the feminine counterpoint to her husband's health-care reforms. Libertarians and conservatives resisted her initiatives and demonstrated less public support for her. To these individuals, the first lady was leading a big government power grab that would lead to even more federal oversight of what citizens served at their tables and put in their mouths.

Michelle Obama also got into some political mudslinging over her antiobesity campaign. On her reality television show, Sarah Palin, former Alaska governor and vice presidential candidate, made s'mores, dedicating the chocolate campfire confection to Michelle Obama. Palin also delivered cookies to a Pennsylvania school in honor of Michelle Obama, proclaiming that the government should not decide what kids eat. Michelle Obama also fought back when Congress wanted to make it optional, not mandatory, for schools to comply with some of the standards or delay the standards. Republicans said that standards were too expensive and that kids were throwing away too much food. Results of a Government Accountability Office survey confirmed this. And school kids took to social media to complain about their lunches, posting photos of the lackluster offerings with the hashtag #ThankYou MichelleObama.[62]

Mostly, Michelle Obama's antiobesity campaign was filled with lighter public relations relatable to moms. In white tennis shoes, she demonstrated "mom dancing" with late-night comedian Jimmy Fallon, which included moves titled, "This Ol' Thing? I Got It at Talbots" and "Getting a Bag from Your Collection of Plastic Bags under the Sink." She appeared with *Sesame Street* puppets Elmo, Rosita, and Big Bird, planting a garden with them on the PBS program. And she flexed her biceps for them at a White House conference where she announced that Sesame Workshop would temporarily waive its licensing fee for produce industry marketing. She also bested Ellen DeGeneres in a push-up contest on DeGeneres's daytime talk show.

Michelle Obama and Jimmy Fallon perform the "Evolution of Mom Dance II" for The Tonight Show with Jimmy Fallon *in New York, New York, on 2 April 2015. Official White House Photo by Chuck Kennedy.*

Then in April 2011, Michelle Obama launched Joining Forces, an initiative to support military families. Though the initiative targeted male and female veterans and spouses alike, it stemmed from Michelle Obama's empathy with military wives. It was also an initiative that de-emphasized race and was not as ideological as the *Let's Move!* initiative. Supporting the military was typically something conservatives did. Barack Obama described the program's impetus:

> I remember how it began. It was during our campaign. Michelle was meeting with women all across the country, listening to their struggles, hearing their stories. And inevitably there were complaints about husbands and—(laughter)—not doing enough around the house and—(laughter)—being confused when you've got to brush the daughter's hair and get that ponytail right. (Laughter.) So they were sharing notes. But in all these conversations, there was one group that just kept on capturing Michelle's heart—and that was military spouses. And she decided

right then and there, if . . . she was given the opportunity to serve as first lady, she would be their voice.

He continued, "So I want every military family to know that Michelle hears you—not just as a first lady . . . but as a wife, and a daughter, and a mom." Barack Obama's words make clear that Joining Forces stemmed from his wife's family ties.[63]

Michelle Obama confirmed this. In discussing her plans for the initiative, she said that as first lady she wanted to focus on what she knew. And as a working mom, she thought she knew about juggling a job and the needs of her family. But she was surprised by the special challenges of military families, from missing birthdays to finding new pediatricians during frequent relocations to facing adoption challenges when moving from state to state. "So here I was, someone who'd always thought of myself as knowledgeable about women's issues. I'd been reading about, thinking about, talking about, and living these issues my entire life and here was one group of women for whom these issues were magnified ten-fold, a hundred-fold—and I had no idea." To Michelle Obama, women's problems were family problems, and military wives experienced them more than anyone.[64]

Michelle Obama did not work alone, however. Joining Forces was a partnership with Jill Biden, wife of the vice president, as well as their husbands. Though primarily attached to the first lady's office and secondarily to the second lady's, this partnership between the four offices was unprecedented. Jill Biden was a self-described proud military mom. Given Jill Biden's link to service families and Michelle Obama's access to the commander in chief, the arrangement made sense. It also confirmed the historical legacy of planting initiatives about the care and well-being of the family inside the first lady's office.

The question driving Joining Forces was, how can the nation support military families? Michelle Obama found answers in "what we do for each other as women," as sisters, girlfriends, mothers, and daughters. "We show up at the door with some food We show up at the door with some chocolate. . . . We take that shift in the carpool. We say, hey, send the kids over to my house right now. I'll take them off your hands," she said. She wanted the nation to reach out the way women reached out.[65]

Joining Forces sought to ease burdens on military families in em-

Michelle Obama and Jill Biden attend a baby shower for pregnant wives of military service members in Camp Lejeune, North Carolina, on 13 April 2011. Official White House Photo by Chuck Kennedy.

ployment, education, and wellness. The first lady took a conservative approach to military family issues by engaging individuals, nonprofits, and businesses. For example, writing in an editorial, she admonished companies for overlooking veterans and military spouses when filling positions. Veterans who enlisted after 11 September 2001 had a higher unemployment rate than the rest of the country. She pointed out how their life experiences—adapting to new environments, multitasking, and bearing the emotional burdens of an empty seat at the dinner table—gave them valuable skills. She also pointed out some of her concrete accomplishments. The Chamber of Commerce had begun holding job fairs for veterans, the Department of Defense started working with private employers through the Military Spouse Employment Partnership, and the Society for Human Resource Management committed to educating professionals about the skills of military spouses.[66]

Yet she could solve only some issues by changing public policy and bureaucratic rules. Thirty-five percent of military spouses, for example, had jobs, such as teachers, nurses, or social workers, that required a professional license. She issued a call to action to the National Governors Association to pass legislation to ease spousal licensing burdens, saying, "All of you are the ones who can make the biggest difference for our troops on this issue. So we need you. We need you to champion these credentialing issues right from the governor's mansion." Because of her efforts, Barack Obama ordered the Department of Defense to establish the Military Credentialing and Licensing Task Force and reformed already existing military transition and employment assistance programs.[67]

The nuts and bolts of the Joining Forces bureaucratic rules reform went on behind the scenes. Meanwhile, Michelle Obama specialized in the personal details, such as throwing Mother's Day teas for military moms, giving military kids a special preview of the White House Christmas décor, and dispensing mothering advice at Joining Forces baby showers.

Conclusion

irst ladies have acted. They have baked cookies and had teas. They have given commencement speeches and radio addresses. They have written articles and books. They have rallied women to causes, testified before Congress, and led major policy reforms. They have renovated the White House and set fashion trends. They have modeled consumer behavior and responded to cries for material assistance. They have traveled by air as diplomats and by train as campaigners. They have hugged babies, read to children, and comforted adults. They have danced on late night television and at state dinners. The job of a first lady is busy, pressure-filled, and pregnant with meaning. As Pat Nixon said, it is the hardest unpaid job in the world.

The first ladyship is a job that defies definition, even though it is endowed with power. The Constitution says nothing about it. Though the courts have ruled that the presidential spouse is a de facto federal official, it is a derivative position. She acts because she is married to the president. Otherwise, few formal guidelines direct what she must do. For that, we must look to the patterns of history.

The first major pattern that one notices is that first ladies have been inextricably linked to American womanhood. Much of what first ladies have done has been focused on women. She has spoken to women during campaigns and received women's groups at the White House. When she has modeled behaviors, whether how to purchase food or how to read to children, these have been directed toward women. The rights and policies she has advocated have pertained to women's interests. She has rested her authority to act in her role as a mother. Her womanhood defines her position. She is a lady, first.

This book has explored how and why first ladies have acted using the lens of women's changing social and political roles, revealing two main patterns in their actions. First, modern first ladies' actions have been shaped by women's expanding roles in the public sphere of politics, government, and policy. Second, their actions have been shaped by women's relationship to the private sphere of home and family. As women's social and political roles have changed, so too have first ladies' actions.

After suffrage, when women were entering the electorate and making their way forward in politics, we see first ladies bolstering their work. During the second wave, when there was a push for women's political and legal equality, first ladies spoke out on behalf of these ideals. And after 1980, when the push for women's rights expanded overseas and translated into rights for other groups in the United States, we see first ladies move and work in these areas. First ladies in each of the three historical eras have acted similarly.

After suffrage and during the Great Depression, World War II, and the postwar era, we see first ladies promoting family stability. During the second wave, we see first ladies responding to trends that made personal issues political. And after 1980, we see motherhood shaping their policies and programs. Here again, first ladies in each of these three historical eras have acted similarly.

Though their actions have been similar, they have not behaved the same, even within each of the three historical areas and within the same political parties. For example, Eleanor Roosevelt gave the press tremendous access, while Bess Truman gave them little. Pat Nixon made her mark as a diplomat, while Betty Ford was not identified with this role. Michelle Obama planted a kitchen garden, while Hillary Clinton had little to do with kitchens or gardens. Each first lady has innovated, moved boundaries, and put her own mark on the office. These differences also raise larger questions about the first lady's freedom and limitations, especially amid a changing cultural consensus about women's roles. To what extent does the first lady have room to exercise leadership and agency? To what extent can she define the position for herself? On the other hand, what rules must she follow? What must she do and not do? Where are her boundaries? Several answers emerge from the preceding account.

First ladies must respond to trends related to women's expanding rights and roles in the public sphere at home and abroad. As chiefly public women, first ladies cannot ignore women's political roles. If they are not inclined to be politically active, they will be inevitably drawn in. They are highly visible female actors within the government, and they have provided a link between the presidency and public for American women. First ladies have helped to bring women closer to classical liberal and democratic ideals, as the country has extended these to more and more groups. First ladies' actions are expected to reflect those changing ideals.

First ladies must not neglect their roles that stem from the private sphere of home and family. While first ladies must respond to women's expanding rights and roles, greater support and less controversy have surrounded first ladies who affirm and model roles in the private sphere and who connect their public sphere activism to their private roles. When Hillary Clinton appeared to reject the traditional trappings of the first lady's role by moving her office into the West Wing and undertaking health-care reform, controversy ensued. She later abandoned this office and refocused on children in an attempt to soften her image. We rarely hear contemporary first ladies advocate for abortion and similar policies that reject motherhood without getting into hot water. When choosing projects and events, first ladies have zeroed in on children and family issues. In all they do, first ladies must take into account the prevailing culture of motherhood and problems related to the family.

First ladies must tread carefully around contemporary domestic feminism. This has been the case especially since 1980. Nancy Reagan ignored feminists. Barbara Bush purposefully did not prioritize the feminist agenda. Even Hillary Clinton did not build her first lady platform around reproductive rights, comparable worth, sexual harassment, domestic violence, and other such issues. First ladies delving into these issues would raise the controversial proposition that women's rights have not been achieved in the United States. It might also undermine the notion that America is superior to many nations in its treatment of women. This is why recent first ladies have received accolades for arguing for women's rights abroad.

First ladies must act in accord with the agendas of their respective political parties and administrations. These agendas can both compel first ladies to act and restrain them from acting. For example, while Barbara Bush harbored more liberal views than the Republican base, she kept her opinions to herself. While this frustrated feminists, Barbara Bush enjoyed widespread popularity for her grandmotherly persona. At the same time, Republicans set out to secure civil rights for disabled Americans, bolstering Barbara Bush's work for that cause. Hillary Clinton's second-term focus on kitchen table issues was in line with the Democratic Party's move toward lumping women's issues with family issues, just as her first-term focus lined up with their celebration of the political woman. No first lady has been a completely free agent to set her own agenda. Since she is unelected, and lacks direct democratic accountability, she has an obligation to support the agenda of her president and party.

First ladies are free to innovate within the aforementioned boundaries. Eleanor Roosevelt gave unprecedented press conferences. Jacqueline Kennedy invented the first lady project. Subsequent first lady projects have ranged from drug abuse, beautification, childcare, literacy, and education to healthy eating. Pat Nixon carved out the first lady's diplomatic role. Hillary Clinton set the precedent of working for women's rights abroad. These innovations, and how they framed them, were in accord with women's roles either in politics or at home during the times they served. They acted in accord with their parties and presidencies and avoided domestic feminist controversy.

First ladies' actions have been and will be molded by their historical time and place. This is the overarching principle. No first lady was completely ahead of her time and no one was behind. We have seen how the actions of first ladies have been intimately shaped by the conditions of women during their formative years. We cannot understand Eleanor Roosevelt's activism apart from her background as a New York City debutante turned social reformer. We cannot understand Bess Truman's comparative reticence without knowing how her small-town Missouri upbringing taught women how to behave in public. Hillary Clinton, Laura Bush, and Michelle Obama, who came of age during and after second wave feminism, all had graduate degrees and independent careers. Though they did not all behave the same, their educational and work experiences infiltrated their first lady actions.

Certainly, there are exceptions, and there have been many instances where first ladies lost support and generated controversy. Eleanor Roosevelt overstepped her bounds with her OCD position. Bess Truman could have been more forthcoming with the hungry women's press corps. Jacqueline Kennedy could have reached out to women's groups. Pat Nixon could have been more educated about the burgeoning women's movement. Betty Ford could have been more conciliatory to the pro-family forces in Republican ranks. Hillary Clinton regretted her West Wing office. These are just some examples, but they each violated one of the principles outlined above.

Since first ladies have been molded by their historical time and place, it is too simple to categorize them as either activist or traditional. We also cannot fairly judge their actions by contemporary standards. To do so would be to ignore women's historical roles. The first lady's story has been interwoven with the story of American women, and these stories are nuanced, complex, and ever changing.

Notes

ABBREVIATIONS USED IN NOTES
DDEL   Dwight D. Eisenhower Presidential Library, Abilene, Kansas
FDRL   Franklin D. Roosevelt Presidential Library, Hyde Park, New York
GBL   George Bush Presidential Library, College Station, Texas
GRFL   Gerald R. Ford Presidential Library, Ann Arbor, Michigan
HHL   Herbert Hoover Presidential Library, West Branch, Iowa
HSTL   Harry S. Truman Presidential Library, Independence, Missouri
JCL   Jimmy Carter Presidential Library, Atlanta, Georgia
JFKL   John F. Kennedy Presidential Library, Boston, Massachusetts
LBJL   Lyndon B. Johnson Presidential Library, Austin, Texas
RNPM   Richard Nixon Presidential Materials, National Archives at College
        Park, Maryland
RRL   Ronald Reagan Presidential Library, Simi Valley, California

INTRODUCTION

1. "The First Lady and Dr. Biden Visit Operation Shower at Camp Lejeune, North Carolina," 13 April 2011, https://www.whitehouse.gov/blog/2011/04/13/first-lady-and-dr-biden-visit-operation-shower-camp-lejeune-north-carolina. "African Queen for a Week," *Time*, 17 January 1972, 12–14. Lou Hoover, radio address, 23 March 1931, box 6, Subject File, Lou Henry Hoover Papers, HHL.

2. "African Queen for a Week," 12.

CHAPTER 1. WOMEN'S CITIZENSHIP

1. "Republican Women Hear Mrs. Hoover's Opinions," n.p., 5 May 1923, box 3, Subject File, Lou Henry Hoover Papers, HHL.

2. Kristi Andersen, *After Suffrage: Women in Partisan and Electoral Politics before the New Deal* (Chicago: University of Chicago Press, 1996).

3. Anne N. Costain, "After Reagan: New Party Attitudes toward Gender," *Annals of the American Academy of Political and Social Science* 515 (May 1991): 114–125; William H. Chafe, *The American Woman: Her Changing Social, Economic, and Political Roles, 1920–1970* (New York: Oxford University Press, 1972), 128–129.

4. "Mrs. Hoover's International Housekeeping," *Literary Digest*, 24 November 1928, 40–46.

5. Lou Hoover to Mary Helm, 6 February 1942, and "Engineering for Women," 26 May 1921, box 70, Subject File, Lou Henry Hoover Papers, HHL.

6. Mary Dougherty, "Mrs. Hoover's Charm and Grace Wins Friends," *New York Journal*, 15 June 1928, box 21, Subject File, Lou Henry Hoover Papers, HHL.

7. Andersen, *After Suffrage*, 71–74,108–109. "Mapping Campaign Activity of Hoover Woman Problem," *Washington Post*, 5 August 1928.

8. Mildred Hollingsworth to Lou Hoover, 14 August 1928, box 21, Subject File, Lou Henry Hoover Papers, HHL.

9. Maurice Thatcher to Lou Hoover, 20 September 1928 and 9 October 1928, box 24, Subject File, Lou Henry Hoover Papers, HHL.

10. Lou Hoover to Caroline Slade, 27 August 1928, box 25, Subject File, Lou Henry Hoover Papers, HHL.

11. "Mrs. Hoover Proving Big Help to G.O.P. during Westward Trek," *Christian Science Monitor*, 16 July 1928, box 35, Subject File, Lou Henry Hoover Papers, HHL.

12. Mrs. George H. Lorimer to Lou Hoover, 29 August 1928, box 24, and "Mrs. Hoover Visits Quaker City Shrine," *Washington Post*, 20 September 1928, box 35, Subject File, Lou Henry Hoover Papers, HHL.

13. Mrs. Martin Kent Northam to Lou Hoover, 16 January 1929, box 21, Subject File, Lou Henry Hoover Papers, HHL.

14. Unsigned impressions recorded by secretary, 16 October 1929, box 109, Subject File, Lou Henry Hoover Papers, HHL.

15. Mrs. Herbert Hoover, Foreword to *Play Day—The Spirit of Sport*, by Ethel Perrin and Grace Turner (n.p.: American Child Health Association, 1929), box 5, Subject File, Lou Henry Hoover Papers, HHL.

16. Douglas B. Craig, *Fireside Politics: Radio and Political Culture in the United States, 1920–1940* (Baltimore, MD: Johns Hopkins University Press, 2000), 242–250.

17. Lou Hoover, radio address, 22 June 1929, box 5, Subject File, Lou Henry Hoover Papers, HHL.

18. Craig, *Fireside Politics*, 248. Robert D. Heinl, "Off the Antenna," *Washington Post*, 30 June 1929.

19. "Mrs. Hoover Tries Out Her Voice on Sound Films to Improve It," *Star*, 5 November 1931, box 46, Lou Henry Hoover Papers, HHL.

20. Herbert Hoover, *The Memoirs of Herbert Hoover*, vol. 2: *The Cabinet and the Presidency, 1920–1933* (New York: MacMillan, 1952), 324; "Governor Upholds First Lady's Critics," *Washington Post*, 6 July 1929; David S. Day, "A New Perspective on the 'DePriest Tea' Historiographic Controversy," *Journal of Negro History* 65, no. 1 (Winter 1980): 6–17.

21. Hoover, *Memoirs*, 188.

22. Sarah Hallenbeck, "Working Together and Being Prepared: Early Girl Scouting as Citizenship Training," in *Women and Rhetoric between the Wars*, ed. Ann George, M. Elizabeth Weiser, and Janet Zepernick (Carbondale: Southern

Illinois University Press, 2013), 79–86; Lou Hoover, remarks, 14 October 1931, box 6, Subject File, Lou Henry Hoover Papers, HHL.

23. Lou Hoover, radio address, 23 March 1931, and Arthur Woods to Lou Hoover, 25 March 1931, box 6, Subject File, Lou Henry Hoover Papers, HHL.

24. "Report on Cases," 13 August 1931, box 82, Subject File, Lou Henry Hoover Papers, HHL.

25. Lenna Yost to Philippi Harding Butler, 5 November 1932, and Lenna Yost to Lou Hoover, 16 September 1932, box 48, Girl Scouts and Other Organizations File, Lou Henry Hoover Papers, HHL.

26. Nancy Beck Young, *Lou Henry Hoover: Activist First Lady* (Lawrence: University Press of Kansas, 2004), 160–161. Andersen, *After Suffrage*, 75, 145.

27. Lou Hoover, "The Woman's Place in the Present Emergency," 27 November 1932, box 6, Subject File, Lou Henry Hoover Papers, HHL.

28. Joseph P. Lash, *Eleanor and Franklin: The Story of their Relationship, Based on Eleanor Roosevelt's Private Papers* (New York: Norton, 1971), 80–81, 97–100; Allen F. Davis, *Spearheads for Reform: The Social Settlements and the Progressive Movement 1890–1914* (New York: Oxford University Press, 1967), 8, 38–39.

29. Lash, *Eleanor and Franklin*, 99–100.

30. Ibid., 175, 208, 218–219.

31. Ibid., 260, 288–291, 309–311; Eleanor Roosevelt, "Women Must Learn to Play the Game as Men Do," *Redbook Magazine*, April 1928, 78–79, 141–142.

32. Chafe, *American Woman*, 39.

33. Box 575, Eleanor Roosevelt Papers, FDRL.

34. Ibid.

35. Ibid.

36. Ibid.

37. Boxes 575 and 578, Eleanor Roosevelt Papers, FDRL.

38. Susan Ware, *Beyond Suffrage: Women in the New Deal* (Cambridge, MA: Harvard University Press, 1981), 50–52.

39. Ruby A. Black, "'New Deal' for News Women in Capital," *Editor and Publisher*, 10 February 1934, box 587, Eleanor Roosevelt Papers, FDRL; Maurine H. Beasley, "The Press Conferences of Eleanor Roosevelt," paper presented at the Annual Meeting of the Association for Education in Journalism and Mass Communication, Corvallis, OR, 1983, http://files.eric.ed.gov/fulltext/ED229770.pdf.

40. Alice Kessler-Harris, *Out to Work: A History of Wage-Earning Women in the United States* (New York: Oxford University Press, 1982), 254; Eleanor Roosevelt, radio address, 24 February 1933, box 3024, Eleanor Roosevelt Papers, FDRL

41. Ware, *Beyond Suffrage*, 106–107.

42. "Educational Camps for Unemployed Women 1934 and 1935," box 331, Eleanor Roosevelt Papers, FDRL.

43. Eleanor Roosevelt, "Resident Schools and Camps for Unemployed Women Statement," n.d. [ca. 1935], box 3032, Eleanor Roosevelt Papers, FDRL.

44. Box 625, Eleanor Roosevelt Papers, FDRL.

45. "Report on the Handling of Mrs. Roosevelt's Mail," 13 April 1939, box 331, Eleanor Roosevelt Papers, FDRL.

46. Rosalyn Terborg-Penn, "Discontented Black Feminists: Prelude and Postscript to the Passage of the Nineteenth Amendment," in *Decades of Discontent: The Women's Movement 1920–1940*, ed. Lois Scharf and Joan M. Jensen (Boston: Northeastern University Press, 1983), 273–274.

47. Eleanor Roosevelt to Dorothy McAllister, n.d. [ca. July 1944], box 721, Eleanor Roosevelt Papers, FDRL.

48. "Friends, Foes of Equal Rights for Women Get Hearing in First Lady's Apartment," *New York Times*, n.d. [ca. February 1944], box 814, Eleanor Roosevelt Papers, FDRL.

49. Eleanor Roosevelt to Rose Schneiderman, box 814, Eleanor Roosevelt Papers, FDRL.

50. Eleanor Roosevelt, "Defense and Girls," *Ladies' Home Journal*, May 1941, box 3040, Eleanor Roosevelt Papers, FDRL.

51. Eleanor Roosevelt, "Shall We Draft Women?" *Liberty*, 13 September 1941, box 3041, Eleanor Roosevelt Papers, FDRL.

52. Doris Kearns Goodwin, *No Ordinary Time: Franklin and Eleanor Roosevelt: The Home Front in World War II* (New York: Simon & Schuster, 1994), 280–281, 324–325.

53. Chafe, *American Woman*, 135–136.

54. Ibid., 136–137, 159–160; Eleanor Roosevelt, "Women in the War Effort," *Flying Times*, 26 January 1943, box 3047, Eleanor Roosevelt Papers, FDRL; Eleanor Roosevelt, "Recording for Office of War Information—Women in Industry," December 1942, Eleanor Roosevelt Papers, FDRL.

55. Eleanor Roosevelt, "American Women in the War," *Reader's Digest*, January 1944, box 3047, Eleanor Roosevelt Papers, FDRL; Chafe, *American Woman*, 145.

56. Eleanor Roosevelt, "Women at the Peace Conference," *Reader's Digest*, April 1944, box 3050, Eleanor Roosevelt Papers, FDRL; "A Summary Statement of the Conference on How Women May Share in Post-War Policy-Making," 14 June 1944, box 113, Eleanor Roosevelt Papers, FDRL.

57. Cynthia Harrison, *On Account of Sex: The Politics of Women's Issues 1945–1968* (Berkeley: University of California Press, 1988), 51–53.

58. Undated correspondence [ca. 1948], box 5, Reathel Odum Papers, HSTL; Helen Worden Erskine, "The Riddle of Mrs. Truman," *Collier's*, 9 February 1952, box 5, Reathel Odum Papers, HSTL.

59. Margaret Truman, *Bess W. Truman* (New York: McMillan, 1986), 1, 4, 7, 21–22.

60. Ibid., 22, 46.

61. Ibid., 104, 113.

62. Ibid., 203, 214.

63. India Edwards Oral History, 16 January 1969, 1–4, 38–40, HSTL.

64. Ibid., 10 November 1975, 4, HSTL; ibid., 16 January 1969, 82–83, 85–89, 99, HSTL; Harrison, *On Account of Sex*, 58.

65. Achsah Dorsey Smith, "Republican Male Dares to Attend Democratic 'Women-Only' Reception," *Times-Herald*, 4 August 1949, and Betty Beale, "Society News," *Washington Daily News*, 4 August 1949, box 40A, Student Research File, HSTL.

66. Undated correspondence [ca. September 1951], box 2, India Edwards Papers, HSTL.

67. "A Typical Day at the White House (Mrs. Truman)," box 5, Reathel Odum Papers, HSTL; India Edwards to Edith Helm, 7 October 1946, box 7, Social Office Files, HSTL.

68. Box 24, Social Office Files, HSTL.

69. Harry Truman to India Edwards, 27 January 1951, box 40A, Student Research File, HSTL; Mary Rickett to Frank McHale, 14 October 1947, box 1, India Edwards Papers, HSTL.

70. J. M. Helm to India Edwards, 29 May 1945, box 7, Social Office Files, HSTL.

71. Jo Freeman, *A Room at a Time: How Women Entered Party Politics* (Lanham, MD: Rowman & Littlefield, 2000), 198.

72. India Edwards Oral History, 16 January 1969, 46–48, 59, HSTL.

73. "Report Made by Mrs. India Edwards," 20 October 1948, and "Mrs. Truman, Margaret Help with Handshakes and Smiles," *Louisville Times*, 1 October 1948, box 3, India Edwards Papers, HSTL; India Edwards, *Pulling No Punches: Memoirs of a Woman in Politics* (New York: Putnam, 1977), 118–119.

74. India Edwards to Bess Truman, 9 August 1946, and Bess Truman to India Edwards, undated correspondence [ca. August 1946], box 1, India Edwards Papers, HSTL.

75. DNC women to India Edwards, 5 December 1952, box 40A, Student Research File, HSTL.

76. India Edwards to Harry Truman, 4 December 1952, box 40A, Student Research File, HSTL.

77. India Edwards to Leisa Bronson, 6 April 1953, box 40A, Student Research File, HSTL; Edwards, *Pulling No Punches*, 203.

78. Freeman, *A Room at a Time*, 104–105, 198.

79. Catherine E. Rymph, *Republican Women: Feminism and Conservatism from Suffrage through the Rise of the New Right* (Chapel Hill: University of North Carolina Press, 2006), 136, 149–151.

80. Susan Eisenhower, *Mrs. Ike: Memories and Reflections on the Life of Mamie Eisenhower* (New York: Farrar, Straus and Giroux, 1996), 10, 13, 20–21.

81. Mamie Eisenhower Oral History, 15 August 1972, 117, DDEL.

82. Mamie Eisenhower Oral History, 20 July 1972, 11, and 15 August 1972, 42, DDEL.

83. Mamie Eisenhower Oral History, 15 August 1972, 89, DDEL.

84. Katherine Howard Oral History, 16 July 1968, 88–89, DDEL.

85. Ibid., 90.

86. Ibid., 436.

87. Ibid., 477.

88. Rymph, *Republican Women*, 151–154.

89. Bertha Adkins Oral History, 18 December 1967, 42–44, DDEL.

90. "Mamie's Working Hard for Ike," *U.S. News and World Report*, 21 August 1953, Vertical File, DDEL.

91. Bertha Adkins to Mamie Eisenhower, 5 May 1953, box 5, Social Office Files, DDEL.

92. See Freeman, *A Room at a Time*, 199.

93. J. B. West, *Upstairs at the White House: My Life with First Ladies* (New York: Coward, McCann and Geoghegan, 1973), 134–135.

94. Mamie Eisenhower Oral History, 16 August 1972, 154–156.

95. Charles Willis to Sherman Adams, 12 March 1954, box 541, White House Central Files, DDEL.

96. Francis Dorn to Wilton Persons, 13 May 1953, box 16, Social Office Files, DDEL.

97. William Ayers to Jack Martin, 25 March 1954, and Jack Martin to Mary Jane McCaffree, 1 April 1954, box 542, White House Central Files, DDEL.

98. Helen Cann Janne to Mary Jane McCaffree, 12 March 1953, box 5, Social Office Files, DDEL.

99. Harrison, *On Account of Sex*, 33–36.

100. Eisenhower, *Mrs. Ike*, 298, 301. Marilyn Irvin Holt, *Mamie Doud Eisenhower: The General's First Lady* (Lawrence: University Press of Kansas, 2007), 107. Eugenia Kaledin, *Mothers and More: American Women in the 1950s* (New York: Macmillan, 1985), 27.

101. "Lady with a Doughnut," *Time*, 18 October 1954, 18; Center for American Women and Politics, "Fact Sheet," http://www.cawp.rutgers.edu/fast_facts /levels_of_office/documents/cong.pdf.

102. "Honoring the Companion's Most Successful Women," *Woman's Home Companion*, n.d., Vertical File, DDEL.

103. Chafe, *American Woman*, 199–201, 218–220; Holt, *Mamie Doud Eisenhower*, 71.

104. Anne Wheaton Oral History, 8 March 1968, 150, DDEL; Harrison, *On Account of Sex*, 61–63.

105. "Biography of Jacqueline Bouvier Kennedy," February 1962, box 10, Pierre Salinger Files, JFKL.

106. Chafe, *American Woman*, 212–214.

107. Harrison, *On Account of Sex*, 74–75, 79.

108. Box 706, White House Central Files, JFKL.

109. Box 19, DNC Press Releases, JFKL.

110. "Campaign Wife," 13 October 1960, box 20, DNC Press Releases, JFKL.

111. "Campaign Wife," 1 November 1960, and DNC press releases, 6 October 1960 and 16 October 1960, box 21, DNC Press Releases, JFKL.

112. "Campaign Wife," 29 September 1960, and DNC press release, 22 September 1960, box 19, DNC Press Releases, JFKL.

113. Box 20, DNC Press Releases, JFKL.

114. "Campaign Wife," 27 October 1960, box 1034, 1960 Campaign, Pre-Presidential Papers, JFKL.

115. Ibid.

116. Jacqueline Kennedy, *Historic Conversations on Life with John F. Kennedy* (New York: Hyperion, 2011), 131; Robert Klara, *The Hidden White House: Harry Truman and the Reconstruction of America's Most Famous Residence* (New York: St. Martin's Press, 2013), 173–179.

117. Press release, 23 February 1961, box 101, Pierre Salinger Files, JFKL.

118. Hugh Sidey, "The First Lady Brings History and Beauty to the White House," *Life*, September 1961, 55–64.

119. Jacqueline Kennedy to Arthur Schlesinger, n.d. [ca. May 1963], box P-6, Papers of Arthur M. Schlesinger Jr., JFKL; Press release, 3 November 1961, box 101, Pierre Salinger Files, JFKL.

120. Kennedy, *Historic Conversations*, 141, 174; Jacqueline Kennedy to Arthur Schlesinger, n.d. [ca. 1962], and 14 February 1962, box W-7, Papers of Arthur M. Schlesinger, Jr., JFKL.

121. Kennedy, *Historic Conversations*, 137–143.

122. Letitia Baldrige, *A Lady, First: My Life in the Kennedy White House and the American Embassies of Paris and Rome* (New York: Penguin Books, 2002), 183.

123. Box 1, William Walton Papers, JFKL.

124. Harrison, *On Account of Sex*, 173.

125. Arthur Goldberg to JFK, 13 December 1961, and Executive Order 10980, box 2, President's Commission on Status of Women Records, JFKL; United States Department of Labor, "Highlights: 1920–1960," n.d., box 1, President's Commission on the Status of Women Records, JFKL.

126. Harrison, *On Account of Sex*, 138–165.

127. Lyndon Johnson to Jacqueline Kennedy, 8 April 1964, box 5, White House Famous Names File, LBJL.

CHAPTER 2. THE STABLE SOCIETY

1. M. L. Wilson, "How New Deal Agencies Are Affecting Family Life," *Journal of Home Economics* 27, no. 5 (May 1935): 274–280.

2. Anne Beiser Allen, *The Life of Lou Henry Hoover* (Westport, CT: Greenwood Press, 2000), 75.

3. Vylla Poe Wilson, "Mrs. Hoover at Reception Wears Train," *Washington Post*, 13 October 1929.

4. Sara M. Evans, *Born for Liberty: A History of Women in America* (New York: Free

Press, 1989), 198–201; Alice Kessler-Harris, *Out to Work: A History of Wage-Earning Women in the United States* (New York: Oxford University Press, 1982), 250–258.

5. Louise Bryant, *Educational Work of the Girl Scouts* (Washington, DC: Government Printing Office, 1921), 3, 14, http://www.gutenberg.org/ebooks/29373.

6. Adele Entz, "Girl Scout Home-Making Activities Stimulated by Aid of Mrs. Hoover," n.d. [ca. 1930], n.p., box 12, Girl Scouts and Other Organizations File, Lou Henry Hoover Papers, HHL.

7. "The National Committee on Volunteer Service Addressed by Mrs. Herbert Hoover," *Red Cross Courier*, 1 January 1930, box 6, Subject File, Lou Henry Hoover Papers, HHL.

8. "Mrs. Hoover Holds Dish-Washing Housewife Has More Courage Than the Big Game Hunter," *New York Times*, 2 October 1930, box 6, Subject File, Lou Henry Hoover Papers, HHL.

9. Lou Hoover, remarks, 14 October 1931, box 6, Subject File, Lou Henry Hoover Papers, HHL.

10. "Mrs. Hoover Urges Living Normal Life," *Washington Post*, 15 October 1931.

11. Vylla Poe Wilson, "Mrs. Hoover Wears Attire Made in U.S.," 14 February 1932, *Washington Post*, box 47, Subject File, Lou Henry Hoover Papers, HHL.

12. "Mrs. Hoover Knits to Help Needy," n.p., 17 November 1932, box 47, Subject File, Lou Henry Hoover Papers, HHL.

13. Lou Hoover, remarks, box 6, Subject File, Lou Henry Hoover Papers, HHL.

14. "Girl Scout Aid to the World Cited by Mrs. Hoover," *New York Herald*, 8 October 1932, box 6, Subject File, Lou Henry Hoover Papers, HHL.

15. Wilson, "New Deal Agencies," 276. Steven Mintz and Susan Kellogg, *Domestic Revolutions: A Social History of American Family Life* (New York: Free Press, 1988), 144.

16. Joseph P. Lash, *Eleanor and Franklin: The Story of Their Relationship, Based on Eleanor Roosevelt's Private Papers* (New York: Norton, 1971), 191–207, 311. Mintz and Kellogg, *Domestic Revolutions*, 119–126.

17. Eleanor Roosevelt, "A Mother's Responsibility as a Citizen," 3 February 1933, box 3024, Eleanor Roosevelt Papers, FDRL.

18. Eleanor Roosevelt, *It's Up to the Women* (New York: Frederick A. Stokes Company, 1933), 2, 7–8, 11–12.

19. Ibid., 95–97, 113.

20. Eleanor Roosevelt, "Ratify the Child Labor Amendment," *Woman's Home Companion*, September 1933, box 3025, Eleanor Roosevelt Papers, FDRL; Wilson, "New Deal Agencies," 275–276.

21. Eleanor Roosevelt, "Women as Consumers," n.d. [ca. 1934], box 3028, Eleanor Roosevelt Papers, FDRL; Eleanor Roosevelt, "Setting Our House in Order," *Woman's Home Companion*, October 1933, box 3025, Eleanor Roosevelt Papers, FDRL.

22. Eleanor Roosevelt, "A Message to Farm Homemakers," 6 June 1934, box 3027, Eleanor Roosevelt Papers, FDRL; Susan Ware, *Holding Their Own: American Women in the 1930s* (Boston: Twayne, 1982), 8–11; Mintz and Kellogg, *Domestic Revolutions*, 144–149.

23. Wilson, "New Deal Agencies," 277–278.

24. Lash, *Eleanor and Franklin*, 398; Eleanor Roosevelt, "My Day," 3 December 1936, https://www.gwu.edu/~erpapers/myday/.

25. Lash, *Eleanor and Franklin*, 417; Eleanor Roosevelt, "My Day," 28 June 1938, https://www.gwu.edu/~erpapers/myday/.

26. Eleanor Roosevelt, "Women in Defense," *Trade Union Courier*, September 1941, box 3041, Eleanor Roosevelt Papers, FDRL.

27. Eleanor Roosevelt, *The Moral Basis of Democracy* (New York: Howell, Soskin & Co., 1940).

28. Eleanor Roosevelt, "Speech on *McCall's* Magazine Consumer Pledge," n.d. [ca. 1942], box 3046, Eleanor Roosevelt Papers, FDRL; Eleanor Roosevelt, "Woman's Contribution to the War," October 1942, box 3045, Eleanor Roosevelt Papers, FDRL; Mintz and Kellogg, *Domestic Revolutions*, 160; Eleanor Roosevelt, "My Day," 5 November 1941, https://www.gwu.edu/~erpapers/myday/.

29. Eleanor Roosevelt, "Women in War Week," 22 November 1942, box 3046, Eleanor Roosevelt Papers, FDRL.

30. Maurine H. Beasley, *Eleanor Roosevelt: Transformative First Lady* (Lawrence: University Press of Kansas, 2010), 181–183.

31. Eleanor Roosevelt, radio address, 8 October 1940, box 3039, Eleanor Roosevelt Papers, FDRL.

32. Eleanor Roosevelt, "Woman's Place after the War," *Click*, April 1944, box 3050, Eleanor Roosevelt Papers, FDRL; Chafe, *The American Woman: Her Changing Social, Economic, and Political Roles 1920–1970* (New York: Oxford University Press, 1972), 176–177, 190–191.

33. Mintz and Kellogg, *Domestic Revolutions*, 153, 173–175; Coleman R. Griffith, "The Psychological Adjustments of the Returned Servicemen and Their Families," *Journal of Home Economics* 36, no. 7 (September 1944): 385–389.

34. Box 3, India Edwards Papers, HSTL.

35. India Edwards, *Pulling No Punches: Memoirs of a Woman in Politics* (New York: Putnam, 1977), 111; Margaret Truman, *Bess W. Truman* (New York: Macmillan, 1986), 18, 132–135.

36. Cynthia Harrison, *On Account of Sex: The Politics of Women's Issues, 1945–1968* (Berkeley: University of California Press, 1988), 4–6; Nanette Kutner, "If You Were Mrs. Eisenhower," *Good Housekeeping*, January 1944, 31.

37. Dorothy Williams to Reathel Odum, undated correspondence, box 5, Reathel Odum Papers, HSTL.

38. "Behind Mrs. Truman's Social Curtain: No Comment," *Newsweek*, 10 November 1947, box 5, Reathel Odum Papers, HSTL.

39. "Back to Normalcy." n.d., n.p., Vertical File, Truman Family File, HSTL.

40. Charlie Ross to Roy Howard, 4 February 1947, President's Personal File 2, HSTL.

41. Unsigned memorandum, 18 May 1945, President's Personal File 2, HSTL; Truman, *Bess W. Truman*, 262.

42. President's Personal File 2, HSTL.

43. Truman, *Bess W. Truman*, 295–296; Evelyn Peyton Gordon, "Spanish Broth at White House," n.p., n.d., Truman Family File, Vertical File, HSTL.

44. Achsah Dorsey Smith, "Republican Male Dares to Attend Democratic 'Women-Only' Reception," *Times-Herald*, 4 August 1949, box 40A, Student Research File, HSTL.

45. "A Typical Day at the White House (Mrs. Truman)," 27 August 1946, box 5, Reathel Odum Papers, HSTL.

46. Box 15, Family Correspondence File, Papers of Harry S. Truman, HSTL.

47. RNC Press Release, 13 October 1956, box 18, Bertha Adkins Papers, DDEL.

48. Mamie Eisenhower Oral History, 20 July 1972, 36–38, 117, and 16 August 1972, 65–68, 147, DDEL; Susan Eisenhower, *Mrs. Ike: Memories and Reflections on the Life of Mamie Eisenhower* (New York: Farrar, Straus and Giroux, 1996), 198–199.

49. Anne Wheaton Oral History, 8 March 1968, 148, DDEL.

50. Katherine Howard Oral History, 13 March 1969, 355, DDEL; Robert Wallace, "They Like Mamie Too," *Life*, 13 October 1952, 149–150.

51. Anne Wheaton Oral History, 31 January 1968, 23–27, 53, and 8 March 1968, 147, DDEL.

52. Transcripts, box 9, Campaign Series, Dwight D. Eisenhower—Papers as President, DDEL.

53. Katherine Howard Oral History, 7 February 1970, 451–453, DDEL; Eisenhower, *Mrs. Ike*, 274.

54. Transcript of press conference, 11 March 1953, box 35, Mamie Doud Eisenhower Papers, DDEL; J. B. West, *Upstairs at the White House: My Life with First Ladies* (New York: Coward, McCann & Geoghegan, 1973), 129–131, 140, 178.

55. Transcript of press conference, 11 March 1953, box 35, Mamie Doud Eisenhower Papers, DDEL.

56. "The President's Lady," *Time*, 19 January 1953, 17; Questions from Ruth Boyer Scott, 27 June 1953, box 35, Mamie Doud Eisenhower Papers, DDEL.

57. Helen Thomas to Mary Jane McCaffree, 2 September 1953, box 35, Mamie Doud Eisenhower Papers, DDEL.

58. Ruth Gmeiner to Mary Jane McCaffree, 20 October 1953, box 35, Mamie Doud Eisenhower Papers, DDEL.

59. Lawrence Lader to Murray Snyder, 29 April 1953, and "Kinds of Letters," undated report, box 35, Mamie Doud Eisenhower Papers, DDEL.

60. Murray Snyder to Mary Jane McCaffree, 31 January 1955, box 35, Mamie Doud Eisenhower Papers, DDEL; Marilyn Irvin Holt, *Mamie Doud Eisenhower: The General's First Lady* (Lawrence: University Press of Kansas, 2007), 64; An-

nett Francis to Clare Francis, 29 November 1955, box 35, Mamie Doud Eisenhower Papers, DDEL.

61. Chafe, *American Woman*, 217; Matilda Taylor to Barbara Eisenhower, 22 December 1952, box 35, Mamie Doud Eisenhower Papers, DDEL.

62. Holt, *Mamie Doud Eisenhower*, 132–134; Eugenia Kaledin, *Mothers and More: American Women in the 1950s* (New York: Macmillan, 1985), 2–4.

63. Dwight D. Eisenhower, "Remarks at the U.S. Savings Bond Conference," 25 February 1959, http://www.presidency.ucsb.edu/ws/?pid=11667.

64. Nancy Robinson to Mary Jane McCaffree, 9 January 1953, and Treasury Department press release, 16 February 1953, box 1, Social Office Files, DDEL.

65. Public service statements, 21 March 1953, May 1953, 30 July 1953, box 41, Mamie Doud Eisenhower Papers, DDEL.

66. Holt, *Mamie Doud Eisenhower*, 140–141; Ruth Montgomery, "Mamie," *Look*, 23 February 1954, Vertical File, DDEL.

67. Jacqueline Kennedy, 1960 television advertisement, http://www.living roomcandidate.org/commercials/1960/mrs-jfk.

68. "A Tour of the White House with Mrs. John F. Kennedy," 14 February 1962, https://www.youtube.com/watch?v=CbFt4h3Dkkw.

69. Carole B. Schwalbe, "Jacqueline Kennedy and Cold War Propaganda," *Journal of Broadcasting and Electronic Media* 49, no. 1 (2005): 111–127.

70. Press release, 17 January 1962, box 101, Pierre Salinger Files, JFKL.

71. Press release, 21 January 1963, box 101, Pierre Salinger Files, JFKL.

72. Andre de Coizart, "Success of Mrs. Kennedy in Europe Defies the Imagination," *La Prensa Libre,* box 705, Subject File, White House Central Files, JFKL; "La Presidente," *Time*, 9 June 1961, 13–15; Jacqueline Kennedy, *Historic Conversations on Life with John F. Kennedy* (New York: Hyperion, 2011), 222–224.

73. Jaume Miravitlles, "Jacqueline Kennedy," *La Nacion*, 18 June 1961, box 705, Subject File, White House Central Files, JFKL.

74. Letitia Baldrige to Mike Mansfield, 10 April 1962, box 705, Subject File, White House Central File, JFKL; Schwalbe, "Cold War Propaganda," 121–122.

75. Kennedy, *Historic Conversations*, 243–245.

76. Ibid., 202, 303, 347.

77. "Biography of Jacqueline Bouvier Kennedy," February 1962, box 10, Pierre Salinger Files, JFKL.

78. Pamela Turnure to Ruth Nathan, 8 November 1962, box 706, Subject File, White House Central Files, JFKL.

79. Kennedy, *Historic Conversations*, 331–332, 341–343.

80. Press release, 19 September 1962, box 101, Pierre Salinger Files, JFKL.

81. Harrison, *On Account of Sex*, 140.

82. Kennedy, *Historic Conversations*, 88–89, 170, 243.

83. Betty Friedan, *The Feminine Mystique* (New York: W. W. Norton, 1997), 408, 416.

CHAPTER 3. EQUALITY

1. Jacqueline Kennedy, *Historic Conversations on Life with John F. Kennedy* (New York: Hyperion, 2011), 85; Esther Peterson Oral History, 25 November 1968, 26, LBJL.

2. Lewis L. Gould, *Lady Bird Johnson: Our Environmental First Lady* (Lawrence: University Press of Kansas, 1999), 1–10.

3. Gould, *Lady Bird Johnson*, 11–18.

4. Robert A. Caro, *The Years of Lyndon Johnson: Means of Ascent* (New York: Alfred A. Knopf, 1990), 56–58.

5. "Forward: The American Female," *Harper's*, October 1962, 117–118.

6. Cynthia Harrison, *On Account of Sex: The Politics of Women's Issues 1945–1968* (Berkeley: University of California Press, 1988), 173–174.

7. Liz Carpenter to Lyndon Johnson, 24 February 1964, box 58, Human Rights 3, White House Central Files, LBJL.

8. Helen Thomas to Liz Carpenter, 16 March 1965, box 67, and Liz Carpenter to Bess Abell, 11 January 1968, box 68, Liz Carpenter Subject Files, LBJL.

9. Box 67, Liz Carpenter Subject Files, LBJL.

10. Liz Carpenter Oral History, 4 April 1969, 33, LBJL; Vera Glaser, "First Lady Rewards the 'Doers,'" *Bulletin* (Philadelphia, PA), 6 July 1964, box 7, Liz Carpenter Subject Files, LBJL.

11. Liz Carpenter to Lady Bird Johnson, undated correspondence [ca. January 1964], and Isabelle Shelton, "Women Doers Are Told History Needs Records," *Washington Star*, 20 February 1964, box 71, Liz Carpenter Subject Files, LBJL.

12. Press release, 29 June 1965, box 16, Liz Carpenter Subject Files, LBJL.

13. Press release, 13 January 1968, box 45, Liz Carpenter Subject Files, LBJL.

14. Press release, 2 April 1968, box 48, Liz Carpenter Subject Files, LBJL.

15. Excerpts from women doers luncheon, 18 January 1968, and "Mrs. Johnson Sorry Furor Obscured Other Ideas," *New York Times*, 20 January 1968, box 45, Liz Carpenter Subject Files, LBJL; Liz Carpenter to LBJ, 15 January 1966, box 58, HU3, LBJL.

16. Mileage tally, 31 October 1964, box 73, Liz Carpenter Subject Files, LBJL.

17. Press release, 16 August 1964, box 79, Liz Carpenter Subject Files, LBJL; *Taylor v. Louisiana*, 419 U.S. 522 (1975).

18. Box 62, President's Personal File 5/Johnson, Lady Bird, LBJL.

19. Liz Carpenter Oral History, 3 December 1968, 11–12, LBJL.

20. Ibid., 11–16, LBJL; Lady Bird Johnson, remarks, 6 October 1964, box 79, Liz Carpenter Subject Files, LBJL; unsigned and undated White House memoranda, box 11, Liz Carpenter Subject Files, LBJL.

21. Liz Carpenter Oral History, 3 December 1968, 13–15, LBJL.

22. Lady Bird Johnson, remarks, 20 August 1964, box 70, and 17 September 1964, box 79, and 24 October 1964, box 80, Liz Carpenter Subject Files, LBJL.

23. Margaret Price to state women's activities coordinators, undated corre-

spondence, and transcript of "tell a friend," box 11, Liz Carpenter Subject Files, LBJL; Margaret Price, memorandum, 29 September 1966, box 30, Liz Carpenter Subject Files, LBJL.

24. Myer Feldman to Jane Grant, 31 December 1963, box 72, Legislation/Human Rights, LBJL.

25. Helen Bentley to Richard Nixon, undated memorandum, box 28, Robert Finch Files, RNPM.

26. Elizabeth Shelton, "Mrs. Nixon: 'We're Already Equal,'" *Washington Post*, 8 May 1969. Jean Witter to Richard Nixon, undated correspondence, and John Brown to Hope Roberts, 24 May 1969, Human Rights 2-5 Women, RNPM.

27. Mary C. Brennan, *Pat Nixon: Embattled First Lady* (Lawrence: University Press of Kansas, 2011), 44–58.

28. Barbara Franklin and Jean Spencer, memorandum, October 1971, box 28, Robert Finch Files, RNPM.

29. Press briefing transcript, 4 May 1970, box 30, Robert Finch Files, RNPM.

30. Christina Wolbrecht, *The Politics of Women's Rights* (Princeton, NJ: Princeton University Press, 2000), 107, 143, 177.

31. Constance Stuart to Pat Nixon's staff, 8 February 1972, box 11, Susan Porter Files, RNPM.

32. Wolbrecht, *Politics of Women's Rights*, 35–36; Barbara Franklin and Jean Spencer, memorandum, October 1971, box 28, Robert Finch Files, RNPM.

33. Marlene Cimons, "Caucus Has No Appeal for Pat," *Los Angeles Times*, 19 August 1971, Outside Women's Organizations File, Anne Armstrong Files, RNPM.

34. Pat Nixon to Lorraine Beebe, 17 April 1972, box 65, Anne Armstrong Files, RNPM.

35. Pat Nixon's staff to Hugh Sloan, 20 August 1970, Human Rights 2-5 Women, RNPM.

36. Barbara Franklin to Anne Armstrong, 9 May 1973, box 35, Anne Armstrong Files, RNPM; Lucy Winchester to Helen Engel, 14 March 1974, box 4, Susan Porter Files, RNPM.

37. Barbara Franklin to Fred Malek, 18 October 1971, box 42, Anne Armstrong Files, RNMP; Julie Nixon Eisenhower, *Pat Nixon: The Untold Story* (New York: Simon & Schuster, 1986), 321.

38. "Support Women: Pat Nixon," *Evening Star*, 9 February 1972, box 45, Anne Armstrong Files, RNPM.

39. Barbara Franklin and Jean Spencer, memorandum, October 1971, box 28, Robert Finch Files, RNPM; Donnie Radcliffe, "First Lady's Campaign," *Washington Post*, 9 August 1972.

40. Schedule proposals, box 40, Anne Armstrong Files, RNPM.

41. Vera Hirschberg, fact sheet, 17 August 1972, box 11, Susan Porter Files, RNPM.

42. Pat Nixon, remarks, 23 August 1972, https://www.youtube.com/watch?v=-w6rmPWJ-gY.

43. Pat Nixon, statement, box 7, Gwendolyn B. King Files, RNPM.

44. Betty Ford, *The Times of My Life* (New York: Harper & Row, 1978), 8, 17–18, 23–26.

45. Ibid., 27–30.

46. Ibid., 38–43.

47. Ibid., 93, 124–125.

48. Press conference transcript, box 1, Sheila Weidenfeld Files, GRFL.

49. "A Conversation with Betty Ford," transcript, 10 August 1975, box 6, Sheila Weidenfeld Files, GRFL; Ford, *Times of My Life*, 201–202.

50. Janet M. Martin, *The Presidency and Women: Promise, Performance & Illusion* (College Station: Texas A&M University Press, 2003), 168–169; Anne Armstrong to Betty Ford, 15 August 1974, box 21, Patricia Lindh and Jeanne Holm Files, GRFL.

51. Patricia Lindh to Betty Ford, 5 March 1976, PP5-1, GRFL.

52. Eileen Shanahan, "Ford Sets up Unit on Women's Year," *New York Times*, 10 January 1975, and Terry O'Donnell, memorandum, 9 January 1975, box 4, Sheila Weidenfeld Files, GRFL.

53. Patricia Lindh to Betty Ford, 17 January 1975, box 4, Sheila Weidenfeld Files, GRFL; Anne Armstrong to Betty Ford, 6 December 1974, box 21, Patricia Lindh and Jeanne Holm Files, GRFL.

54. Memoranda, box 3, PP5-1, GRFL; Department of State bulletin, box 47, Sheila Weidenfeld Files, GRFL.

55. Betty Ford, remarks, 25 October 1975, box 19, Sheila Weidenfeld Files, GRFL.

56. Jane Mansbridge, *Why We Lost the ERA* (Chicago: University of Chicago Press, 1986), 4–6.

57. STOP ERA, "You Can't Fool Mother Nature," box 47, Sheila Weidenfeld Files, GRFL.

58. Phyllis Schlafly to Betty Ford, 16 September 1974, box 336, Name File, Social Files, GRFL.

59. Betty Ford, memoranda, Box 37, Sheila Weidenfeld Files, GRFL; "Alton's Own Challenges Betty on ERA," *Chicago Tribune*, 11 February 1975, box 21, Patricia Lindh and Jeanne Holm Files, GRFL; UPI, 14 February 1975, box 47, Sheila Weidenfeld Files, GRFL.

60. "Betty Ford Pushes for ERA," *Milwaukee Journal*, 7 February 1975, and Associated Press, "Mrs. Ford Widens Her Campaign," box 21, Patricia Lindh and Jeanne Holm Files, GRFL.

61. Mansbridge, *Why We Lost the ERA*, 177; Doug Bailey to Sheila Weidenfeld, 15 April 1975, box 47, Sheila Weidenfeld Files, GRFL.

62. Donald Deuster to Betty Ford, 5 February 1975, box 47, Sheila Weidenfeld Files, GRFL.

63. Grace Boulton to Betty Ford, 14 February 1975, and Mary Louise Smith to Grace Boulton, 26 February 1975, and Mailgram to Gerald Ford, 22 August 1975, box 47, Sheila Weidenfeld Files, GRFL.

64. "ERA Loses in Senate by 21 to 17," 25 April 1975, *Fort Lauderdale News*, box 21, Patricia Lindh and Jeanne Holm Files, GRFL.

65. Associated Press, "Mrs. Ford Gets Missouri Vote," 6 February 1975, box 21, Patricia Lindh and Jeanne Holm Files, GRFL.

66. "Mrs. Ford's Mail 3–1 against ERA," *News* (Mexico City), 21 February 1975, box 21, Patricia Lindh and Jeanne Holm Files, GRFL; Doris Hjorth to Betty Ford, 21 February 1975, box 47, Sheila Weidenfeld Files, GRFL.

67. Jacqueline Trescott, "Reddy for ERAmerica," *Washington Post*, 29 March 1976, box 9, Sheila Weidenfeld Files, GRFL; "A Special Message from Betty Ford," *Redbook*, July 1976, box 23, Betty Ford Papers, GRFL; Betty Ford to ERA vigil, 27 August 1976, box 2, Frances K. Pullen Files, GRFL.

68. Susan Porter to Betty Ford, 5 January 1977, box 11, Susan Porter Files, GRFL.

69. Rosalynn Carter, *First Lady from Plains* (Boston: Houghton Mifflin, 1984), 10–12, 20–29, 73, 76–77, 95–97, 101–103.

70. Martin, *The Presidency and Women*, 206–209.

71. Rosalynn Carter, remarks, 26 April 1979, box 9, Mary Finch Hoyt Files, JCL.

72. Paul Costello to Rosalynn Carter, 18 January 1979, box 8, Mary Finch Hoyt Files, JCL; Rosalynn Carter, undated note, box 48, Kathy Cade Files, JCL; Mary L. Clark, "Carter's Groundbreaking Appointment of Women to the Federal Bench: His Other 'Human Rights' Record," *Journal of Gender, Social Policy & the Law* 11, no. 3 (2003): 1131–1163.

73. Press release, 15 May 1978, box 4, Mary Finch Hoyt Files, JCL.

74. Kathy Cade to Rosalynn Carter, 28 January 1977, box 17, Kathy Cade Files, JCL.

75. Kathy Cade to Rosalynn Carter, 1 February 1977, box 17, Kathy Cade Files, JCL.

76. Rosalynn Carter, remarks, 8 September 1977, box 3, Mary Finch Hoyt Files, JCL.

77. Sara Evans, *Born for Liberty* (New York: Free Press, 1989), 306–307; Georgie Anne Geyer, "Women at Odds," *Los Angeles Times*, 23 November 1977, box 3, Mary Finch Hoyt Files, JCL.

78. Rosalynn Carter, remarks, 18 November 1977, box 3, Mary Finch Hoyt Files, JCL.

79. Robert Grant letter, 10 April 1978, box 3, Mary Finch Hoyt Files; Mail analysis by Hugh Carter, 31 January 1979, box 1, Kathy Cade Files, JCL.

80. Rosalynn Carter, remarks, 15 May 1978, box 4, Mary Finch Hoyt Files, JCL.

81. Liz Carpenter to Rosalynn Carter, 19 April 1978, and John Fary to Marco Domico, 12 May 1978, and Rosalynn Carter to John Fary, 5 June 1978, box 16, Kathy Cade Files, JCL.

82. Kathy Cade to Mary Hoyt, undated correspondence, and Fact Sheet on

ERA Extension Meeting, 18 September 1978, box 31, Mary Finch Hoyt Files, JCL.

83. Mail analysis by Hugh Carter, 31 January 1979, box 1, Kathy Cade Files, JCL.

84. Martin, *Presidency and Women*, 224. Sarah Weddington to Rosalynn Carter, 28 May 1979, box 23, Kathy Cade Files, JCL.

85. Timeline of Rosalynn Carter's ERA activities, box 17, Kathy Cade Files, JCL. Donnie Radcliffe, "The ERA Summit," *Washington Post*, 24 October 1979.

86. List of Rosalynn Carter's calls, and Sarah Weddington to Jimmy and Rosalynn Carter, 19 January 1980, box 16, Kathy Cade Files, JCL.

87. List of Rosalynn Carter's calls, 10 June 1980, box 16, Kathy Cade Files, JCL.

88. Jonathan Harsch, "Illinois ERA Vote," *Christian Science Monitor*, 23 June 1980, http://m.csmonitor.com/1980/0623/062344.html.

CHAPTER 4. THE PERSONAL IS POLITICAL

1. Cynthia Harrison, *On Account of Sex: The Politics of Women's Issues 1945–1968* (Berkeley: University of California Press, 1988), 196–200.

2. Lady Bird Johnson, remarks, 31 March 1964, box 78, Liz Carpenter Subject Files, LBJL.

3. Lady Bird Johnson, remarks, 25 February 1966, box 83, Liz Carpenter Subject Files, LBJL.

4. Eric Goldman to Liz Carpenter, 21 April 1964, box 78, Liz Carpenter Subject Files, LBJL; Lady Bird Johnson, remarks, box 78, Liz Carpenter Subject Files, LBJL.

5. Lady Bird Johnson, remarks, 24 June 1964, box 78, Liz Carpenter Subject Files, LBJL.

6. Margaret Mead, "Mrs. Lyndon B. Johnson: A New Kind of First Lady?" *Redbook Magazine*, July 1965, box 62, PP5/Johnson, Lady Bird, LBJL.

7. Lady Bird Johnson, *A White House Diary* (New York: Holt, Rinehart and Winston, 1970), 235.

8. Liz Carpenter Oral History, 4 April 1969, 32, LBJL; Johnson, *White House Diary*, 310.

9. Lady Bird Johnson, remarks, 5 May 1965, box 72, Liz Carpenter Subject Files, LBJL.

10. Liz Carpenter Oral History, 4 April 1969, 4–10, LBJL.

11. Lady Bird Johnson, remarks, 11 February 1965, box 1, Beautification Files, Social Files, LBJL; Johnson, *White House Diary*, 240; Lewis Gould, *Lady Bird Johnson: Our Environmental First Lady* (Lawrence: University Press of Kansas, 1999), 56.

12. Lady Bird Johnson, remarks, 9 June 1964, box 78, Liz Carpenter Subject Files, LBJL.

13. Liz Carpenter Oral History, 4 April 1969, 33–34, LBJL; Liz Carpenter to Evelyn Rolleri, 27 February 1964, box 127, Liz Carpenter Alpha File, LBJL.

14. Liz Carpenter Oral History, 27 August 1969, 1–2, LBJL.

15. Press release, 5 February 1965, box 7, Liz Carpenter Subject Files, LBJL; Vera Glaser, press clipping of syndicated column, n.p., n.d. [ca. June 1964], box 71, Liz Carpenter Subject Files, LBJL.

16. Mary C. Brennan, *Pat Nixon: Embattled First Lady* (Lawrence: University Press of Kansas, 2011), 108–109.

17. Marilyn Irvin Holt, *Mamie Doud Eisenhower: The General's First Lady* (Lawrence: University Press of Kansas, 2007), 134; "Mrs. Nixon Foreign Travel," box 19, Susan Porter Files, RNPM.

18. Press Release, 24 June 1970, box 45, Susan Porter Files, RNPM; Julie Nixon Eisenhower, *Pat Nixon: The Untold Story* (New York: Simon & Schuster, 1986), 291–293.

19. "A New Pat," *Newsweek*, 17 January 1972, box 7, Susan Porter Files, RNPM.

20. "African Queen for a Week," *Time*, 17 January 1972, 12–14; "Pat Nixon Scholarships," box 45, Susan Porter Files, RNPM.

21. Eisenhower, *Pat Nixon*, 329–333.

22. Barbara Franklin to Julie Eisenhower, 15 February 1972, Human Rights 2-5 Women, RNPM.

23. Eisenhower, *Pat Nixon*, 334–335; "Ladies' Day in Moscow," *Newsweek*, 5 June 1972, 31.

24. Richard Nixon, "Remarks at the First Annual Awards Dinner of the National Center for Voluntary Action," 10 February 1972, http://www.presidency.ucsb.edu/ws/index.php?pid=3739; Peter Michel to Barbara Franklin, 9 March 1972, box 35, Anne Armstrong Files, RNPM.

25. Jane Mansbridge, *Why We Lost the ERA* (Chicago: University of Chicago Press, 1986), 5.

26. Christina Wolbrecht, *The Politics of Women's Rights* (Princeton, NJ: Princeton University Press, 2000), 40; "The Phyllis Schlafly Report," August 1973, box 336, Social Files, GRFL.

27. Mrs. Earl Staub to Pat Nixon, 21 February 1973, and Mrs. Frank Hershman to Pat Nixon, 16 April 1973, and Susan B. Tovey to Pat Nixon, undated correspondence, Jill Ruckelshaus, Patricia Lindh, and Jean Spencer File, Anne Armstrong Papers, RNPM.

28. Wolbrecht, *Politics of Women's Rights*, 40, 158; *Roe v. Wade*, 410 U.S. 113 (1973).

29. Isabelle Shelton, "Pat Is Pressed," *Evening Star*, 19 September 1972, and Donnie Radcliffe, "First Lady's Campaign," *Washington Post*, 9 August 1972, box 46, Barbara Franklin Reference File, Anne Armstrong Files, RNPM.

30. Brennan, *Pat Nixon*, 162–164.

31. Betty Ford, remarks, 25 October 1975, box 19, Sheila Weidenfeld Files, GRFL.

32. Press conference transcript, 4 September 1974, and "Mrs. Ford Reaffirms Her Stand for Abortion," *Detroit News*, 5 September 1974, box 1, Sheila Weidenfeld Files, GRFL.

33. "A Conversation with Betty Ford," transcript, 10 August 1975, box 6, Sheila Weidenfeld Files, GRFL.

34. Sara M. Evans, *Tidal Wave: How Women Changed America at Century's End* (New York: Free Press, 2003), 29, 45; "A Conversation with Betty Ford," transcript, 10 August 1975, box 6, Sheila Weidenfeld Files, GRFL.

35. "The Ordeal of Political Wives," *Time*, 7 October 1974, 15–21.

36. "Betty Ford: Facing Cancer," *Time*, 7 October 1974, 13–14; John Robert Greene, *Betty Ford: Candor and Courage in the White House* (Lawrence: University Press of Kansas, 2004), 49–52.

37. Betty Ford, *The Times of My Life* (New York: Harper & Row, 1978), 202.

38. Betty Ford, remarks, 25 October 1975, box 19, Sheila Weidenfeld Files, GRFL; Winzola McLendon, "Betty Ford Talks about Homemaking," *Good Housekeeping*, August 1976, 26–35; "Personalities," *Washington Post*, 23 August 1976.

39. Susan Porter to Sheila Weidenfeld, 1 May 1975, and Betty Ford, remarks, 26 September 1975, box 7, Sheila Weidenfeld Files, GRFL.

40. John Robert Greene, *The Presidency of Gerald R. Ford* (Lawrence: University Press of Kansas, 1995), 67.

41. Press conference transcript, 4 September 1974, box 1, Sheila Weidenfeld Files, GRFL.

42. Betty Ford, remarks, 20 November 1974, box 2, Sheila Weidenfeld Files, GRFL.

43. "From Betty Ford: Tips on Fighting Inflation," *U.S. News & World Report*, 23 December 1974, box 39, Sheila Weidenfeld Files, GRFL.

44. Gail Perrin, "Betty Ford's Recipes," *Boston Evening Globe*, 2 April 1975, box 38, Sheila Weidenfeld Files, GRFL.

45. Dorothy McCardle, "With an Eye toward Economizing," *Washington Post*, 14 November 1974, box 39, and Frances Spatz, "Economic Edibles from Betty Ford," *Chicago Tribune*, 27 April 1975, box 38, Sheila Weidenfeld Files, GRFL.

46. Dorsey Connors, "Brown-Bagging at the White House," *Chicago Sun-Times*, 3 November 1975, box 38, Sheila Weidenfeld Files, GRFL.

47. Paul Findley to Gerald Ford, 27 September 1974, box 3, PP5-1, GRFL; Texas ranchers to Betty Ford, 5 November 1974, box 38, Sheila Weidenfeld Files, GRFL.

48. Wolbrecht, *Politics of Women's Rights*, 41–43.

49. Robert Shogan, "Nancy Reagan Disagrees with Betty Ford on Sex," *Los Angeles Times*, n.d. [ca. September 1975], box 12, Susan Porter Files, GRFL.

50. "Personalities," *Washington Post*, 23 August 1976, box 39, and "Wouldn't Advise on Presidential Appointments," *Indianapolis Star*, 23 April 1976, box 24, Sheila Weidenfeld Files, GRFL.

51. Judy Klemesrud, "Wives in '76 Campaign Find the Going Difficult," *New York Times*, 12 April 1976, box 37, Sheila Weidenfeld Files, GRFL.

52. Unsigned and undated 1976 campaign memorandum, box 1, Mary Finch Hoyt Files, JCL.

53. "Betty v. Rosalynn," *U.S. News & World Report*, 18 October 1976, 22.

54. "She's Running for First Lady," *Time*, 11 October 1976, 27.

55. "We've Worked Hard—I've Done All I Could Do," *U.S. News & World Report*, 18 October 1976, 24–25.

56. Jimmy and Rosalynn Carter, remarks, 17 February 1977, box 1, Mary Finch Hoyt Files, JCL.

57. Rosalynn Carter, congressional testimony, 7 February 1979, box 29, Kathy Cade Files, JCL; Rosalynn Carter, remarks, 7 October 1980, Mary Finch Hoyt Files, JCL.

58. "Out on Her Own," *Newsweek*, 13 June 1977, 15–18.

59. Transcript of interview, 21 June 1977, box 3, Mary Finch Hoyt Files, JCL.

60. Meg Greenfield, "Mrs. President," *Newsweek*, 20 June 1977, 100.

61. Department of State briefing, 8 September 1977, box 30, Mary Finch Hoyt Files, JCL.

62. Rosalynn Carter, *First Lady from Plains* (Boston: Houghton Mifflin, 1984), 164; transcript, n.d. [ca. December 1977], box 3, Mary Finch Hoyt Files, JCL.

63. Wolbrecht, *Politics of Women's Rights*, 47.

CHAPTER 5. WOMEN'S RIGHTS AND HUMAN RIGHTS

1. Mary Hawkesworth, "The Semiotics of Premature Burial: Feminism in a Postfeminist Age," *Signs* 29, no. 41 (Summer 2004): 961–985.

2. Sara M. Evans, *Tidal Wave: How Women Changed America at Century's End* (New York: Free Press, 2003), 213–214; Hawkesworth, "Premature Burial," 961–962.

3. Rebecca E. Klatch, *Women of the New Right* (Philadelphia: Temple University Press, 1987), 31–54; William Fine, "Nancy Reagan Face-Off," *Ladies' Home Journal*, October 1980, 111–112.

4. Fine, "Face-Off," 111–112.

5. James G. Benze, "Nancy (Anne Frances Robbins Davis) Reagan," in *American First Ladies: Their Lives and Their Legacy*, ed. Lewis L. Gould (New York: Garland Publishing, 1996), 583–591.

6. Fine, "Face-Off," 111–112.

7. Aric Press, "The ABC's of Reagan Style," *Newsweek*, 24 November 1980, 53–54; Leslie Bennetts, "Nancy Reagan," *New York Times*, 21 January 1981.

8. Marjorie Hunter, "$209,508 China Purchase Is Defended by President," *New York Times*, 2 October 1981.

9. Maxine Cheshire, "Nancy Reagan and Bulgari Jewels at the Wedding," *Washington Post*, 30 July 1981. "For Nancy, the Time of Her Life—Despite a Sour British Press," *U.S. News & World Report*, 10 August 1981, 27; Itinerary of Nancy Reagan's visit to England, box 5, Joseph Canzeri Files, RRL.

10. Fred Fielding to Michael Deaver, 8 September 1981, OA 114.19, Peter Rusthoven Files, RRL.

11. Sheila Tate to Ann Wrobleski, 8 January 1982, box 40, Michael Deaver Files, RRL; press release, 17 October 1988, OA 18941, Kathleen Koch Files, RRL.

12. Max Friersdorf, 13 February 1981, OA 13528, White House Office of Legislative Affairs Files, RRL.

13. Michael Uhlmann to Edwin Harper, 11 June 1982, Human Rights 016 Women, 086697, RRL.

14. Ibid.

15. "Key Points: What the Reagan Administration Is Doing for Women," undated memorandum, Human Rights 016 Women 073662, RRL; "Nancy Reagan's Role as She Sees It," *U.S. News & World Report*, 1 June 1981, 46–47.

16. Muffie Brandon to Michael Deaver, 3 November 1981, box 40, Michael Deaver Files, RRL; "A *Newsweek* Poll on the President's Lady," *Newsweek*, 21 December 1981, 25; Richard Wirthlin to Nancy Reagan, 21 October 1981, box 40, Michael Deaver Files, RRL.

17. Nancy Reagan, UPI Feature, 21 December 1981, box 434, Speechwriting Files, RRL; Richard Wirthlin to Michael Deaver, 2 June 1982, box 40, Michael Deaver Files, RRL.

18. Fred Barnes, "Nancy's Total Makeover," *New Republic*, 16 September 1985, 16.

19. Nancy Reagan, remarks, 25 July 1984, OA18721, First Lady Projects Office Files, RRL.

20. Beth Weinhouse, "Nancy Reagan: Traditional First Lady," *Ladies' Home Journal*, July 1985, 138.

21. Barbara Bush, *Barbara Bush: A Memoir* (New York: Charles Scribner's Sons, 1994), 1, 5–6, 21, 26.

22. Ibid., 72.

23. Ibid., 135.

24. Joyce Purnick, "Barbara Bush: Supportive, Not a Maker of Waves," *New York Times*, 18 July 1980.

25. "Bush's Wife Assails Ferraro," *New York Times*, 9 October 1984.

26. Liz Carpenter, "The President's Lady," *Washington Post*, 1 October 1989.

27. Bush, *Barbara Bush*, 274–275.

28. Christina Wolbrecht, *The Politics of Women's Rights* (Princeton, NJ: Princeton University Press, 2000), 58–59.

29. Richard Halloran and Clifford D. May, "Washington Talk," *New York Times*, 1 March 1989.

30. Lois Romano, "Doing Her Own Things," *Washington Post*, 30 May 1989.

31. "Notes from Mrs. Bush's Briefing on Learning Disabilities," / August 1989, OA 00862, Ann Brock Files, GBL.

32. George Bush, Remarks to National Leadership Coalition on AIDS, 29 March 1990, http://www.presidency.ucsb.edu/ws/?pid=18309.

33. Lois Romano, "The Hug That Says It All," *Washington Post*, 23 March 1989.

34. Bush, *Barbara Bush*, 334.

35. Ibid., 423; Susan Porter to Anna Perez, 3 October 1990, OA 06927, First Lady's Press Office Files, GBL.

36. Robert A. Bernstein, "Family Values and Gay Rights," *New York Times*, 26 June 1990; Jeffrey Schmalz, "Gay Politics Goes Mainstream," *New York Times*, 11 October 1992.

37. Laura B. Randolph, "Barbara Bush Speaks Out," *Ebony*, September 1989, 52–60.

38. Donnie Radcliffe, "Walking Hand in Hand," *Washington Post*, 17 February 1989; "First Lady Barbara Bush Honors Frederick Douglass," *Jet*, 12 March 1990, 22.

39. Randolph, "Barbara Bush Speaks Out," 56.

40. Judith Culp, "Bush Has Support of Blacks," *Washington Times*, 21 September 1990.

41. "Thomas 'Superb,' First Lady Says," *USA Today*, 10 October 1990; Bush, *Barbara Bush*, 436.

42. Jo Freeman, "Feminism vs. Family Values: Women at the 1992 Democratic and Republican Conventions," *PS: Political Science and Politics* 26, no. 1 (March 1993): 21–28; Evans, *Tidal Wave*, 228.

43. Hillary Rodham Clinton, *Living History* (New York: Simon & Schuster, 2003), 1–15.

44. Ibid., 16–43.

45. Ibid., 44–61.

46. Ibid., 62–85.

47. Ibid., 94–95.

48. Ibid., 110.

49. Evans, *Tidal Wave*, 226–229.

50. Bill Clinton, "Remarks and an Exchange with Reporters on Health Care Reform," 25 January 1993, http://www.presidency.ucsb.edu/ws/index.php?pid=46378.

51. *Association of American Physicians and Surgeons et al v. Hillary Rodham Clinton*, 997 F. 2d 898 (1993); MaryAnne Borrelli, "The First Lady as Formal Advisor to the President: When East (Wing) Meets West (Wing)," *Women & Politics* 24, no. 1 (2002): 25–45.

52. Clinton, *Living History*, 298–299.

53. "The Four Global Women's Conferences," Beijing: Beijing +5 Background, First Lady's Press Office Files, Clinton Digital Library, http://clinton.presidentiallibraries.us/items/show/2672.

54. Boutros Boutros-Ghali to Hillary Clinton, 19 May 1995, Beijing Women's Conference, Office of the Chief of Staff Files, Clinton Digital Library, http://clinton.presidentiallibraries.us/items/show/2634; Hillary Clinton, remarks, 5 September 1995, First Lady's Press Office Files, Clinton Digital Library, http://clinton.presidentiallibraries.us/items/show/2655.

55. "Report to the President from the U.S. Delegation," 25 October 1995, Beijing Follow-Up: Women [1], Domestic Policy Council Files, Clinton Digital Library, http://clinton.presidentiallibraries.us/items/show/2641.

56. Ibid.

57. Maggie Williams to Hillary Clinton, undated memorandum [ca. September 1995], Beijing Radio Actuality, First Lady's Press Office Files, Clinton Digital Library, http://clinton.presidentiallibraries.us/items/show/2654.

58. Clinton, *Living History*, 280–281.

59. Hillary Clinton's remarks at Beijing + Five, 5 June 2000, First Lady's Press Office Files, Clinton Digital Library, http://clinton.presidentiallibraries .us/items/show/2664.

60. Glyn Davies to Maggie Williams, 1 April 1997, Vital Voices [1], First Lady's Office Files, Clinton Digital Library, http://clinton.presidentiallibrar ies.us/items/show/2690; Hillary Clinton, remarks, 11 July 1997, HRC Foreign Speeches, First Lady's Office and Speechwriting Files, Clinton Digital Library, http://clinton.presidentiallibraries.us/items/show/2753.

61. Hillary Clinton, Vital Voices Speeches, First Lady's Office and Speechwriting Files, Clinton Digital Library, http://clinton.presidentiallibraries.us /items/show/2736.

62. Hillary Clinton, remarks at Beijing + Five, 5 June 2000, Beijing, First Lady's Press Office Files, Clinton Digital Library, http://clinton.presidentiallibraries .us/items/show/2664.

63. Clinton, *Living History*, 500–501.

64. Laura Bush, *Spoken from the Heart* (New York: Scribner, 2010), 52–58, 78–79, 92–95, 143–144.

65. Laura Bush, radio address, 17 November 2001, http://georgewbush-white house.archives.gov/news/releases/2001/11/20011117.html.

66. Bush, *Spoken from the Heart*, 234–238.

67. Ibid., 251–252; Martha Brant, "West Wing Story: The First Lady's Grace," *Newsweek*, 27 November 2001.

68. Laura Bush, remarks, 8 March 2002, http://georgewbush-whitehouse .archives.gov/news/releases/2002/03/20020308-15.html.

69. Laura Bush, remarks, 20 March 2002, http://georgewbush-whitehouse .archives.gov/news/releases/2002/03/20020320-26.html.

70. Bush, *Spoken from the Heart*, 311–318; Laura Bush, remarks, 30 March 2005, http://georgewbush-whitehouse.archives.gov/news/releases/2005/03 /20050330-1.html.

71. Bush, *Spoken from the Heart*, 319.

72. Ibid., 328–334. Laura Bush, press briefing, 13 July 2005, http://georgew bush-whitehouse.archives.gov/news/releases/2005/07/20050713-1.html.

73. Bush, *Spoken from the Heart*, 392–394, 410–411; Laura Bush, interview with Jonathan Karl, 9 June 2008, http://georgewbush-whitehouse.archives.gov /news/releases/2008/06/20080609-13.html.

74. Republican Party Platform of 2000, 31 July 2000, http://www.presi dency.ucsb.edu/ws/?pid=25849.

75. "Mrs. Laura Bush's Leadership," http://georgewbush-whitehouse.ar chives.gov/infocus/bushrecord/factsheets/leadership.html.

76. Laura Bush, remarks, 14 March 2008, http://georgewbush-whitehouse .archives.gov/news/releases/2008/03/20080314-12.html.

77. Michelle Obama, remarks, 28 April 2009, https://www.whitehouse.gov /the-press-office/remarks-first-lady-sojourner-truth-bust-unveiling.

78. Michelle Cottle, "Leaning Out: How Michelle Obama became a Feminist Nightmare," *Politico Magazine*, 21 November 2013, http://www.politico.com /magazine/story/2013/11/leaning-out-michelle-obama-100244.

79. Peter Slevin, *Michelle Obama: A Life* (New York: Alfred A. Knopf, 2015), 38–39, 57, 70, 90, 99, 141–142, 171, 174, 242–243.

80. Todd Rho'Dess, "Obama's 2008 Deracialized Campaign in the Context of the African American Struggle," *Race, Gender & Class* 18, no. 3/4 (2011): 110–122.

81. DeNeen L. Brown and Richard Leiby, "The First Lady's Ambassadors of Success," *Washington Post*, 20 March 2009.

82. Tamara Jones, "Michelle Obama Gets Personal," *MORE Magazine*, February 2012, http://www.more.com/michelle-obama-mentor.

83. Michelle Obama, "My College Story Can Be Yours," *Education Week*, 11 June 2014, http://www.edweek.org/ew/articles/2014/06/11/michelle-obama -my-college-story-can-be-yours.html.

84. Vanessa Freidman, "Michelle Obama Hosts Fashion Education Workshop," *New York Times Blogs*, 8 October 2014.

85. Katherine Skiba, "A Grand Debut for the First Lady," *U.S. News & World Report*, June 2009, 20–23.

86. Michelle Obama, remarks, 24 September 2014, https://www.whitehouse .gov/the-press-office/2014/09/24/remarks-first-lady-united-nations-global -education-first-initiative.

87. Michelle Obama, remarks, 3 March 2015, https://www.whitehouse.gov /the-press-office/2015/03/03/remarks-president-and-first-lady-launch-let -girls-learn-initiative.

88. Michelle Obama, remarks, 10 May 2014, https://www.whitehouse.gov /the-press-office/2014/05/10/weekly-address-first-lady-marks-mother-s-day -and-speaks-out-tragic-kidna.

89. Jane Perlez, "In Beijing Talk, Michelle Obama Extols Free Speech," *New York Times*, 23 March 2014.

CHAPTER 6. MOTHERHOOD AND FAMILY POLITICS

1. Kristin Luker, *Abortion and the Politics of Motherhood* (Berkeley: University of California Press, 1984), 158–191.

2. Anne N. Costain, "After Reagan: New Party Attitudes toward Gender," *Annals of the American Academy of Political and Social Science* 515 (May 1991): 114–125.

3. Rebecca E. Klatch, *Women of the New Right* (Philadelphia: Temple University Press, 1987), 23–30, 45.

4. Paul Recer and Patricia Avery, "The Race for First Lady," *U.S. News & World Report*, 20 October 1980, 27–29.

5. Gloria Steinem, "Finally a 'Total Woman' in the White House!" *Ms.*, March 1981, 13–14. "Mrs. Reagan's Answers to Interview Questions for *First Monday* Magazine," OA 11526, First Lady Press Office Files, RRL.

6. John Lang and Patricia Avery, "For the First Lady, a Role That Keeps Growing," *U.S. News & World Report*, 29 July 1985, 24–25.

7. Carlton Turner, internal memoranda, 29 July 1981 and 15 July 1981, box 57, Carlton Turner Files, RRL.

8. Nancy Reagan, remarks, 24 June 1986, box 57, Carlton Turner Files, RRL.

9. Luaine Lee, "Reagan to TV Executives," *Herald* [Brownsville, Texas], 2 November 1986, OA 18721, First Lady Projects Office Files, RRL.

10. Nancy Reagan, 24 February 1986, OA 18020, Office of Public Affairs Files, RRL.

11. Nancy Reagan, "Guest Editorial on Youth Abuse of Drugs and Alcohol," box 57, Carlton Turner Files, RRL.

12. Ann Wrobleski, 9 November 1981, box 434, Speechwriting, Series III, RRL; Ronald and Nancy Reagan, "National Television Address on Drug Abuse and Prevention," 14 September 1986, OA 18721, First Lady Projects Office Files, RRL.

13. Nancy Reagan, Remarks to United Nations, 21 October 1985, OA 18020, Office of Public Affairs Files, RRL; Nancy Reagan to Javier Pérez de Cuéllar, 18 November 1986, box 28, Carlton Turner Files, RRL.

14. Margaret Carlson, "The Silver Fox," *Time*, 23 January 1989, 22–26.

15. "'I've Got George Bush,'" *Newsweek*, 23 January 1989, 25.

16. Jo Freeman, "Feminist Activities at the 1988 Republican Convention," *PS: Political Science and Politics* 22, no. 1 (March 1989): 39–47.

17. "'I've Got George Bush,'" *Newsweek*, 23 January 1989, 25.

18. Barbara Gamarekian, "Barbara Bush Announces Formation of Literacy Foundation," *New York Times*, 7 March 1989.

19. Barbara Bush, *Barbara Bush: A Memoir* (New York: Charles Scribner's Sons, 1994), 309–310; Donnie Radcliffe, "Mrs. Bush and the Seeds of a Literacy Summit," *Washington Post*, 26 September 1989.

20. Barbara Bush, "Parenting's Best Kept Secret: Reading to Your Children," *Reader's Digest*, October 1990, 67–70.

21. Donnie Radcliffe, "A Sound Idea for Barbara Bush's Favorite Cause?" *Washington Post*, 16 January 199; Donnie Radcliffe, "Barbara Bush and Her Freshman Year," *Washington Post*, 21 January 1990.

22. "Millie's Book," *Good Housekeeping*, August 1990, 95–99; Donnie Radcliffe, "Barbara Bush, Not Letting Go of Literacy," *Washington Post*, 25 November 1992.

23. Sara M. Evans, *Tidal Wave: How Women Changed America at Century's End* (New York: Free Press, 2003), 214–215.

24. Fox Butterfield, "At Wellesley, A Furor over Barbara Bush," *New York Times*, 4 May 1990.

25. Kathleen Fury, "Letter to the First Lady," *Working Woman*, February 1999, 136.

26. Carla Kaplan, *Erotics of Talk: Women's Writing and Feminist Paradigms* (New York: Oxford University Press, 1996), 123–125.

27. Barbara Bush, "Choices and Change: Your Success as a Family," *Vital Speeches of the Day* 56 (1 July 1990): 549.

28. Shirley Green to Susan Porter Rose, 1 June 1990, Events Files, GBL.

29. Freeman, "Feminism vs. Family Values," 21–22.

30. Republican Party Platform of 1992, 17 August 1992, http://www.presidency.ucsb.edu/ws/?pid=25847.

31. Barbara Bush, Address to the Republican National Convention, 19 August 1992, http://www.c-span.org/video/?31360-1/republican-national-convention-address.

32. Hillary Rodham Clinton, "In France, Day Care Is Every Child's Right," *New York Times*, 7 April 1990.

33. Freeman, "Feminism vs. Family Values," 21; Hillary Rodham, "Children under the Law," *Harvard Educational Review* 43, no. 4 (November 1973): 487–514.

34. Alessandra Stanley, "A Softer Image for Hillary Clinton," *New York Times*, 13 July 1992.

35. Henry Muller and John F. Stacks, "'First, We Have to Roll Up Our Sleeves,'" *Time*, 4 January 1993, 35–37.

36. Meg Greenfield, "Did She Take the Hill?" *Newsweek*, 11 October 1993, 72; William H. Chafe, *Bill and Hillary: The Politics of the Personal* (New York: Farrar, Straus and Giroux, 2012) 205–215; Laura Bush, *Spoken from the Heart* (New York: Scribner, 2010), 165.

37. Jo Freeman, "Change and Continuity for Women at the Republican and Democratic Conventions," *Off Our Backs* 27, no. 1 (January 1997): 14–23; Hillary Rodham Clinton, *Living History* (New York: Simon & Schuster), 364.

38. Hillary Rodham Clinton, *It Takes a Village: And Other Lessons Children Teach Us* (New York: Simon & Schuster, 1996), 17, 39–51, 102.

39. Walter Isaacson, "'We're Hoping That We Have Another Child,'" *Time*, 3 June 1996, 28.

40. Clinton, *Living History*, 380; Hillary Rodham Clinton, "Comfort and Joy," *Time*, 3 February 1997, 63.

41. Hillary Clinton, "Press Briefing on White House Conference on Early Childhood Development and Learning," 14 April 1997, Background—Early Childhood Development [1], First Lady's Press Office Files, Clinton Digital Library, http://clinton.presidentiallibraries.us/items/show/2669.

42. Hillary Clinton, "Prescription for Reading Announcement," 16 April

1997, Background—Early Childhood Development [1], First Lady's Press Office Files, Clinton Digital Library, http://clinton.presidentiallibraries.us/items/show/2669.

43. Bill and Hillary Clinton, 23 October 1997, FLOTUS Statements and Speeches, First Lady's Press Office Files, Clinton Digital Library, http://clinton.presidentiallibraries.us/items/show/8205.

44. Sally S. Cohen, *Championing Child Care* (New York: Columbia University Press, 2001), 217–229.

45. Clinton, *Living History*, 466–477; Clinton, *It Takes a Village*, 41–43.

46. Hillary Rodham Clinton, *An Invitation to the White House* (New York: Simon & Schuster, 2000).

47. "Excerpts from Laura Bush's Speech to the G.O.P. Convention," *New York Times*, 1 August 2000.

48. Laura Bush, 26 July 2001, http://georgewbush-whitehouse.archives.gov/news/releases/2001/07/20010726-16.html.

49. Martha Brant, "Comforter in Chief," *Newsweek*, 3 December 2001, 34; Laura Bush, "Letter to Elementary School Students Following Terrorist Attacks," 12 September 2001, http://georgewbush-whitehouse.archives.gov/news/releases/2001/09/letter2.html#.

50. Laura Bush, "Remarks before Senate Education Committee," 24 January 2002, http://georgewbush-whitehouse.archives.gov/news/releases/2002/01/20020124-15.html.

51. "Fatherhood Movement: Can It Reduce the Number of Fatherless Children?" *CQ Researcher* 10, no. 21 (2 June 2000): 473–496.

52. Bush, *Spoken from the Heart*, 349–350.

53. Laura Bush, "President and Mrs. Bush Discuss Helping America's Youth at White House Conference," 27 October 2005, http://georgewbush-whitehouse.archives.gov/news/releases/2005/10/text/20051027-3.html; Bush, *Spoken from the Heart*, 349–354.

54. Harriette Cole, "The Real Michelle Obama," *Ebony*, September 2008, 72–84; Michelle Obama, Speech to the Democratic National Convention, 4 September 2012, http://www.npr.org/2012/09/04/160578836/transcript-michelle-obamas-convention-speech.

55. Cole, "The Real Michelle Obama," 72–84.

56. Harriette Cole, "First Lady Style," *Ebony*, January 2009, 108–109.

57. Michelle Obama, *American Grown: The Story of the White House Kitchen Garden and Gardens across America* (New York: Crown Publishers, 2012), 9.

58. Ibid.

59. Amy Dubois Barnett, "Mom in Chief," *Ebony*, May 2012, 106–111.

60. Michelle Obama, remarks, 2 June 2011, https://www.whitehouse.gov/the-press-office/2011/06/02/remarks-first-lady-food-icon-announcement.

61. Barack and Michelle Obama, "Remarks by the President and First Lady at the Signing of the Healthy, Hunger-Free Kids Act," 13 December 2010, https://

www.whitehouse.gov/the-press-office/2010/12/13/remarks-president-and
-first-lady-signing-healthy-hunger-free-kids-act.

62. Peter Slevin, *Michelle Obama: A Life* (New York: Alfred A. Knopf, 2015),
337.

63. Barack Obama, "Remarks by the President at Launch of Joining Forces,"
12 April 2011, https://www.whitehouse.gov/the-press-office/2011/04/12/re
marks-president-vice-president-first-lady-and-dr-biden-launch-joining.

64. Michelle Obama, "Remarks by the First Lady at the Women's Conference,"
26 October 2010, https://www.whitehouse.gov/the-press-office/2010/10/26
/remarks-first-lady-womens-conference-with-california-first-lady-maria-sh.

65. Ibid.

66. Michelle Obama, "How the Military Boosts the Bottom Line," *U.S. News
Digital Weekly*, 28 July 2011.

67. Michelle Obama, "Remarks of the First Lady to the National Governors
Association," 25 February 2013, https://www.whitehouse.gov/photos-and
-video/video/2013/02/25/first-lady-and-dr-biden-speak-national-governors
-association#transcript.

Bibliographic Essay

In writing this book, I have benefited from the work of political scientists, historians, biographers, and journalists who have gone before me. The volumes that have been written about first ladies range from the scholarly to the sensational and the individual to the institutional. Happily, first lady scholarship has advanced considerably, with more and more authors relying on primary source material to further understanding of the position.

Those wishing to begin researching first ladies would do well to start with Lewis L. Gould's encyclopedic *American First Ladies: Their Lives and Their Legacy*, 2nd ed. (New York: Routledge, 2001), which contains biographic as well as bibliographic essays on individual first ladies. In addition, the works comprising the University Press of Kansas's Modern First Ladies series have relied on primary source material, and all have contributed greatly to the body of knowledge on individual first ladies. On the modern first lady's office, see also Carl Sferrazza Anthony, *First Ladies*, vol. 2: *The Saga of Presidents' Wives and Their Power* (New York: William Morrow, 1991); Betty Boyd Caroli, *First Ladies: From Martha Washington to Michelle Obama*, 4th ed. (New York: Oxford University Press, 2010); Myra Gutin, *The President's Partner: The First Lady in the Twentieth Century* (New York: Praeger, 1989); Robert Watson and Anthony Eksterowicz, eds., *The Presidential Companion: Readings on the First Ladies*, 2nd ed. (Columbia: University of South Carolina Press, 2006); Robert Watson, *The Presidents' Wives: Reassessing the Office of First Lady* (Boulder, CO: Lynne Rienner Publishers, 2000); Jill Abraham Hummer, "First Ladies and the Cultural Everywoman Ideal: Gender Performance and Representation," *White House Studies* 9 (2009): 403–422; MaryAnne Borrelli, "The First Lady as Formal Advisor to the President: When East (Wing) Meets West (Wing)," *Women and Politics* 24 (2002): 25–45; Gil Troy, *Mr. and Mrs. President: From the Trumans to the Clintons* (Lawrence: University Press of Kansas, 2000); Molly Meijer Wertheimer, *Inventing a Voice: The Rhetoric of American First Ladies of the Twentieth Century* (Lanham, MD: Rowman & Littlefield, 2004); Anthony J. Eksterowicz and Kristen Paynter, "The Evolution of the Role and Office of the First Lady: The Movement toward Integration with the White House Office," *Social Science Journal* 27 (2000): 547–562; Lewis L. Gould, "Modern First Ladies in Historical Perspective," *Presidential Studies Quarterly* 15 (1985): 537–538; Betty Houchin Winfield, "From a Sponsored Status to Satellite to Her Own Orbit: The First Lady News at a New Century," *White House Studies* 1 (2001): 21–32.

On the modern presidency, see Samuel Kernell, *Going Public: New Strategies of Presidential Leadership*, 4th ed. (Washington, DC: CQ Press, 2007); Theodore J. Lowi, *The Personal President* (Ithaca, NY: Cornell University Press, 1979); Richard Neustadt, *Presidential Power and Modern Presidents: The Politics of Leadership from Roosevelt to Reagan* (New York: Free Press, 1990); Stephen Skowronek, *The Politics the Presidents Make* (Cambridge, MA: Harvard University Press, 1993). On White House organization, see John P. Burke, *The Institutional Presidency: Organizing and Managing the White House from FDR to Clinton*, 2nd ed. (Baltimore, MD: Johns Hopkins University Press, 2000); Stephen Hess and James P. Pfiffner, *Organizing the Presidency*, 3rd ed. (Washington, DC: Brookings Institution Press, 2002); Bradley H. Patterson, *The White House Staff: Inside the West Wing and Beyond* (Washington, DC: Brookings Institution Press, 2000); Charles E. Walcott and Karen M. Hult, *Governing the White House: From Hoover through LBJ* (Lawrence: University Press of Kansas, 1995).

On women in politics and history, see Christina Wolbrecht, *The Politics of Women's Rights* (Princeton, NJ: Princeton University Press, 2000); Sara M. Evans, *Tidal Wave* (New York: Free Press, 2003); William H. Chafe, *The American Woman* (New York: Oxford University Press, 1972); Rebecca E. Klatch, *Women of the New Right* (Philadelphia: Temple University Press, 1987); Theda Skocpol, *Protecting Soldiers and Mothers: The Political Origins of Social Policy in the United States* (Cambridge, MA: Harvard University Press, 1992); Cynthia Harrison, *On Account of Sex: The Politics of Women's Issues* (Berkeley: University of California Press, 1988). On women and the presidency, see Janet Martin, *The Presidency and Women* (College Station: Texas A&M University Press, 2003); Michaele L. Ferguson, "'W' Stands for Women: Feminism and Security Rhetoric in the Post-9/11 Bush Administration," *Politics and Gender* 1 (2005): 9–38; MaryAnne Borrelli and Janet Martin, eds., *The Other Elites: Women, Politics, and Power in the Executive Branch* (Boulder, CO: Lynne Rienner Publishers, 1997).

There is a substantial literature on gender, representation, and political institutions. See, for example, Wendy Brown, *Manhood and Politics: A Feminist Reading in Political Theory* (Totowa, NJ: Rowman & Littlefield, 1988); Georgia Duerst-Lahti and Rita Mae Kelly, eds., *Gender, Power, Leadership, and Governance* (Ann Arbor: University of Michigan Press, 1996); Jane Mansbridge, "Should Blacks Represent Blacks and Women Represent Women? A Contingent 'Yes,'" *Journal of Politics* 61, no. 3 (August 1999): 628–657; MaryAnne Borrelli, *The President's Cabinet: Gender, Power, and Representation* (Boulder, CO: Lynne Rienner Publishers, 2002); Jill S. Greenlee, *The Political Consequences of Motherhood* (Ann Arbor: University of Michigan Press, 2014).

Lou Hoover's papers are housed at the Herbert Hoover Presidential Library in West Branch, Iowa. They are extensive (141 linear feet and over 220,000 items) and cover her girlhood through postpresidential years. Nancy Beck Young's *Lou Henry Hoover: Activist First Lady* (Lawrence: University Press of Kansas, 2004) portrays her as an innovator and key transitional figure in modern womanhood. Lou Henry Hoover did not write memoirs, but her husband's *The Memoirs of Herbert Hoover*, vol. 2: *The Cabinet and the Presidency 1920–1933* (New York: Macmillan, 1952) is useful for understanding their work in Washington.

Eleanor Roosevelt's papers are stored at the Franklin D. Roosevelt Library in Hyde Park, New York. The collection is extensive (1095 linear feet and over 2 million pages). Her "My Day" column is an excellent source for understanding her daily activities and has been digitized through George Washington University. While numerous biographies of Eleanor Roosevelt have been written, Joseph P. Lash's *Eleanor and Franklin* (New York: Norton, 1971) is the most comprehensive work on her White House years, though Lash writes from the perspective of a personal friend. Susan Ware's *Beyond Suffrage: Women in the New Deal* (Cambridge, MA: Harvard University Press, 1981) highlights Eleanor Roosevelt's influence within bureaucratic reform circles. See also Doris Kearns Goodwin, *No Ordinary Time: Franklin and Eleanor Roosevelt: The Homefront During World War II* (New York: Simon & Schuster, 1994).

Bess Truman left no main body of papers. The Harry S. Truman Library in Independence, Missouri, contains traces of her correspondence. Material on Bess Truman can be found in the papers of Reathel Odum and Alonzo Fields, as well as the Social Office Files and the President's Personal File. The papers of India Edwards, as well as the India Edwards Oral History, are useful in understanding her relationship to Democratic women. See also India Edwards, *Pulling No Punches: Memoirs of a Woman in Politics* (New York: Putnam, 1977) for information on the climate of women's politics during the Truman administration, as well as the President Truman's Response to Women's Issues collection in the Student Research File at the Truman Library. Margaret Truman wrote her mother's official biography, *Bess W. Truman* (New York: Macmillan, 1986). Sara L. Sale's *Bess Wallace Truman: Harry's White House "Boss"* (Lawrence: University Press of Kansas, 2010) illuminates her role as a behind-the-scenes power. Harry Truman's letters to Bess have been published in *Dear Bess: The Letters from Harry to Bess Truman 1910–1959* (New York: W. W. Norton, 1983).

The papers of Mamie Doud Eisenhower are housed at the Dwight D. Eisenhower Library in Abilene, Kansas. They encompass her life from 1894 to 1973 and total approximately 596,000 pages. The Mamie Eisenhower Oral History is also available at the Eisenhower Library and online, though it does not dwell extensively on her White House years. The papers of Mary Jane McCaffree, her social secretary, are available, as are the extensive Social Office Files, which detail her role as an entertainer and liaison. On women in the Eisenhower administration, the papers and oral histories of Bertha Adkins, Katherine Howard, and Anne Wheaton of the Republican National Committee are good sources. Granddaughter Susan Eisenhower wrote *Mrs. Ike: Memories and Reflections on the Life of Mamie Eisenhower* (New York: Farrar, Straus and Giroux, 1996), which is the most comprehensive biography of her. Marilyn Irvin Holt's scholarly biography *Mamie Doud Eisenhower: The General's First Lady* (Lawrence: University Press of Kansas, 2007) reveals how Mamie Eisenhower was an ideal fit for 1950s America.

Jacqueline Kennedy's seven interviews with Arthur Schlesinger Jr., published as *Historic Conversations on Life with John F. Kennedy* (New York: Hyperion, 2011), are a useful source for researchers. While the interviews focus on John F. Kennedy and deal less with her first lady activities, much insight into Jacqueline Kennedy can still be gleaned. The Jacqueline Bouvier Kennedy Onassis Personal Papers are housed at the John F. Kennedy Library in Boston, Massachusetts, and are opened in part. These include the staff files of Mary Gallagher, Pamela Turnure, Letitia Baldrige, and Nancy Tuckerman, as well as audiovisual materials. "A Tour of the White House with Mrs. John F. Kennedy," produced by CBS News, is also available. Letitia Baldrige's *A Lady, First: My Life in the Kennedy White House and the American Embassies of Paris and Rome* (New York: Penguin Books, 2002) documents social life from Baldrige's point of view. See also Letitia Baldrige, *Of Diamonds and Diplomats* (Boston: Houghton Mifflin, 1968). Barbara Perry's scholarly biography *Jacqueline Kennedy: First Lady of the New Frontier* (Lawrence: University Press of Kansas, 2004) focuses on her White House years and illustrates the impact she had on cultural life amid the Cold War.

The Lyndon B. Johnson Library in Austin, Texas, houses Lady Bird Johnson's personal papers, including the originals of her diary, about one-seventh of which she published in *A White House Diary* (New York: Holt, Rinehart and Winston, 1970). The Social Files contain about 1,000 cubic feet of material generated during the White House years, including the Beautification Files, Liz Carpenter Subject Files, Liz Carpenter Alpha File, and Bess Abell White House Social Office Files. The Liz Carpenter Oral History is also useful for understanding the role of women in the Johnson administration. Lewis L. Gould's *Lady Bird Johnson: Our Environmental First Lady* (Lawrence: University Press of Kansas, 1999) focuses on her beautification efforts.

As of 2010, the Nixon Presidential Materials are housed at the Richard Nixon Presidential Library in Yorba Linda, California, with the exception of some audiovisual materials still held at the National Archives in College Park, Maryland. The papers of Pat Nixon's staff members, Gwendolyn B. King, Susan Porter, and Lucy Winchester, are available for research, as are the First Lady's Press Office Files. The papers of Anne Armstrong and Barbara Franklin are useful for understanding the role of women in the Nixon administration. The library also has exit interviews of many staff members who worked with Pat Nixon. The most comprehensive biography of Pat Nixon is Julie Nixon Eisenhower's *Pat Nixon: The Untold Story* (New York: Simon & Schuster, 1986).

Betty Ford has candidly recounted her life in two memoirs. Written with Chris Chase, *The Times of My Life* (New York: Harper & Row, 1978) covers her upbringing through the White House years, and *Betty: A Glad Awakening*

(Garden City, NY: Doubleday, 1987) details her postpresidential struggle with addiction. Betty Ford's papers (10.8 linear feet and about 21,600 pages) are housed at the Gerald R. Ford Library in Grand Rapids, Michigan, and are open for research. The files of her staff members Frances Kaye Pullen, Susan Porter, and Sheila Rabb Weidenfeld are useful for understanding her White House activities. The files of Patricia Lindh and Jeanne Holm provide background on women's politics during the Ford administration. See also Sheila Rabb Weidenfeld, *First Lady's Lady: With the Fords at the White House* (New York: G. P. Putnam's Sons, 1979) and MaryAnne Borrelli, "Competing Conceptions of the First Ladyship: Public Responses to Betty Ford's *60 Minutes* Interview," *Presidential Studies Quarterly* 31 (2001): 397–414. John Robert Greene's *Betty Ford: Candor and Courage in the White House* (Lawrence: University Press of Kansas, 2004) provides a concise and insightful account of Betty Ford's White House years, covering her feminism, breast cancer treatment, and addiction.

On Rosalynn Carter, the Records of the First Lady's Office at the Jimmy Carter Library are mostly open for research. They encompass 402 linear feet and 746 containers. They are arranged by suboffices: Press Office, Social Office, Scheduling Office, Correspondence Office, Projects Office, Secretary's Office. The Records of the Office of the Assistant to the President for Women's Affairs are useful for understanding the impact of feminism on the Carter administration. Rosalynn Carter's autobiography, *First Lady from Plains* (Boston: Houghton Mifflin, 1984) provides useful background information.

Nancy Reagan's papers are not currently open for research at the Ronald Reagan Library in Simi Valley, California. Nor have the records of the Office of the First Lady been fully processed. However, the Reagan Library does have a good bit of material on Nancy Reagan open for research, but it is scattered across collections. Researchers should consult their Freedom of Information Act Topic Finding Aid, "First Lady—Role of," for more information. Since her records remain mostly closed, there are no biographies of Nancy Reagan that are extensively based on her personal papers. Her autobiography, *My Turn: The Memoirs of Nancy Reagan* (New York: Random House, 1989), written with William Novak, has been criticized as not entirely accurate. See also James G. Benze, *Nancy Reagan: On the White House Stage* (Lawrence: University Press of Kansas, 2005).

Barbara Bush's papers and staff member office files are housed at the George Bush Library in College Station, Texas and have not been entirely processed. However, there are some folders open for research across the Office of the First Lady collection. Donnie Radcliffe, who covered Barbara Bush for the *Washington Post*, wrote *Simply Barbara Bush: A Portrait of America's Candid First Lady* (New York: Warner Books, 1989). Barbara Bush kept extensive diaries, and her autobiography *Barbara Bush: A Memoir* (New York: Charles Scribner's Sons, 1994), which records her White House years, is based on those. See also Rosanna Hertz and Susanna M. Reverby, "Gentility, Gender, and Political Protest: The Barbara Bush Controversy at Wellesley College," *Gender and Society* 9 (October 1995): 594–611.

The Clinton Digital Library of the William J. Clinton Presidential Library provides unprecedented digital access to researchers. Their Freedom of Information Act Collection includes the series entitled First Lady's Work on Children's Issues and Women's Rights, Health Care Task Force, and Hillary Rodham Clinton's New York Senate Campaign. The files of Hillary Clinton's staff members—Lissa Muscatine, Neera Tanden, Patti Solis Doyle, Ruby Shamir—as well as the Speechwriting Files have been digitized. Hillary Clinton's autobiography *Living History* (New York: Simon & Schuster, 2003) covers her girlhood through her Senate campaign. Biographies of Hillary and Bill Clinton abound; however, many books on the Clinton marriage are sensationalized. See William Chafe's *Bill and Hillary: The Politics of the Personal* (New York: Farrar, Straus, and Giroux, 2012) for an assessment of their personal and political relationship. See also Barbara Burrell, *Public Opinion, the First Ladyship, and Hillary Rodham Clinton* (New York: Routledge, 2001).

The George W. Bush Presidential Library has not yet processed materials related to Laura Bush's work. However, it has made available online the archived White House website. Its section on Laura Bush retains all of the information it did on the day George W. Bush left office. All of her speeches and press releases can be found there, in addition to audiovisual materials. Laura Bush's autobiography *Spoken from the Heart* (New York: Scribner, 2010) recounts her life from her girlhood in Texas through her White House years.

Michelle Obama's speeches and remarks can be found on the White House website. A number of books have been written about Michelle Obama. Peter Slevin, who covered Michelle Obama for the *Washington Post*, wrote *Michelle Obama: A Life* (New York: Alfred A. Knopf, 2015), which ties her Chicago upbringing to her work as first lady.

Index